Accelerating Literacy for Diverse Learners

Classroom Strategies That Integrate Social/Emotional Engagement and Academic Achievement, K–8

SECOND EDITION

SOCORRO G. HERRERA

SHABINA K. KAVIMANDAN

DELLA R. PEREZ

STEPHANIE WESSELS

Foreword by
Ester J. de Jong

TEACHERS COLLEGE PRESS

TEACHERS COLLEGE | COLUMBIA UNIVERSITY
NEW YORK AND LONDON

Templates, rubrics, and checklists as noted below are available for free download from the Teachers College Press website: tcpress.com/accelerating

- Picture This, template, page 35
- Pictures and Words, template, student academic behavior checklist, pages 43, 192
- Mind Map, student assessment rubric, page 193
- Listen Sketch Label, template, student academic behavior checklist, pages 57, 194
- Story Bag, template, student assessment rubric, pages 64, 195
- DOTS, templates, student academic behavior checklist, pages 77, 78, 196
- Pic-Tac-Tell, template, student assessment rubric, pages 94, 197
- Vocabulary Quilt, template, student academic behavior checklist, pages 104, 198
- Thumb Challenge, student academic behavior checklist, page 199
- U-C-ME, template, student assessment rubric, pages 136, 200
- Extension Wheel, template, student assessment rubric, pages 144, 201
- Hearts, templates, pages 152, 153
- Active Bookmark, template, student academic behavior checklist, pages 161–162, 202
- Tri-Fold, template, page 176
- Word Drop, template, page 183

Video clips illustrating teachers' implementation of the strategies listed below are available for viewing online at coe.k-state.edu/cima/biographycrt

- Linking Language
- DOTS
- Foldable
- Vocabulary Quilt
- U-C-ME
- Extension Wheel

Published by Teachers College Press, 1234 Amsterdam Avenue, New York, NY 10027

Text Design: Lynne Frost

Library of Congress Cataloging-in-Publication Data

Names: Herrera, Socorro Guadalupe, author.
Title: Accelerating literacy for diverse learners : classroom strategies that integrate social/emotional engagement and academic achievement / Socorro G. Herrera, Shabina K. Kavimandan, Della R. Perez, Stephanie Wessels ; foreword by Ester J. de Jong.
Description: Second Edition. | New York : Teachers College Press, [2017] |
Previous edition published: New York : Teachers College, Columbia University, 2013, under title Accelerating literacy for diverse learners : strategies for the common core classrooms, K-8. | Includes bibliographical references and index.
Identifiers: LCCN 2017014377 (print) | LCCN 2017022818 (ebook) | ISBN 9780807776155 (ebook) | ISBN 9780807758595 (paperback : acid-free paper)
Subjects: LCSH: Language arts (Elementary)—Curricula—United States. | Language arts (Middle School)—Curricula—United States. | Children with social disabilities—Education—United States. | Minorities—Education—United States.
Classification: LCC LB1576 (ebook) | LCC LB1576 .H3396 2017 (print) | DDC 371.829—dc23
LC record available at https://lccn.loc.gov/2017014377

ISBN 978-0-8077-5859-5 (paper)
ISBN 978-0-8077-7615-5 (ebook)

Printed on acid-free paper
Manufactured in the United States of America

For Dawn, Kevin, Jesse, and Isamari. May you continue to explore the world and dream throughout your lifetime!

—Socorro Herrera

For my kids, Ayan Farhan and Anya Suresh, who teach me so much about language and literacy every single day.

—Shabina Kavimandan

For my daughter, Ruth, who inspires me every day through her love of reading and life, and for my husband, Miguel, who has supported me on this journey.

—Della R. Perez

For the students who share their experiences and knowledge with me on a daily basis and to my family for all of their love and support.

—Stephanie Wessels

Together, we also dedicate this book to all of the outstanding educators we have had the pleasure to work with and who have shared their insights and expertise to make this book a reality.

Contents

Foreword, *by Ester J. de Jong*   vii

Preface   ix

PART I   Theoretical Foundations, Framework, and Action   1

Why It's Important   1
But Say It Isn't So: No Ruby Slippers Within Political Contexts   2
Making It Happen   2
The Framework: Activating, Connecting, and
   Affirming Student Learning   6
The Strategies Versus Activities Debate   7
Meeting of the Minds: Students and Teachers as Equal Partners   9
Transformative Comprehensible Input   9
Putting All the Pieces Together   11
Transformative Thinking: Letting Go of Our Socialized Self   13
Conclusion   14

PART II   BDI Strategies: Creating an Ecology of Care and Rigor   15

1   Images as Catalysts for Culturally Driven Connections   17

Linking Language   19
Picture This   28
Pictures and Words   36
Mind Map   44
Listen Sketch Label   50
Story Bag   58

**2   Rigor: Leveraging Words
Toward Academic Achievement**   65

DOTS   68
Foldable   79
Pic-Tac-Tell   87
Vocabulary Quilt   95
Thumb Challenge   105
Magic Book   111
IDEA   118

**3 Comprehension: It's Not Real
Until It's Rehearsed and Written** 124

U-C-ME 127

Extension Wheel 137

Hearts 145

Active Bookmark 154

Mini Novela 163

Tri-Fold 169

Word Drop 177

**PART III   Empowering Ourselves to Dismantle
Both Visible and Invisible Walls** 185

Why Are We Stuck? 185

Teachers as Agents of Change 185

A Glimpse of What's Possible 186

Change Begins with Each of Us 187

Student Knowledge Is ALWAYS Evolving 188

Lesson Planning and Lesson Delivery Are Not Mutually Exclusive 188

A Final Word 189

Appendix: Strategy Rubrics and Checklists 191

1   Images as Catalysts for Culturally Driven Connections

Pictures and Words: Student Academic Behavior Checklist 192

Mind Map: Student Assessment Rubric 193

Listen Sketch Label: Student Academic Behavior Checklist 194

Story Bag: Student Assessment Rubric 195

**2   Rigor: Leveraging Words
Toward Academic Achievement**

DOTS: Student Academic Behavior Checklist 196

Pic-Tac-Tell: Student Assessment Rubric 197

Vocabulary Quilt: Student Academic Behavior Checklist 198

Thumb Challenge: Student Academic Behavior Checklist 199

**3   Comprehension: It's Not Real
Until It's Rehearsed and Written**

U-C-ME: Student Assessment Rubric 200

Extension Wheel: Student Assessment Rubric 201

Active Bookmark: Student Academic Behavior Checklist 202

References 203

Index 208

About the Authors 214

Foreword

CULTURALLY AND LINGUISTICALLY DIVERSE (CLD) students constitute the norm in most of our classrooms today. Some of these students are U.S.-born children of immigrants; others are immigrant children. Some grow up in mixed immigration status households with documented and undocumented members in the same family. Against the backdrop of anti-immigrant rhetoric and policies, it is easy to forget that these students come with the same hopes, dreams, and desires to better this world as other students. In an era of high-stakes accountability systems that measure achievement in English only, it is easy to overlook the culturally and linguistically rich experiences that CLD students bring to their learning tasks. Now more than ever, teachers need to be able to advocate for and implement policies and practices that build and extend CLD students' linguistic and cultural resources.

Meeting the needs of our diverse students and preparing them for the future therefore places a great demand on the preparation of teachers. Mainstream teachers, English as a second language teachers, and bilingual teachers need to be able to work with students who have engaged in multiple and diverse language, literacy, and cultural experiences. Helping teachers develop the knowledge and skills they need to advocate for and create effective and equitable learning environments for CLD students has been recognized as a national challenge and imperative (de Jong & Harper, 2005). While there are many books that aim at helping teachers teach English language learners (ELLs), *Accelerating Literacy for Diverse Learners* is unique in that it places the bilingual student front and center and then extends and integrates theoretical principles and practices from this starting point.

The book also places teachers as decisionmakers at its core. On a daily basis, teachers make instructional decisions about their curriculum, their pedagogy, and their assessment practices (de Jong, 2011). They create informal norms in their classrooms regarding their own language use and decisions about which language(s) their students are encouraged or permitted to use and when. They also decide on whether and how to use materials in languages other than English, for example, using bilingual books or selecting books in students' native languages for their classroom libraries. Teachers also establish classroom participation structures by defining how their students are expected to participate in the classroom and what constitutes appropriate interaction among students and between the teacher and the student. Such norms can position students as passive receivers or active constructors of knowledge and learning. Through their decisions, teachers can thus create or may close down spaces for student learning and participation. They can organize their classrooms in ways that affirm or can potentially destroy their students' identities. This book provides teachers a powerful framework to guide their decisionmaking processes in support of their students' sociocultural, linguistic, cognitive, and academic biographies. The book presents a varied set of strategies that actively engage students in communicating, displaying, sharing, analyzing, reflecting on, and using their own understandings to develop new understandings and gain access to a high-quality curriculum.

With this biography-driven approach to CLD teaching and learning, Socorro Herrera and her colleagues remind us that teaching is so much more than knowledge or a set of activities. Teaching is a matter of the heart—of understanding, first and foremost, who our students are as human beings. This, in turn, will enable us to design our instruction in ways that affirm, strengthen, and challenge our students.

—Ester J. de Jong, EdD
Professor, ESOL/Bilingual Education & Director
School of Teaching and Learning, University of Florida
President, TESOL International Association (2017–2018)

Preface

IN RECENT YEARS, the growth in the numbers of culturally and linguistically diverse (CLD) students in schools, as well as increasing diversity of all kinds among students in classrooms, has raised awareness of the need to differentiate both classroom instruction and instructional strategies for varying student populations. In our prior texts, especially *Biography-Driven Culturally Responsive Teaching* (Herrera, 2016), we have argued that an explicit focus on instructional strategies is needed in today's complex classrooms. As educators, we often have to be reminded that it's not all about the lesson plan or structured strategies for talk—although talk is essential to learning. However, students often lack the words to be full participants in making their voices heard. Having a tool in their hand to scaffold the language not only increases participation but also increases learning. The foundation of the strategies described in this book is the teacher's efforts to be intentional in providing opportunities for students to make public the language and knowledge they have in relation to what is being taught. Teachers plan and deliver lessons keeping the biography of the learner as a central tenet of their teaching. They document what students are producing and weave it into the existing curriculum. Such attention to the CLD student's biography reduces both inaccurate assumptions about what students know (and do not know) and redundancies in teaching.

Early, extensive, and ongoing attention to the dimensions of students' biographies—the sociocultural, the cognitive, the linguistic, and the academic dimensions—encourages student–teacher partnerships in the attainment of rich learning and literacy development objectives. The value of the sociocultural dimension, in particular, cannot be overestimated, as it often tends to determine what students find meaningful in classroom strategies for differentiated instruction. Moreover, this dimension speaks to the social/emotional needs of learners and to the imperative

for us as teachers to support each child's development of a positive self-concept that reflects:

- Confidence in his or her academic abilities to learn and succeed,
- Assurance that his or her perspective matters,
- Conviction that his or her culture and native language are inherently valuable, and
- Belief that he or she is a contributor to the learning of the classroom community.

Students' engagement in school-based learning increases when they see tangible actions on the part of teachers to build relationships with them and address these foundational social/emotional needs (Guthrie, Rueda, Gambrell, & Morrison, 2009). Their sense of personal belonging in turn promotes students' ability to make meaningful connections to the content (Boston & Baxley, 2014). Educational neuroscience especially stresses the importance of such *meaningful learning* to the student's success in the classroom and beyond (Sousa, 2011).

This text, like our earlier resource for secondary educators (Herrera, Kavimandan, & Holmes, 2011), offers K–8 teachers strategies for academic learning and literacy development that are grounded in, and build upon, the four dimensions of the student biography. Each of the strategies is intentionally designed to *explore students' hearts and minds* as a means of creating a learning experience that is both meaningful and authentic. Each strategy has been *classroom tested with CLD students* in grade-level and ESL classrooms. A systematic, classroom observation–based study of 239 teachers in 41 different schools in one Midwestern state suggests that when teachers deliberately incorporate such strategies into their lessons, those teachers demonstrate higher-quality instruction (Herrera, Perez, Kavimandan, Holmes, & Miller, 2011). Specifically, teachers using a biography-driven instructional strategy showed significantly higher levels of meeting universal standards of effective pedagogy (Tharp & Dalton, 2007). These standards are emphasized throughout the book and include instructional practices such as these:

- Drawing on students' prior knowledge and background experiences related to language and literacy development.
- Leveraging student assets to facilitate a community of learners in which individuals' personal connections with the content are shared, respected, and used to advance learning.
- Communicating clear standards and expectations for challenging activities while also monitoring students' affective responses and providing scaffolds to support success.
- Prompting students to articulate their thoughts and then revoicing student connections in ways that promote elaboration, critical thinking, and a shared sense of community.

This book offers both teachers and teacher educators a valuable resource and reference for their ongoing efforts to enhance their teaching and professional capacities for delivering highly differentiated classroom instruction that maximizes biography-driven strategies. In addition to detailed descriptions of the research-based rationale and methods for enacting each strategy, printed and online resources are provided. For many strategies, templates for use in the classroom, as well as rubrics and checklists to assist the teacher in assessing student progress, appear in the book and are available for free download from the Teachers College Press website: tcpress.com/accelerating. Real-world implementation of six of these biography-driven strategies with diverse learners in grade-level classrooms is illustrated in video clips that are available for viewing online at coe.k-state.edu/cima/biographycrt.

Acknowledgments

The Center for Intercultural and Multilingual Advocacy (CIMA) is filled with colleagues, graduate students, and undergraduates who all, in one way or another, shared a part of their lives to make this project possible. Throughout this process, our colleagues have provided us with valuable insights and feedback. Special thanks go to Melissa Holmes and Sheri Meredith, who were steadfast in their attention to detail as they provided constructive criticism, helped us refine and clarify our thoughts, and encouraged us through to the end. Without their support, this project would still be an unfinished dream. We are indebted to Ray Martinez, whose creative photographic outlook allowed us to capture in both pictures and video teachers' successful use of these strategies.

We also owe special thanks to the many administrators and teachers across the state of Kansas and in numerous other states who opened their school and classroom doors to us for extensive conversations regarding cultural and linguistic diversity in America's classrooms. Their unwavering dedication to the field was a constant source of motivation. Their perspectives and their willingness to discuss both their challenges and their successes contributed tremendously to the heart and soul of this book.

Finally, to the many BESITOS students who have passed through the College of Education at Kansas State University and are continually striving in the field to provide all students with the education they deserve, regardless of current or past political agendas, your willingness to share your lives as advocates for students and families has certainly paved the way for generations of students to turn their dreams into reality.

PART I

Theoretical Foundations, Framework, and Action

AS SCHOOLS AND DISTRICTS across the country race toward a continually moving target of increasing academic achievement for all, the students most in need of effective classroom instruction continue to be left behind with regard to both opportunity to learn and community membership. These realities manifest themselves in demonstrated gaps in learning and achievement among certain groups of students. For the last 2 decades, the Center for Intercultural and Multilingual Advocacy (CIMA) has posed the following questions in an attempt to identify what often keeps professional development from accomplishing its intended goals: educators' application of theory to practice or, more specifically, their higher levels of implementation of scientifically based strategies that support content and language learning for all students.

- What explicit supports do teachers need in order to be successful in diverse classrooms where students vary in level of language proficiency, cultural background, and academic foundations to learn?
- What do "opportunity" and "respect" look, feel, and sound like in classrooms that hold high expectations for all?
- In what ways can conditions be created for all learners to be active participants in the learning community?
- What implications do lesson activities and strategies have for student interaction, higher-order thinking, and academic achievement?
- What instructional strategies have the greatest potential—through effective teacher implementation— for assimilation by students as personal learning strategies?
- How can a teacher utilize students' languages, cultures, and academic backgrounds to promote their higher-order thinking and support them in reaching high levels of participation, discussion, and learning?

These are but a few of the questions for which we have gathered data across the country for nearly 20 years. These data have informed our own teaching and learning and have provided us with evidence from classroom practice that gives us the confidence to say, "What you will find in this book works in classrooms!" This book was written for teachers, with teachers, and by teachers. Herrera (2016) details the scientific underpinnings of the instructional method that is the focus of our work: biography-driven instruction. The theory that frames actions in classroom practice has been documented clearly for decades. Our work in this book represents the next step in planning and delivering lessons that are grounded in and guided by the biography of the learner. Biography-driven instruction supports teachers in holding the highest expectations for students and in nurturing citizens of the future who will use their own agency to achieve their highest potential. The comprehensive method provides the framework and tools needed for bridging between students' biographies and grade-level vocabulary and academic concepts. This framework and an array of field-tested strategies and tools for ensuring equal community participation, individual accountability, and the academic advancement of all learners comprise the essence of this book.

Why It's Important

Now, more than ever, there is a need to ensure that educators become decision-makers within their classrooms and that they are equipped with the best research, reflective about their practice, and dedicated to not just teaching but *knowing* and *reaching* their community of learners. Teachers are charged with implementing ever-increasing levels of rigor in instruction, resources used, and assessment, and with promoting higher-order thinking in every classroom, every day! These expectations are imposed at the same time that our classrooms are becoming increasingly diverse in language, culture, socioeconomic status, mobility, and so much more.

For example, more than 400 languages in addition to English are represented in U.S. schools (Goldenberg & Wagner, 2015). Although Spanish-speaking students make up 77% of the total K–12 culturally and linguistically diverse student population, Arabic, Chinese, and Vietnamese are among the other top languages, each constituting approximately 2% (U.S. Department of Education, 2016). The diversity of languages and cultures will continue to impact educators across the United States, as an estimated 40% of school-aged students are expected to speak a language other than English by the year 2030 (Bhattacharya & Quiroga, 2009). We choose to use the term *culturally and linguistically diverse (CLD)* to describe the students for whom this book is targeted. This term, for us, provides the reader with a more realistic picture of what classroom diversity looks like across the country. Within any classroom, one will find students who "wear" different labels and receive different services. For these students, and particularly for those whose first language is not English, the strategies in this book provide essential support systems that ensure critical scaffolding for their linguistic and academic learning.

But Say It Isn't So: No Ruby Slippers Within Political Contexts

Teaching as a form of political action has often limited the execution of best practice since the dawn of the modern era. Bound by school culture, as well as district, state, and national agendas, the life of educators is always in flux waiting for what we call the "flavor of the day," that is, the new curriculum or new program that often touts what educators need to do to respond to the changing needs of culturally and linguistically diverse students. However, the end results are limited to short-term bumps on standardized tests, which leave students anxious, frustrated, and believing that they will never be good enough. At the same time, such initiatives leave teachers feeling overwhelmed and disillusioned with the results and, oftentimes, the damage. We wait for the next super solution or quick fix, hoping that the next program or set of re-envisioned standards will emerge as the saving grace for all our system's failings. These agendas are often superimposed on teachers—professionals who have the knowledge, skill, passion, and commitment to think for themselves. When provided with a general roadmap, strong leadership, and the freedom to teach, teachers bring learning to life and all learners benefit. This book is about taking the next step and doing what's best for students in our classrooms, despite the political contexts that surround us.

The Common Core State Standards (National Governors Association Center for Best Practices & Council of Chief State School Officers [NGA & CCSSO], 2010) have set the bar that "all students must be able to comprehend texts of steadily increasing complexity as they progress through school" (p. 2). Every classroom must be focused on ensuring that all students, regardless of background, spend more time reading in the content areas. The key to achieving these goals is an explicit focus on instruction in academic vocabulary in ways that move learners beyond being passive recipients of word explanations and definitions to being active constructors of word knowledge who understand how words work in different contexts and for different purposes. This type of academic language learning requires teachers to have a deep understanding of not only the instructional content but also their students' biographies. Teachers must create classroom conditions in which all members of the learning community see both their own background knowledge and ongoing discourse as central to generating ideas, testing hypotheses, reaching consensus, and applying their knowledge to the future. Although the future of the Common Core standards is unknown, a quick glance at national and state standards of the past provides us with clear evidence that standards change very little over time. Each set strives to provide a clear guide, a roadmap of where our journey in the classroom should take us. Therefore, regardless of which academic standards we use—those of the past or the reconfigured standards of the future—the overarching goals will continue to be the same. For teachers, the question becomes: *How will we set conditions that promote reaching these standards for ALL students, especially those who do not learn from traditional ways of teaching?*

At the end of the day, increasing student achievement is as much about the *how* of teaching and learning as it is about the *what*! The goal of this book is to provide pre-K–8 teachers with an explicit framework for lesson delivery and a set of strategies within a biography-driven method of instruction (Herrera, 2010, 2016). These biography-driven instructional strategies assist teachers in providing all learners with the tools, skills, and knowledge necessary to support their own learning within a grade-level, standards-based, and standards-driven curriculum.

Making It Happen

Fundamental to moving forward in meeting the academic, linguistic, and social needs of all learners is understanding the paths they have traveled before they arrive in our classrooms. The "histories" they bring serve to inform our instructional practice in ways that allow us to better establish the necessary conditions for all learners to be part of a classroom learning community that together negotiates meaning, challenges positions, and constructs new meaning from text. This type of teaching and learning dynamic begins with the single step of our creating opportunities for learners to make public both their personal and academic experiences, perspectives, and knowledge.

CLD students come to school with a wealth of knowledge and experiences (Rea & Mercuri, 2006). As educators, we realize this, but we often fail to plan for opening the lesson from a building background, asset perspective. We need to let go of the assumption that the content and language we are going to introduce are completely new or beyond the students' reach, because otherwise we wouldn't need to teach it. Often we assume a deficit perspective and begin to teach based on our assumptions about what the learner is missing, language limitations, or academic gaps. We attempt to build background by filling in the perceived gaps using our own cultural experiences and language. An experience Socorro Herrera had while observing a class illustrates the problem:

> I once observed a teacher who was teaching about the importance of sequence in writing. She proceeded to lecture her students about a cooking show she watched everyday. During the show, she shared, it was important for the chef to follow the sequence of the recipe if he was to understand it and ensure that what he was cooking would turn out as planned. She had the group repeat the word *sequence* and then repeat why it was important to follow the sequence if you wanted your writing to be organized and to turn out as planned. This lesson took more than 20 minutes, with a thumbs up response at the end to check for understanding.
>
> As I watched the lesson and observed the students, I knew that they were on autopilot. All of the students were Mexican American, and if they were watching television at home, I was pretty certain they would not be watching a cooking show—maybe a telenovela, but not a cooking show. I also knew that if the teacher had just provided a few minutes for the *students* to generate instances when a person would have to use sequence for something, she could have harvested a bounty of ideas from which to make connections to the writing process.

Key to our work is providing a strategy that invites the learner in when we open our lessons. Asking students to share the knowledge they already possess related to the topic or vocabulary we are going to introduce is essential. When asked, most teachers agree that using prior knowledge in the lesson is critical for "hooking" students into learning. Yet we educators often fall short of holding every student accountable for sharing and documenting what he or she knows so that this knowledge is available for our joint use when we cross the bridge into the lesson with our students.

In our work with teachers, most share with us that they generally incorporate isolated, and at times fragmented, activities and strategies into their teaching, and they cite time constraints and scripted programs as the reason for not taking time to listen to every student's voice. They realize that they are missing opportunities to invite the learner into the lesson, yet they struggle to see how providing such opportunities will translate to greater learning outcomes. In this book, we challenge teachers to think of the "activation" of background knowledge systems (Herrera, Kavimandan, & Holmes, 2011) as a nonnegotiable phase of the lesson that validates the potential of every learner. The process of activating and accessing students' background knowledge throughout the lesson is as important as interaction during the lesson and assessment of student learning at the end of the lesson.

We ask teachers to re-envision the opening moments of a lesson, moving beyond the typical KWL (know/want to know/learned), picture walk, or whole-group response to visuals and toward strategies that provide insights into every child's multiple layers of background knowledge. Applying strategies that provide a forum for every student to be an active participant at the beginning of the lesson increases the likelihood that teachers will use what students already know to take every learner to the zone of proximal development (Vygotsky, 1978), as well as to validate, respect, and invite every learner into the lesson. When teachers have knowledge of what students know both in and out of school, they are better prepared to create conditions and situations that scaffold learning socioculturally, linguistically, cognitively, and academically.

Biopsychosocial Histories, Communication, and Cognition in Action

Grounded in the communicative and cognitive approaches of teaching and learning, the biography-driven instruction (BDI) method (Herrera, 2016) situates teaching and learning within the biopsychosocial histories of the learner and the teacher. That is, it asks teachers to consider the biological, psychological, and sociological influences at play for each person in the classroom learning community (Herrera, Cabral, & Murry, 2013). Student learning is a complex and dynamic process that has been the focus of study for hundreds of years. Science and practice-based theory has documented core or foundational principles for effective instruction within any classroom setting. Among these is the need to be student centered (Dewey, 1938; Marzano &

Toth, 2014; Tomlinson et al., 2003), to build relationships (Boston & Baxley, 2014; Guthrie, Rueda, Gambrell, & Morrison, 2009; Noddings, 2005; Sleeter, 2011) and contextualize instruction within the lived experiences of the learner (Gay, 2010; Tharp & Dalton, 2007; Wyatt, 2015). These are just a few of the first critical concepts that teachers need to understand in order to be effective in classroom practice. Who the student is, where he or she comes from, and how she or he fits into the culture of the school are essential factors to understand before effective lessons can be planned and delivered.

Building on the work of Thomas and Collier (e.g., 1995, 1997), Herrera and Murry have developed the concept of the *CLD student biography* (see Herrera, 2016; Herrera, Cabral, & Murry 2013; Herrera & Murry, 2016; Herrera, Perez, & Escamilla, 2014). This concept accounts for the challenges and processes associated with each of the four dimensions of the student: the sociocultural, linguistic, cognitive, and academic dimensions. These dimensions are interrelated and influence the individual child's way of viewing, interpreting, and interacting in the world. Biography-driven lessons incorporate structured opportunities for students to articulate their perspectives and to make connections between the past and their present learning. Because lessons are connected to each dimension of students' biographies, they promote lasting, meaningful links to the content and language as well as students' future applications of learning. Following is a brief overview of each of the dimensions of the CLD student biography.

Sociocultural Dimension

The sociocultural dimension is at the heart of the CLD student's biography, as it reflects the student's funds of knowledge (home) and prior knowledge (community). It consists of the intersection between social institutions (e.g., home, school), affective influences (e.g., self-esteem, anxiety, motivation), and social interactive phenomena (e.g., bias, prejudice, discrimination). In short, the sociocultural dimension is about a student's life, love, and laughter (Herrera, 2016).

Socioculturally, the family and community in which the CLD student is being raised have a huge impact on how he or she initially defines literacy (Herrera et al., 2014). For example, a CLD student raised in a family where oral story-telling practices are woven into the fabric of traditions is no less literate than a student who spends hours each week at the library. Educators in schools, where the tapestry of learners is as rich and as varied as the stories they know, must begin to define "literacy" in ways beyond the act of reading from a book.

Teachers in biography-driven classrooms respect students for the varied backgrounds they bring and provide all learners with a "canvas of opportunity" for sharing the literacy opportunities they have at home. These opportunities may include visual representations of knowledge and learning. At the opening of the lesson, during the lesson, and at the close of the lesson students are provided with multiple opportunities to "make public" their connections to the academic language and content being taught. Students' depth of understanding thus becomes transparent not only for the learner but also for the teacher, who can then use these insights to guide each learner to higher levels of linguistic and academic development. In short, a teacher's working knowledge of the sociocultural dimension is contingent upon the classroom conditions that he or she creates to encourage students to share their knowledge and experiences and know that such contributions will be respected, valued, and built upon in the learning process.

Linguistic Dimension

Educational perspectives that overlook or minimize the role of students' linguistic assets in their development of English language proficiency and learning have led to classroom practices such as "teaching to the test" and drill-and-practice techniques to increase language knowledge, vocabulary development, and conceptual understanding. Tests and more tests have been developed to monitor, sometimes on a weekly basis, the language growth of English language learners. Such an emphasis on testing leads to a narrowed curricular focus and frequently results in students remaining at the lower levels of thinking and learning. Resulting classroom practices do little to maximize L1 (native language) to L2 (target language, English) transfer, rarely allow students to use their native language to build a conceptual foundation for learning, and seldom focus on meaningful interaction. A shift in thinking can open doors for educators to understand how the native language, which is intertwined with a student's culture, influences how students comprehend, communicate, and express their knowledge, their process thinking, and themselves.

The native language reflects the core of each student, as it is the vehicle he or she first used to communicate and express his or her needs. Depending on the individual school and classroom, this native language is either acknowledged and validated as an essential part of the CLD student biography or is ignored and disregarded based on the belief that it inhibits the student's acquisition of English. However, research has shown that when the native language is used as a foundation for English language development, we are able to accelerate our students' acquisition of English (Collier & Thomas, 2009; Cummins, 1981, 1989; Thomas & Collier, 2002, 2012). By encouraging students to draw upon their native language in their academic endeavors, we affirm their personal identities, support their expression of content understanding and learning, and promote the cross-linguistic transfer of literacy knowledge and skills needed to comprehend academic, grade-level curricula (Cummins, 1989; Herrera, 2016; Herrera et al., 2014; Thomas & Collier, 2012).

Key aspects of any language that shape literacy development and that have implications for learning (Herrera et al., 2014) include the following:

- *Phonology.* The sounds of the native language, which may or may not exist in the English language.
- *Syntax.* The order in which words are put together in the native language, which again can be very different from English word order.
- *Morphology.* The structure of words and the meaning of word parts.
- *Semantics.* The meaning of words in context.

Knowing about each of these aspects can support us as we approach literacy instruction with CLD students. This knowledge provides us with a backdrop for understanding how students use language to articulate their views, pose questions, and comprehend what is being communicated or taught. The art of observing the student's ways of knowing and how this knowledge is expressed or made public has the potential to teach us about the cognitive paths the learner is taking. With these insights, we can better orchestrate instruction to ensure that each learner has the linguistic support necessary to achieve each lesson's goals.

Cognitive Dimension

The cognitive dimension highlights how students know, think, and apply. As defined by Gipe (2014), cognition refers to "the nature of knowing, or the ways of organizing and understanding our experiences" (p. 5). The lived experiences of CLD students vary greatly and dramatically influence the way they make sense of the world. For example, the lived experiences of a CLD student who has fled his country with a parent due to religious persecution are very different from those of a CLD student who was born and raised in the United States. Understanding how the experiences lived by each of these students provide him or her with a unique lens for interpreting events and information is critical.

As a result of individual differences in how they know and think, students also differ in the way they learn and apply new knowledge. Consider the varied responses students might provide if asked to summarize a passage of text. Each student, based on how he or she knows and thinks about the topic, might perceive certain details to be of greater or lesser importance. Each of these processes—knowing, thinking, and applying—is influenced by the funds of knowledge, prior knowledge, and academic knowledge specific to each individual student.

- *Funds of knowledge* relate to "those historically developed and accumulated strategies (e.g., skills, abilities, ideas, practices) or bodies of knowledge that are essential to a household's functioning and well-being" (ERIC Clearinghouse on Languages and Linguistics, 1994, p. 1; see also Greenberg, 1989; Moll, Amanti, Neff, & Gonzalez, 1992; Vélez-Ibáñez & Greenberg, 1992).
- *Prior knowledge* relates to the knowledge that students gain through their interactions with the community or communities in which they live and through their environments, including the natural world, recreational reading, television, and the Internet.
- *Academic knowledge* relates to the school-bound skills and knowledge students gain through their academic experiences in the United States, as well as those in the country of origin (or any other country in which the student received education). Students can also gain academic knowledge in unconventional ways, such as through informal apprenticeships. For example, a student who learns how to build a house from a parent might possess cognitive skills that can support him or her in solving mathematical problems. (*Note:* The same student may or may not have the academic vocabulary needed to verbally express the mathematical reasoning and problem-solving processes.)

Together, these existing knowledge systems make up a student's *background knowledge,* and they create unique pathways for the learner (Herrera, 2016).

Educators often talk about learning styles and learning strategies, yet we seldom connect how each of these may be molded by the language, culture, experiences, and academic background of the learner. Taking students to the zone of proximal development (Vygotsky, 1978) in the classroom requires us to ensure that they have a certain level of "struggle" and challenge. This constructive imbalance requires the learner to use all available pathways—new and old—to solve the problem. Learning results when students take information and make it their own. Our reward as teachers comes from seeing the student make meaning of the information and use it for more than simply answering a question on a test! Academic success begins with students knowing that they have learned something and that the effort they have put in was worthwhile.

Academic Dimension

The academic dimension of the CLD student biography encompasses students' access, engagement, and hope. It relates to both present and past school experiences, educational and support programs, and curricula that have played a part in a student's education. The climate of the educational settings in which a student has participated—as well as the attitudes, perspectives, and expectations of teachers—help form a student's perceptions about his or her abilities and place in school. Such factors play a pivotal role in the student's motivation to engage in the learning process. They also affect whatever degree of hope the learner has that his or her effort will lead to English language development and academic achievement.

When it comes to literacy development, the academic dimension plays a particularly pertinent role. Academic literacy, as defined by Gipe (2014), is the instructional literacy children have been exposed to through personal experiences with books and other forms of written or spoken language. Often students come with academic knowledge that is discounted because it was taught using ways that differ from those currently dictated. Frequently, math teachers will comment, "Students can get the correct answer, but they cannot show the steps we are required to check." In a similar way, students' academic knowledge in science is not tapped into or used to bridge to the current curriculum. As a result, students are left feeling as though they are blank slates. As noted in our discussion of the sociocultural dimension of the CLD student biography, many CLD students may not have experienced the more traditional exposure to "text" that is recognized within the U.S. public school setting. Yet literacy development and academic learning that are guided and supported by the teacher's reflective actions, selection of materials, and orchestration of the community of learners have the potential to lead to the type of learning that is always moving students forward.

The Framework: Activating, Connecting, and Affirming Student Learning

In this book we provide a framework that serves as an overlay to lesson planning and a guide for lesson delivery. The framework is intended to help stimulate a discussion among paraprofessionals, ESL teachers, content-area teachers, administrators, and other educators regarding academic vocabulary development, comprehension, and the acceleration of literacy and academic achievement for *all* students. The framework is meant to be descriptive rather than prescriptive, as it is not meant to replace existing curricular programs but rather to provide tools that more explicitly bring CLD students into the learning equation. The framework further provides the essential elements necessary to be a culturally responsive educator. Toward this end, we describe what we see as essential processes of effective instruction through presentation of specific actions that take place throughout three phases that make up the lesson.

Our framework supports attainment of learning goals throughout the following three phases of linguistic and academic development within the lesson: Activation, Connection, and Affirmation. These phases of development align with the three general stages of the lesson: opening, work time, and closing. Each phase is action oriented toward achieving the goals of activating and documenting students' background knowledge, utilizing what is produced to make connections to new content, and using artifacts to affirm linguistic and academic growth.

Activation: A Canvas of Opportunity

In the *Activation* phase (opening of the lesson), the goal is to create a risk-free environment for our students so they can draw from their funds of knowledge, prior knowledge, and academic knowledge and identify links to the lesson. From the outset, we must create conditions that encourage learners to take risks at their own pace without being judged for their linguistic variations or background knowledge. The first step in creating opportunities to make public what is known in relation to the stated objective is to let go of our assumption as teachers that our students could not possibly be able to produce anything that would be of value. At this time, group configurations reflect our consideration of the biographies of the students who will come together to share before anything new is introduced. We use our knowledge of students' cognitive and academic dimensions to consider differences in academic readiness. We also take into account possible differences in student perspectives resulting from influences of culture and community. Value and respect for one another are critical at this point, when student expression is the goal. Throughout this phase we assume the role of strategic observer, taking in whatever students share and internally brainstorming ways we might be able to connect students' thoughts and ideas with the lesson.

By introducing the topic or vocabulary using visuals and specific strategies that activate students' background knowledge, we provide students with the opportunity to make public both their experiential and academic knowledge. A risk-free environment allows all students to represent what they know in words and/or in pictures and to use whatever language(s) are available as resources to express what they know. By documenting what every student knows and thinks, we make the information available for incorporation into the lesson. By using student voice for explanation of new vocabulary and revealing connections between what students have shared and the lesson text, we promote greater levels of engagement and academic achievement. To motivate and engage learners, Activation first lets them see themselves as contributors to the lesson. Our responsibility as teachers is to be aware of what has been shared and to hold ourselves accountable for using that information in constructive ways throughout the lesson.

Connection: The Broad and Narrow Strokes of Learning

In the *Connection* phase (work time of the lesson), we act as facilitators in students' construction of meaning and knowledge. Student knowledge/words from the Activation phase are explicitly called out by the teacher to serve as links to the new lesson. This foundational knowledge and language support student connections to new vocabulary and concepts as well as their progress toward meeting the expected outcomes of the lesson. In this phase, we as teachers orchestrate the teaching–learning process by balancing individual students' biographies (identified assets and needs), learning goals/objectives, and the community of learners. Selecting strategies that support this orchestration has the potential for decreasing the frustration that many teachers have with prescriptive programs, limited time frames, and communities of learners with diverse language and academic needs. Supporting students in making connections involves actions by the teacher that balance rigor, relevance, and biography.

As we teach and students negotiate their learning through talk and writing, we revoice (reiterate for the entire class) the connections they make between their background knowledge and the content. Discussed in depth later in this chapter, revoicing helps to ensure that all students receive the comprehensible input they need to achieve language acquisition (Krashen, 1985) as well as the cognitive and academic challenge they need to be stretched (via their zone of proximal development; Vygotsky, 1978) to their highest learning potential. We confirm/disconfirm students' understandings of the relationships among content concepts and related academic vocabulary. We are able to model for students our own ways of approaching a task, thinking about a passage of text, or relating a vocabulary term to existing schemas. Through the strategies that we as teachers select, students are able to practice and apply various cognitive, metacognitive, and social/affective learning strategies, individually and with peers. Students come to understand which strategies can be used to achieve specific

purposes. As a result, students are better able to internalize the strategies and apply procedural knowledge regarding their use to future applications within and across content areas.

Affirmation: A Gallery of Understanding

In the *Affirmation* phase (closing of the lesson), students need to have evidence of what they have learned throughout the lesson. A strategy that has been used through all three phases of the lesson to ensure that the language and academic building blocks produced by students are documented provides such evidence of vocabulary/language growth and conceptual understanding. Positive self-concept related to learning, for many students, does not come from grades or periodic positive statements. Rather, it comes from frequent words of affirmation and application of authentic assessments that evaluate what students have gained from the lesson. This type of assessment is both formative during the lesson and summative at the end of the lesson. Effective strategies can serve as tools for documenting both language and academic growth for every student. Students who are guided to make decisions about what is important throughout the lesson, and who are explicitly provided evidence of what they have learned at the end of the lesson, are more likely to be engaged and motivated to continue learning in the future.

The Strategies Versus Activities Debate

On a daily basis, teachers sift through innumerable strategies in order to provide meaningful input to students. Some of the common ones teachers report using are visuals, modeling, round-robin reading, chunking, highlighting, graphic organizers, Cornell notes, picture walks, turn and talk, and Kagan structures (often used as strategies). In this section, we aim to enter into a dialogue with our fellow teachers on some of the unique characteristics of strategies as tools for learning. During our interactions with teachers, our conversations often revolve around lesson planning, lesson cycles, and most importantly the use of strategies. We regularly pose questions regarding the ways teachers use strategies throughout the lesson cycle, namely during the opening, work time, and closing of the lesson. Most teachers are able to share the different strategies that are being used during different parts of the lesson; however, what they are not able to articulate is how the same strategy evolves throughout the lesson to give students a connected pathway for learning and understanding.

We all likely have had the experience of going to professional development sessions and carrying back bags full of strategies with us. We brainstorm how we might include this or that strategy in the classroom the next day or the next week. We might even engage in self-talk that sounds something like: *If I do this strategy with my students, then . . .* Or, *When I do this strategy, I will . . .* As you read about strategies in this section, ask yourself: *Do I consider my students' learning and growth as a by-product of* my teaching, *or do I consider students' learning and growth as a by-product of the way the lesson unfolded and the* teaching and learning processes *that took place?*

What's in a Name?

Within the field of education, there is great inconsistency in the use of terms such as *strategies, techniques, activities, methods,* and so forth. This can lead to confusion among educators as we engage in larger conversations focused on pedagogy and instruction. More importantly, this inconsistency can result in fragmented, limited opportunities for our students to engage with the language and content of our curricula. In an effort to be transparent about our own views regarding how to plan and implement effective lessons in CLD classrooms, we would like to differentiate between strategies and activities.

BDI strategies provide our students with a road map and guidance *throughout* the lesson. The different actions/processes/activities that we include during the life cycle of the strategy are what make learning meaningful and the content comprehensible for our learners. Strategies are more than just isolated tools and structures used to teach a skill or accomplish a task. Instead, strategies are process-oriented frames that make possible the public exchange of ideas among the teacher(s) and students in the classroom community from the onset of the lesson. Through this dynamic interplay of action and response, teachers and students become reciprocal partners in learning. When strategies are implemented as process-oriented tools, a teacher's orchestration of the lesson consistently focuses on being responsive to students' behaviors, cognitive processing, and evolving needs.

In a lesson where strategies of this type are used to guide instruction, opportunities for interaction are naturally built in. Student grouping structures are geared to promote the exchange of knowledge, experiences, and information as part of high-level academic conversations among students. The teacher's use of strategies is intentional and well thought out. Students see the strategy as a springboard to interact with challenging questions being posed by the teacher and inquiries of real importance to the classroom of learners.

Strategies of this kind allow us to yield (or stop altogether) in response to challenges that might arise for stu-

dents. As teachers, our close observation of students and their learning processes alerts us to the need to modify what we are doing or change course on the way to our destination. Students frequently give us signs that additional opportunities to talk with a partner or negotiate the meaning of a concept with a small group are needed. When we see the strategy as a medium that guides the flow of the lesson and provides a structure for overall lesson implementation, we see that the purpose of these opportunities (activities) is to continually move us—our entire learning community—in the direction of achieving our lesson objectives.

Activities, on the other hand, are point-in-time tools that teachers use in the classroom to provide learners with opportunities to explore alternative perspectives on a topic, negotiate the meaning of a concept, and practice key vocabulary. They are included to help learners briefly exchange information and extend upon their understanding. Activities also allow students to explore applications of learning within the safe context of partner or small-group work. We use different activities as implementation components of the larger intentional strategy that is guiding our overall lesson.

Because we are creatures that crave novelty, it is easy at times to get students to participate in new activities that deviate from our standard instruction. Perhaps these activities even incorporate cooperation and talk among students. Yet, we must challenge ourselves to consider the honest answers to questions such as the following:

- How does the activity require my students to think more deeply and critically about the content?
- In what ways does the activity incorporate scaffolds to ensure that all students can engage from their unique linguistic, sociocultural, and academic vantage points?
- How does the activity require students to collaborate with one another in ways that ensure that each member is an equal contributor to the learning process?
- What products or evidence will result from the activity that the students and the teacher can then use to move learning forward?
- How does the activity prompt students to reflect on their use of resources (background knowledge, peers, standard curricular materials and text, real world materials, Internet, etc.) to support their personal learning?

On the other hand, we often are quick to dismiss students' lack of excitement in the class as a lack of overall motivation or desire to engage in a particular classroom activity. What we fail to reflect upon is whether the implementation of the many actions during the course of the lesson gives students opportunities

- To bring forth the knowledge, skills, and experiences they came equipped with,
- To discuss with others and exercise their critical thinking about the topic and the relationship between the topic and their own lives, and
- To reflect on their learning process, including the effectiveness of the learning strategy(ies) they used to reach their goals.

Taken together, these objectives might sound daunting. However, if we were to step back and take a moment to reflect upon the three types of opportunities we need to provide for students, we would realize that they are not new. These goals, supported by research, are goals that we as teachers have held for ourselves for some time. We acknowledge that children enter school, and our own classrooms, with personal histories and particular strengths. Our job as teachers is to recognize these assets and use them as foundations for our students' learning. Strategies provide us with the mechanism for ensuring that the teaching–learning process truly is reciprocal, responsive to students' needs, relevant to the learner, and effective in meeting our goals for language, literacy, and academic development.

Meeting of the Minds: Students and Teachers as Equal Partners

Teachers are experts on their content areas; students are experts on their lives. The student and the teacher each possess knowledge and understandings that the other needs to reach the common goal of personal and professional (in the case of the student, academic) success. As discussed earlier in this chapter, before teachers can expect their students to gain the targeted concepts, vocabulary, and academic language from a given lesson, they must first activate students' existing knowledge. The teacher then helps students make connections between their existing knowledge and the new content. The teacher supports learners as they extend their understandings and, as necessary, reroutes them to accurate understandings. Vygotsky (1978) asserts the importance of collaboration and interaction among peers during this process. He conceptualizes the *zone of proximal development* as the most effective instructional level, which is attained when the learner is stretched beyond his or her current independent level of skill through the help and interaction of more capable peers (along with the teacher). Similarly, Krashen (1985) uses the term *i+1* to describe the developmental process of language acquisition, whereby the learner begins at a particular level ("i") and is able to move to the next stage of development ("+1") when provided with comprehensible input. Building on the work of Krashen, we have adopted his "i" to identify the level of the student and used it to represent the "i"ndividual student biography.

Teachers who strive to provide students with comprehensible input frequently shelter their instruction by using the traditional components of hands-on activities, cooperative learning, guarded vocabulary, and visuals (Herrera & Murry, 2016). Although these instructional components have potential for making content more comprehensible at the surface level, they generally are insufficient for helping CLD students connect with the academic vocabulary and concepts on a personal level. Such individual schematic connections—or links to a student's sociocultural, linguistic, cognitive, and academic biography—are essential to a student's full understanding and ownership of the material (N. J. Anderson, 1999; Donovan & Bransford, 2005; Herrera et al., 2014; Maria, 1990; Rumelhart, 1980; Sousa, 2011).

Traditional methods of providing second language learners with comprehensible input can also fall short of developing students' academic literacy skills needed for success in grade-level and content-area classrooms (Calderón, 2007). This means that students must acquire academic vocabulary. Without such vocabulary, CLD students are prevented from full participation in the curriculum, and their ability to discuss, interpret, analyze, critique, debate, and apply concepts (both orally and in writing) is hindered.

What is needed, then, is a re-envisioning of what it means to provide students with comprehensible input. The previously referenced means of providing comprehensible input, along with others that are discussed in the following section, must be implemented in the context of the CLD student biography and with the explicit intent to build understanding. The framework modeled in this book is grounded in the notion of transformative comprehensible input provided throughout the opening, work time, and closing phases of the lesson. As you read the strategies presented in this book, you will see many references to using visuals, grouping, guarded vocabulary, and hands-on activities. Through the incorporation of photos and real-world examples, we have attempted to help you experience what these four components of comprehensible input look, feel, and sound like in classroom practice when they are used to maximize learning!

Transformative Comprehensible Input

Krashen (2009) reminds us that even more than planning to provide *comprehensible* input, we need to think about the actions necessary to ensure *comprehended* input. The end result of comprehension is what's at stake for our students. Our language will inherently include $i+1$ structures if we work together with our students to arrive at mutual understanding. Through the use of strategies we can achieve truly comprehensible input. However, the BDI strategies have to be used intentionally throughout the lesson to help students activate their existing understanding, move toward greater knowledge about the content, develop greater facility with the English language, and reflect upon their progress and overall learning process.

To ensure that instruction promotes students' personal connections to the content and acquisition of academic language and vocabulary, teachers can employ strategic grouping configurations, revoice students' connections, and confirm/disconfirm learning throughout the instructional process. Each of these processes is foundational to facilitating a learning community that works together to achieve together, utilizing the strengths of each member to advance understanding. Walqui (2000) describes an effective classroom environment as one in which "teachers and students together construct a culture that values the strengths of all participants and respects their interests, abilities, languages, and dialects. Students and teachers shift among the roles of expert, researcher, learner, and teacher, supporting themselves and each other" (p. 1). Our goal, then, is to create within our classroom a true community of learners.

Group Configurations That Teach

Planning for and using student groups to move the lesson forward requires teachers to be active/intentional facilitators, always considering the *why* in relation to student processing. The use of various group structures (e.g., partner, small group) and the configuration of those student arrangements (i.e., which students are placed together) are guided by the learning goals/objectives of the lesson and the situational talk that happens as a result of how students are processing what they are learning.

The strategies in this book use the acronym $i+TpsI$ (pronounced "I plus tipsy") to help teachers think about the "ebb and flow" of classroom talk. These opportunities for talk encompass moving from learner (i = individual) to teacher, teacher to learners (T = teacher-directed, text-driven, total-group), student to student (p = pairs/partners), and students in groups (s = small teams) debating, discussing, rationalizing, and coming to consensus on learning. Throughout the lesson cycle, the teacher serves as a guide, scribe, facilitator, and supporter of student and classroom discourse. By the end of the lesson, individual students (I) are equipped to apply the new material in personally meaningful ways while demonstrating individual accountability.

When planning for student groups, teachers can reflect on each dimension of the CLD student biography by considering the following types of questions:

Sociocultural

- How can I maximize students' possible leadership and decision-making skills resulting from the roles they play in their families?
- How might each student's possible knowledge of community resources and challenges be used to make real-world applications to the text or lesson?
- How can I draw upon the insights that students might bring based on their countries of origin and/or knowledge of international travel?

Linguistic

- How can I best utilize and develop my students' levels of English language proficiency?
- How will I allow for cross-linguistic insights to be shared among the students given their native language proficiencies?
- How might I consider students' preferred modes of expression?

Cognitive

- How can I allow for cross-cultural perspectives on processes or events to be shared by students so that a deeper level of understanding is gained?
- How might I encourage students to use their inductive or deductive reasoning skills?
- How will I structure student groups to enhance learners' creative and imaginative thinking (and thereby enhance group motivation)?

Academic

- How can I maximize students' family literacy practices to make the process of academic vocabulary development more relevant?
- How will I provide opportunities for students' academic knowledge gained in another country to be used in the class's construction of knowledge?
- How might I encourage students to make text-to-text or text-to-world connections?

Putting students together in ways that advance each learner's holistic development requires "on-your-toes" thinking and planning and continual observation of student responses to evolving learning situations. Our responsiveness to students as we consider their biographies and the learning goals during lesson delivery becomes part of our habits of mind.

Revoicing Student Connections

Revoicing is the act of observing students, listening to what they have to say, and re-uttering their understanding by repeating, rephrasing, expanding upon, summarizing, and reporting what was shared (Forman, Larreamendy-Joerns, Stein, & Brown, 1998; Herrera, 2016; Krussel, Springer, & Edwards, 2004; Kwon, Ju, Rasmussen, Park, & Cho, 2008). Teachers also can revoice student gestures, as this type of revoicing broadens the discussion for the class, especially for those whose current level of English proficiency makes it difficult for them to fully articulate their thoughts (Shein, 2012). Revoicing allows teachers to combine their content-area expertise with their knowledge of individual students in order to help students successfully navigate the grade-level content and academic vocabulary. Although teachers can use revoicing throughout the lesson, it is predominantly employed as an instructional tool in the work time phase. Through revoicing, teachers acknowledge students' background knowledge and then use these insights as well as new learning to scaffold students' thinking to a greater depth of understanding.

As students share from their lived experiences and bring their funds of knowledge, prior knowledge, and academic knowledge into the public realm of the classroom, they look to their peers and their teacher for assurance that what they know is important to the construction of meaning. Revoicing acknowledges each student's membership in the intellectual community and has the potential to increase the individual's self-esteem (O'Connor & Michaels, 1996). Teachers use revoicing to help solidify and expand upon students' schematic connections to the content and vocabulary. They further use revoicing as the lesson progresses to make critical connections between concepts and the language and ideas produced by students. This repetition of key conceptual relationships, academic terms, and language structures in the context of natural discussion provides students with opportunities to hear and comprehend the concepts, vocabulary, and language multiple times and from multiple perspectives.

Confirming/Disconfirming Student Learning

Teachers confirm and disconfirm learning in the work time and closing phases of the lesson to validate students' thinking and effort while redirecting them where needed. During the lesson, teachers are continually assessing students in informal ways to gauge their understanding of the content and related vocabulary. The manner in which we disconfirm learning is especially critical. We must strive to disconfirm misconceptions in ways that uphold the dignity of the student and encourage community members to learn from one another. We need to sensitively identify building blocks of student knowledge that can continue to be used in the construction of a more accurate understanding. In this way, we help students celebrate their incremental gains toward mastery of the content and language.

At the end of the lesson, teachers use authentic assessments to document what students have learned. In doing so, they continue to keep in mind the CLD student biography. They consider the varied starting points of each individual learner. Progress matters! Every additional piece of knowledge constructed, each additional vocabulary word committed to memory, and each additional instructional strategy that the student incorporates into his or her own bag of *learning strategies* becomes another piece the CLD student can then use for future learning. Documenting student learning throughout the lesson provides both the student and the teacher with concrete evidence of what was gained.

Putting All the Pieces Together

The BDI strategies described in this book follow the Activate–Connect–Affirm framework and support the core of teachers' biography-driven lesson delivery by accomplishing the following:

- Inviting learners into the lesson by providing a canvas of opportunity that allows all students to be active contributors in the classroom community.
- Providing the teacher with words/information from each student's background knowledge (funds of knowledge, prior knowledge, and academic knowledge) to use during the lesson.
- Providing the teacher with a frame for creating opportunities for interaction and academic talk throughout the lesson.
- Supporting students with a tool in their hand that they can use for engaging with others and building academic vocabulary and conceptual knowledge.
- Providing the teacher with concrete evidence of students' processing and learning throughout the lesson.
- Scaffolding students' participation in the lesson and ownership of their learning process.
- Incorporating tools that the teacher can use to authentically assess and celebrate student progress and achievement.

To illustrate how all of the components of a BDI strategy work together to ensure the student's and teacher's shared responsibility and mutual accountability for learning, Figure 1 provides an overview of the DOTS strategy (see pages 68–78 for detailed exploration of this strategy).

FIGURE 1
DOTS Strategy

I am responsible to . . .

DETERMINE   OBSERVE   TALK   SUMMARIZE, SOLVE, SYNTHESIZE

When: Before, During, & After

How: Activate, Connect, Affirm

STUDENT (D)
- Determine what I know about the topic/vocabulary before the lesson starts
- Decide what I am learning during the lesson to document what is important as evidence of my learning
- Evaluate what I learned and how I learned it

STUDENT (O)
- Observe for clues the teacher provides on what is important and relevant
- As I read the text, be observant for what the message is and what meaning I bring to the text
- Use selective attention and document my observations, as evidence of what I have learned and where I found the information

STUDENT (T)
- Use the tool as a resource to
- Use the vocabulary to discuss my conceptual understanding
- Listen to others and clarify by asking questions
- Consider others' perspectives
- Build consensus
- Plan, elaborate, clarify, and make connections

STUDENT (S)
- Use the tool as a resource to summarize, solve, and/or synthesize the information in writing in order to share what I have learned

TEACHER (D)
Determine what the student knows—before, during, and after the lesson—by activating, connecting, and affirming knowledge/assets from all knowledge systems. Use the information for *i* +1 (language) and ZPD (academic development) through instructional conversations

TEACHER (O)
- Observe affective filters and information processing by continuously using the DOTS chart to formatively assess
- Use the vocabulary, student talk, and student notes for decision making about scaffolds that would support student learning in the moment

TEACHER (T)
- Set conditions for academic talk to occur (intentional)
- Select structures and grouping configurations that are intentional and based on the needs of each learner
- Provide structured opportunities as springboards for academic talk, and ask higher-order questions based on student processing of information
- Use the tool to revoice using the students' words
- Make meaningful links for the classroom community using the students' words

TEACHER (S)
Use the tool as a resource to help students summarize, solve, and/or synthesize the information in writing to provide meaningful opportunities to share what has been learned

12

DOTS begins with all students working to individually *determine* ("**D**") what they know about the topic by documenting their background knowledge using the A–Z boxes of the DOTS chart. In this Activation phase, students record their ideas using words (in the native language and/or in English) and pictures. These multiple points of entry to the topic allow all students to engage in the lesson. From what students produce, teachers likewise determine which points might best be highlighted to support connections to the content and make instruction relevant for learners.

As the class gets into the Connection phase of the lesson, students *observe* ("**O**") for key points and ways that the target vocabulary words are used in context. They document the connections they make to the text, knowing that these notes will continue to support their meaning-making processes throughout the lesson. They also draw lines on their DOTS charts to link the words and ideas from their background knowledge to the key vocabulary of the lesson in order to demonstrate how their new understandings build upon the knowledge they brought to the lesson. Similarly, the teacher's close observation of student learning provides insights into the ways individual students are processing and making sense of the information. The results of this ongoing formative assessment support the teacher in differentiating and scaffolding instruction.

Student and teacher *talk* ("**T**") also is essential in the Connection phase as well as the remainder of the lesson. Students share their perspectives and collaborate with peers in pairs and small teams, using their DOTS charts as personalized scaffolds for learning. The teacher listens to students' conversations and continues to observe for links that they document on their learning tool. The teacher uses instructional conversations and revoices student connections and ideas in order to affirm understanding, clarify misconceptions, and advance the learning of the entire class.

In the Affirmation phase, the completed DOTS chart becomes a tool that students use to support them as they *summarize*, solve, and synthesize ("**S**") their learning. They complete authentic writing and other tasks that allow them to demonstrate what they have learned, linguistically and academically. Teachers also use the DOTS chart to support students' development of metacognitive skills, challenging students to reflect on their learning process and consider how their background knowledge provided a foundation for their continued learning. Together, the members of the classroom community are able to celebrate their collective progress and new understandings, given the evidence of growth demonstrated through the multiple activities of the strategy.

All of the BDI strategies provided in this book are designed to support the same sort of reciprocal flow of action between the teacher and the students. Because our ability to be culturally responsive in our instruction first requires students to *produce* something (talk, writing, drawings) to which we can then respond, a safe, nonthreatening environment is central to the success of these strategies. Moreover, the tools that students use to support their learning are just that—*their* tools. The ways in which students make sense of the curriculum will not match our own. We each draw upon our unique biography-based schemas to construct meaning and interpret the world.

Transformative Thinking: Letting Go of Our Socialized Self

The journey of becoming a competent culturally responsive (at times referred to as *culturally relevant* or *critical care*) teacher requires a shift in paradigm that often contradicts the culture or political agenda of schools in which we educators find ourselves. As we move forward in a sea of diversity, our response to the moral imperative to challenge the models of the past is what will set us apart from those who continue to teach the same way they were prepared for in college and taught in schools. Key to the success of culturally and linguistically diverse students is removing the barriers that have long stood in the way of their academic engagement and achievement. This begins with educators taking the time to get to know their students and shaping their teaching around what they learn from their community of learners (Sleeter, 2011).

Preparation for becoming a culturally responsive educator, not only in thought but also in action, requires us to audit our own histories by examining *what* we think and *why* we think it. That is, we must critically reflect on our own socialization in and out of school (Herrera, 2016; Herrera & Murry, 2016). We each carry our own meaning perspectives related to what is possible. We either do our best to move these forward through our efforts to create more caring and effective classrooms, or we stay stuck in the often debilitating language of school cultures and the sociopolitical climate that surrounds us.

Meaning perspectives are a product of prior socialization, particularly our primary socialization in our home culture and language, but also our secondary and tertiary socialization in societal institutions. The schools we attended and the preservice program through which we received our professional preparation are the primary influences that have framed our thinking about what it means to be a teacher. At the end of the day, we become teachers in systems that either support or hinder our professionalism—and sometimes they do a little of both! Regardless, we choose how to navigate these difficult spaces in ways that will ensure that those who are most often marginalized by the type of education they receive become engaged in meaningful and authentic ways. Through our actions, our pedagogy and instructional practices can lift rather than limit CLD learners.

Taking up the challenge to turn possibilities into reality requires us to explore our capacities as professionals and our untested volition about what is best for kids, beginning with the methods, frameworks, strategies, and techniques that we use in classroom practice. Current agendas have scripted even the smallest aspects of what we do as teachers, sometimes down to the minute. The time has come to rise above the sociopolitical agendas, question and test the assumptions that derive from our socializations, and make decisions as professionals. When we move forward with an agenda that is not prescriptive but is grounded in emancipatory action, professionalism, and love for children as learners and as developing human beings, we can create shared spaces where our own passion for teaching is honored and all students thrive.

Conclusion

In these introductory remarks, we have tried to provide a glimpse into an educational context where thoughtful reflection is the cornerstone of teaching. There is a need for all of us to critically examine our own perspectives about the students we teach and the learning opportunities we provide in our classrooms. The strategies that follow are meant to be a starting point—a resource to use as you gain new insights into your learning community and create an environment where students can explore meaning and find ways to connect with text and with one another.

Any kind of strategy application must begin with an analysis of the students' needs and one's own site-specific realities. As you read each BDI strategy, contemplate how you might adapt the strategy or add your own creative spin to make it work for *your* students and *your* curriculum. We encourage you to make these strategies your own—reflecting upon your classroom at every step along the way and using the CLD student biography as the lens through which you view lesson planning, implementation, and assessment.

We encourage you to ask yourself: *How can I use these strategies to set conditions that lead to more academic talk and higher-order thinking through the use of challenging activities?* In our work, we have drawn from the Standards for Effective Pedagogy and Learning developed by the Center for Research on Education, Diversity & Excellence (e.g., CREDE, 2002, 2014). We encourage teachers to use strategies that lead to *joint productive activity* that involves teacher, students, and peers working jointly to produce evidence of learning and progress toward common learning goals. We strive to ensure that our classroom conditions and situations are driven by *instructional conversations* and the discourse that results by encouraging students to make their thinking public. We scaffold *challenging activities* that accelerate learning for all students, rather than remediating and dumbing down the curriculum. Finally, every lesson is grounded in *language and literacy development* and *contextualized* in the lives of the students we teach. Our research has documented the great promise that biography-driven instruction has for increasing the academic success of CLD learners. We are excited for you to try these strategies and experience for yourself the freedom and re-ignited passion for teaching that result when you create, imagine, dialogue, and construct knowledge alongside your community of learners.

PART II

BDI Strategies: Creating an Ecology of Care and Rigor

IN PART II, we provide the reader with strategies that can be used by K–8 educators to support CLD students in being confident and engaged contributors in their learning community. These strategies are designed to increase achievement by attending to the social/emotional dimension of learners while simultaneously accelerating students' language acquisition, vocabulary and literacy development, and content comprehension. The BDI strategies are powered by students' own experiences and knowledge and provide teachers with an action plan for implementing culturally responsive pedagogy in the context of daily lessons. The strategies are organized into three chapters:

* *Chapter 1: Images as Catalysts for Culturally Driven Connections.* This chapter includes strategies that use images to spark students' imaginations and ignite students' connections with their background knowledge (i.e., funds of knowledge, prior knowledge, and academic knowledge). These strategies also support students in developing visual literacy skills as they engage with the content they are studying.
* *Chapter 2: Rigor: Leveraging Words toward Academic Achievement.* This chapter includes strategies that guide students to greater depths of understanding related to content, language, and literacy. Students use hands-on tools to develop metacognitive skills and take ownership of their learning.
* *Chapter 3: Comprehension: It's Not Real Until It's Rehearsed and Written.* This chapter includes strategies that guide students to greater depths of understanding related to content, language, and literacy. Students use hands-on tools to develop metacognitive skills and take ownership of their learning.

The description of each strategy follows the same organization and includes the following introductory elements:

* *Strategy Artifact.* Each strategy elaboration begins with a photo that reflects a "moment in time" during implementation of the strategy.
* *Teacher Testimonial.* A K–8 teacher shares his or her thoughts regarding implementation of the strategy and its benefits for students.
* *Where Theory Meets Practice.* Each strategy is founded on key theories and current research regarding culturally responsive pedagogy, second language acquisition, literacy development, teaching/learning dynamics, and brain-based learning.
* *Materials and Resources.* A list of materials needed to perform each strategy is provided. Many strategies employ only basic classroom materials. For others, a template included in the strategy description is also used as a hands-on tool for students. Additional resources provided are also noted, including instructions for constructing tools used in the strategies, assessment rubrics and checklists, and video clips of strategy implementation.

The same guiding elements are provided for each strategy to help educators follow the flow of strategy activities. As described in Part I, the three phases of a lesson are *Activation* (opening), *Connection* (work time), and *Affirmation* (closing). In like manner, implementation of the strategies progresses through these three phases. For each phase, we provide:

* A separate set of directions.
* One or more visuals depicting a student artifact or student involvement related to the particular phase of strategy implementation.
* A reminder of the *i+TpsI* group configuration(s) used in that portion of the lesson. The *i+TpsI* mnemonic, as explained in Part I, reminds teachers to always

consider the sociocultural, linguistic, cognitive, and academic dimensions of their students' biographies when making decisions about opportunities for student interaction.

* A section that explains the benefits of the strategy activities for CLD students.

Where applicable, sections of "Author Talk" are also included to provide educators with opportunities for critical reflection on classroom practice as well as insights that teachers across the country have shared with us regarding practical adaptations and modifications of the strategy.

Finally, strategies include the following wrap-up elements:

* *Spotlight: Early Literacy Connection.* Some strategies include this feature, which demonstrates how the strategy can be used to promote CLD students' early experiences with oral language, reading, and writing. Because these experiences vary considerably from one child to another, this feature allows educators to promote important literacy connections in the home.
* *It's the "i" Thing.* Given the need to differentiate instruction for CLD students, this section appears in some strategies and highlights considerations for maximizing the strategy to address the unique needs of individual learners.
* *One Classroom's Perspective.* This element uses words and pictures to capture the progression of the strategy from one classroom's perspective. The featured teacher provides a first-hand description of his or her implementation of the strategy with students throughout the lesson to target the critical concepts, academic vocabulary, and learning objectives of the lesson.
* *Templates.* Some strategies require templates for use during the lesson. When applicable, the template specific to the strategy is provided at the end of the strategy description. The templates are also available for free download and printing from tcpress.com/accelerating.
* *Instructions.* Some strategies require construction of hands-on tools for use during the lesson. When applicable, detailed illustrated instructions for creation of these tools are provided.

* *Rubrics and Checklists.* Sample assessment tools for some strategies are provided in the Appendix. Student assessment rubrics and student academic behavior checklists are provided as examples of formative and summative assessments that can be created for use in conjunction with the strategies presented in this book. The rubrics and checklists are also available for free download and printing from tcpress.com/accelerating.
* *Video Clips of Exemplary Teaching.* Video clips highlighting teachers' implementation of selected strategies are available for viewing online at coe.k-state.edu/cima/biographycrt. Each clip illustrates an educator's use of a biography-driven strategy with diverse learners in a grade-level classroom. The clips exemplify the Activation, Connection, and Affirmation phases of the lesson. They provide an inside look at how teachers have used the strategies to meet the needs of individual learners in their site-specific classrooms. Just as no two classrooms are alike, the implementation of a particular strategy as modeled by the teacher in a video clip might not reflect how you would choose to implement the strategy with your learners. We challenge you to use the modeled strategies as a source of inspiration for your own ideas about how best to implement these strategies in your professional practice.

We realize that, for some teachers, the amount of information provided for each strategy may initially seem overwhelming. We also understand that some teachers prefer a "nutshell" overview of strategies they are considering for implementation with their particular group of learners. To accommodate the various needs and purposes of our readers, we have provided all information that is essential to carrying out each strategy in boxes with banners incorporating icons that reflect the gist of each phase: Activation (light bulb), Connection (links), Affirmation (applauding hands). We can assure you that everything you absolutely need is *in the boxes.* The full strategy description provides the elaboration, details, and nuances of classroom application that teachers are continually requesting when we share these strategies in the field. Use those elements that you find most applicable, return to others as needed, and share with other educators what works for you!

CHAPTER 1

Images as Catalysts for Culturally Driven Connections

THE STRATEGIES PRESENTED in this chapter explore the power of images as catalysts for students' vocabulary development, comprehension, critical thinking, and, most importantly, for their personally meaningful, culturally relevant associations to the content. The benefits of using visuals will come as no surprise to many teachers. Images have often been used in our schools and classrooms as a way to help students make connections, start conversations, and gain new vocabulary. Most packaged curricula being used in schools come with a wide array of visuals already aligned to a set of vocabulary words that are tied to a theme or a topic for the week. Teachers use these cards at the beginning of each lesson to pre-teach vocabulary and in some instances even to help students make associations to the larger context of the story or the content. However, what we hear from teachers is that the conversations that occur in classrooms through the use of these vocabulary word cards remain essentially inorganic and largely opaque because the conversations and the dialogue merely lead to regurgitation of information. Students can say what the image is and how it relates to the word. Oftentimes, a connection is already there and the students are merely copying the association between a particular word and its respective picture.

Where Do We Go From Here?

Let's consider a parallel scenario in which a teacher provides a visual to students and shares with them the topic of the lesson. From there, students are asked to use the images as true catalysts to jump-start their *individual* understanding of the topic. Students document their own connections to the visuals before having conversations on how a particular visual is connected to the topic/word/concept of the day or the week. Throughout this process, students connect to the visual at their own level. They interpret the visual through their own cultural and linguistic lens to find connections to their knowledge systems, which reflect the trove of experiences and knowledge gained through interactions within family, community, and school settings. Students are able to integrate their personal experiences and imagination with the social experiences of the classroom. Think of the rich academic conversations that occur when we have such a wealth of experiences to draw upon as we support students in developing multifaceted understandings of key words and concepts!

This process-oriented approach to using visuals capitalizes on the ability of our brain to read, interpret, and use information presented in pictorial or graphic images (such as visuals in books). It scaffolds tasks for our students by allowing them to engage with visuals from their own frame of reference, promoting connections to their individual schemas. Regardless of what a visual might mean to us, as teachers, it is what the visual means to *students* that we must document and use as a springboard for learning.

Because context is pivotal to our interpretation of visuals, the links that students make to visuals used at the beginning of the lesson will continue to evolve as they dig deeper into the content in the remainder of the lesson. The strategies included in this section highlight how visuals can be used through the life cycle of a strategy to scaffold students' interaction with the key concepts and vocabulary throughout the lesson. Classroom scenarios and instructional tips are provided to support you in bringing visuals to life as you explore the world through the curriculum with your community of learners.

Picturing the Path to Visual Literacy

According to Tillmann (2012), visual literacy generally refers to the capacity to "understand, apply, analyze, evaluate and create visual material as essential parts of a whole" (p. 9). Simply put, visual literacy includes the ability to "think, learn, and express oneself in images" (Braden, 1996, as cited in Tillmann, p. 10). Students' ability to create visual material that represents their thinking, a key element of visual literacy (Brumberger, 2011), opens new doors for their communication and collaboration with others.

The strategies in this section ask students to interpret visuals provided to them as well as generate their own visuals to support their learning. Both types of visuals are important for supporting students' comprehension and retention (Sousa, 2011). Proficient readers create mental images from all of their senses when they read (Harvey & Goudvis, 2007; Tompkins, 2007). Through our instruction, we strive to facilitate CLD students' ability to combine the author's words with their own background knowledge to create mental images that enhance their understanding of the words, concepts, and larger text (Harvey & Goudvis, 2007). Mental images, however, can be fleeting and easily forgotten while students are grappling with the sociocultural, linguistic, cognitive, and academic demands of the lesson. For this reason, the strategies in this section provide opportunities for students to document these images as valuable resources to support their language and content comprehension throughout the lesson.

Such opportunities are especially critical for English learners, who must contend with the often decontextualized language of the lesson and text. Visuals can scaffold CLD students' entry to the lesson, allowing them to make public the background knowledge that they bring to the topic without being hindered by language. Images also can be used to support individual expression related to new learning and students' communication of ideas with peers. The more students use the language for authentic purposes, the more they acquire the language. Linguistic advances happen through the connected, reciprocal dialogue that occurs in the classroom among students and between the students and the teacher. As noted in the title of this chapter, visuals can serve as catalysts for these conversations. Visuals produced by students are especially powerful when used by the teacher during instructional conversations to revoice connections between students' ideas and the curriculum. In this way, the teacher's actions demonstrate to all students that their ideas matter, that they will be supported to participate as full members of the learning community, and that they can be successful at learning the content, vocabulary, and academic language of the lesson.

Through the use of BDI strategies, we focus our teaching on our greatest resources—our students! As Benson and Lunt (2011) remind us, "children naturally have very particular and important insights to offer in helping us to develop our understanding of teaching and learning" (p. 679). The strategies included in this section help students make their voices heard as they share their knowledge, experiences, and cognitive processes (which inform our teaching actions and decisions) and become engaged in the joy of learning.

Strategies in Practice

In this chapter you will find descriptions of the following six strategies, which explicitly create conditions that encourage learners to use visuals to further their content and language learning and to support their active participation in the lesson:

- Linking Language
- Picture This
- Pictures and Words
- Mind Map
- Listen Sketch Label
- Story Bag

STRATEGY

Linking Language

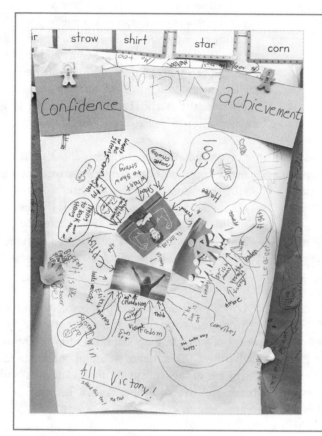

This visuals-based strategy really helps my students focus on the topic and the vocabulary words. Each and every student in my class is able to find some kind of a connection to the topic of the day. The conversations are good, and students find that they have a lot to say. I have used visuals before in my strategies, but this way the students begin making their connections themselves. I was amazed at how many associations my kids made. We have used the strategy multiple times now, and it is always exciting for students. I am able to see what my students bring with themselves from their prior knowledge and the direction they are able to take with it.

—*Susan Cunningham, 2nd-Grade Teacher*

Where Theory Meets Practice

It is often said that a picture paints a thousand words. The question then becomes in classroom practice: *Whose words paint the picture?* Visuals frequently are used in classrooms to support the learner by building background, introducing a new topic, developing vocabulary, sparking new ideas, reinforcing ideas, and strengthening the content. For many educators, their implementation of visuals happens because they see visuals as tools to make learning transparent and meaningful for students. However, even in these situations, teachers start by introducing the concept and associating it with a predetermined and identified visual. The relationship that exists between the concept and the visuals has already been determined by the teacher, which means that students become passive recipients of stimuli that they then are expected to process through the cultural lens of

the teacher, without putting much of their own cognitive thought into this initial connection.

When teachers in culturally and linguistically diverse settings predetermine the connection at the very onset of the lesson, students' voices, ways of knowing, and language are discounted before the lesson begins. English learners need some kind of medium from the very beginning that allows them to create their own connections to the content and the visuals. As they create their own connections and share their own words and images, students engage in a visual learning process that supports their cognitive operations of viewing, interpreting, expressing, inquiring, and preparing to become participants in classroom learning. In discussing the benefits of visual learning, Aisami (2015) states:

The research outcomes on visual learning make complete sense when we consider that our brain is mainly an image processor (much of our sensory cortex is devoted to vision), not a word processor. In fact, the part of the brain used to process words is quite small in comparison to the part that processes visual images. Words are abstract and rather difficult for the brain to retain, whereas visuals are concrete and, as such, more easily remembered. . . . Visuals have been proven to engage students in the learning process, and images stimulate their critical and creative thinking. (p. 542)

What is needed then, instead of a teacher-led connection to the visual, is an avenue for students to connect to vocabulary and concepts (the lesson content) using their own schemas, built-in knowledge systems, and ways of thinking. While reading and preparing to write, visuals can become increasingly meaningful for students when they think of their own vocabulary associations, their own inferences, and their own connections to the visuals. With strategies such as Linking Language, students use images to personally connect to the content from the very beginning of the lesson. They develop skills for asking questions of self, making connections to their knowledge systems, thinking metacognitively, inferring, and visualizing.

In this strategy, the connections established in the opening of the lesson are then taken into the work time of the lesson, and additional connections are made to strengthen students' understanding of the content. Linking Language sets the stage for students' active participation and is a springboard for their discussion and articulation of thought and understanding about the content. It also promotes discussion regarding the ways visual representations (e.g., charts, pictures, graphs) support reading and writing. Linking Language is a strategy that allows teachers to maximize the use of visuals throughout the lesson. This continued use of visuals helps advance CLD students' academic literacy development, thinking, content-based connections, and understanding.

To implement this strategy, the teacher uses pictures from the specific content, identifies critical concepts, and plans how the visuals will be used to elicit connections, activating students' existing knowledge and vocabulary prior to instruction. The pictures are used to provide all learners with an opportunity to participate and engage in the lesson by drawing upon their experiences, language, and knowledge systems to process and make public what they know. For the teacher, the information that students document and discuss serves as a bridge between the content and learners' background knowledge.

Linking Language helps educators gain meaningful insights into their students' schemas and knowledge systems that can then be used throughout the lesson to aid learners in attainment of the lesson's goals. Lent (2012) emphasizes the essential role of the teacher in leveraging students' knowledge to support learning:

Once you have gained insights about what your students know, you can create lessons that target specific learning, something textbooks simply cannot do. It takes a teacher who knows his [or her] students to differentiate, and the more you assess background knowledge and teach to your students' strengths, the better you will become at focusing your instruction. (pp. 37–38)

Linking Language incorporates cooperative learning, writing, and vocabulary and concept development as a means of providing opportunities for differentiating and furthering CLD students' academic understanding. Consistent use of the strategy promotes students' ability to use visuals effectively to support their learning in all content areas.

MATERIALS & RESOURCES

Materials Needed: Blank poster paper • pictures for key vocabulary words • vocabulary words on precut strips of paper • sticky notes • paper • markers/colored pencils

Video: A video clip illustrating implementation of this strategy is available for viewing online at coe.k-state.edu/cima/biographycrt

ACTIVATION: A Canvas of Opportunity

Directions:

i (individual)

- Depending on your essential question, planned outcomes, objectives, and identified skills, select three or four pictures that illustrate key concepts or ideas from the lesson. Pictures can be taken from the Internet, clip art, or magazines, or pictures from the textbook can be used.
- Tape each picture in the center of a large piece of chart paper, allowing enough room for students to write what they see, feel, and think about the picture. If using a textbook, place the textbook in the center of the chart paper.
- Place the students in groups of three to five students, and station one group at each of the posters. Make sure to group students strategically so that, if needed, students can brainstorm ideas with each other or ask each other for help.
- Instruct the students to individually write or draw everything they think of, see, or feel when they look at the picture. Encourage English learners to write in their native language if they prefer.
- Allow only 1–2 minutes for students to write. (Depending on the make-up of your class, you may decide to provide more time.)
- Then have the whole group rotate to the next chart/picture.
- Continue until all groups have been to each picture.
- As students are writing or drawing their ideas, rotate around the room so you can guide students through the process. This also is your time to document some of the students' initial connections, which can be utilized during the lesson.

Instructional Tips:

- Take notice of the kinds of things that students are writing, as these initial words/phrases can become a springboard for you to help connect your students' ideas with each other, connect ideas to the larger content, and reroute conversations as needed. This is also a time for teachers to attend to their English learners, reluctant learners, and students who might need assistance or clarification of the task.
- Strategic questioning, such as asking students what they see or probing the ways they are making connections, leads them to draw or write what they share. Such scaffolding from the teacher at this point in the lesson can help students focus their specific ideas and thoughts related to the visuals. This is also the time when students are reading/interpreting the visual, so questions from the teacher can help promote comprehension of the image itself.

Author Talk: Activation

The terms *scaffolding* and *comprehensible input* have been used in the field of education for a long time. These concepts provide teachers with specific ideas to make learning accessible and meaningful for their students. Yet for teachers the question becomes: *Are we pausing enough in our day-to-day reality to reflect on the way we select and use scaffolds with our students?* Visuals are one means through which we consistently scaffold instruction for learners and aim to provide comprehensible input. For English learners, visuals represent a very non-threatening way to make connections to the content. In this strategy, visuals provide a gateway to students' empowerment as active members of

the learning community. As observers in pre-K–8 classrooms across multiple states, we have been privileged to witness the power of Linking Language in providing students with full access to the curriculum and a sense of belonging to the classroom community.

The more we have observed this strategy in practice, the more we have noticed the "energy" change within the classroom as the teacher prepared the students for application of the strategy. We have noticed students immediately becoming more alert as the teacher explained the directions for the strategy. It was almost as if students were undergoing a mental shift as they saw that this was their opportunity to tell the teacher what they knew. And because they all understood that there was no "right" or "wrong" answer, the stress that is usually associated with a pre-test to determine what students know about a topic was nowhere to be found. Close observation of the CLD students revealed that they often had an even higher level of confidence because they were allowed to draw or write in their native language. By removing the pressure to produce something in English, particularly if they were not yet proficient in English, their affective filters were lowered and their motivation was high. Throughout the lesson as links were made, students' skills in listening, articulating their views, reading, and engaging in the learning process were increased.

In talking to teachers, we have learned that this strategy provided them with a great deal of insight about their students. Many of them commented that if it had not been for the Linking Language strategy, they would not have known half the things they did about their students' background knowledge. In fact, several teachers indicated that once they learned how much their students already knew about a particular topic, they were able to spend significantly less time on identified vocabulary in the curriculum and focus on other academic vocabulary that the students did not know. Using insights into students' background knowledge as a springboard to instruction inspires students as well as the teacher to fully engage in the lesson.

Activating the "*i*"
How does this process activate CLD students' existing knowledge?

- **Sociocultural:** The visuals provide students with a stimulus for connecting to their existing knowledge systems. They provide a built-in scaffold for students to relate their experiences and backgrounds to the content. Connections become "real" when students actually draw or write them.
- **Linguistic:** The strategy provides a natural platform for students at all levels of language proficiency to engage in the lesson. Visuals serve as a scaffold as students examine, interpret, express, and document what is known.
- **Academic:** Linking Language provides students with a nonthreatening opportunity to demonstrate their existing knowledge about the academic content being taught.
- **Cognitive:** This phase encourages students to cognitively stretch their imagination, think deeper, and make schematic links to content.

 CONNECTION: The Broad & Narrow Strokes of Learning

Directions:

T (Total Group), p (partner), s (small group)

 Bridging to the Content— Drawing the *i* into the Lesson

At this phase of the lesson, the Linking Language posters have become personalized learning tools for students, supporting them as they continue to infer, visualize, and understand their own connections to the content. Remind students that you have noted the language and first set of ideas documented, and that these will serve as possible links to the skills, language, and concepts they are going to learn in the lesson.

- Once all groups have returned to their original posters, have them review all of the information that was placed on the poster and identify common ideas/vocabulary

by circling them and linking them together with a line. This step of the strategy is critical in helping students identify any specific themes that might help them relate to the content of the lesson.

CONNECTION: The Broad & Narrow Strokes of Learning (continued)

- Share with students the target vocabulary for the lesson. As you say each word, tape its strip of paper to the chalkboard/wall for all to see.
- Have students discuss in their group which of the target vocabulary words best matches the picture on their poster.
- As a class, discuss ideas about the best match for each poster. Upon reaching consensus, have a student representative from each group come up and remove the appropriate word's strip and tape it to his or her group's poster.
- Have students look for connections between the target vocabulary and the common ideas/words they recorded on the poster. Ask them if they see a theme related to the connections they have made.
- Have each group share out these connections, as well as other links they made, to the rest of the class.

Instructional Tips:

- Encourage student conversations to also consider the ideas and words on the posters that were *not* linked together. Have students locate ideas and words that add a new element or level of understanding related to the target vocabulary.
- Post the posters at the front of the room, so students have access to all of the words as they proceed through the lesson.

 ### Digging into Text

- As you share the text with students during the Connection phase of the lesson, invite and encourage them to use this information to think in new ways about the content.
- Provide numerous opportunities for discussion with peers. These regular opportunities for collaboration as partners and in small groups promote students' abilities to make connections and inferences.

- Stop at regular intervals to have students discuss and think critically about how their own initial words, drawings, and connections on the posters relate to the text they are reading.
- Encourage students to add to the Linking Language posters throughout the lesson by using sticky notes to add new information (e.g., specific vocabulary words, new concepts) they learn.
- As you finish the text/content, have students summarize in their small groups how the content relates to the posters and determine any new ideas they might want to add.

Instructional Tips:

- Encourage students to refer to peers' ideas and ask questions of one another as they get into the lesson and begin to read, write, and think more deeply about the content.
- Ask questions that require critical thinking in order to promote nuanced understandings of the content among students.
- Remember to stop at regular intervals and discuss as a class how the classroom community's ideas, opinions, and thinking are aligned with the essential questions/identified skills. Have them work toward building consensus based on evidence.
- Use total group, partner, and small group interactions to respond situationally to learning as it unfolds.
- Hold students individually accountable by having them share their new connections to the topic, concepts, or language of the lesson through sticky notes and discussions.
- Encourage students to refer back to the posters throughout the lesson as they move incrementally toward a more robust use of academic language to express their ideas, rehearse information and skills, write, ask questions, and solidify their understanding.

Connecting to the "*i*+1"
How does this process move CLD students from the known to the unknown?

- **Sociocultural:** Because individuals interpret visuals through the lens of their own cultural schemas, this phase provides unique opportunities to weave together the students' cultural perspectives. As the class makes new connections to the content, the teacher can use concrete examples from individual students to demonstrate that all cultures are valued and contribute equally to attainment of the learning objectives.

- **Linguistic:** The teacher-provided and student-created visuals on the posters serve as a springboard for literacy development and additional content connections. The posters support students' ongoing practice of all four literacy skills: listening, speaking, reading, and writing.

- **Academic:** Linking Language emphasizes categorization and analysis of themes, in addition to the lesson's target skills. The accumulated words and ideas on the posters document for the classroom community the learning that is taking place. With visuals that provide scaffolding related to the topic, all students have access to difficult content and are able to engage in academic tasks.

- **Cognitive:** Cognitive processes are strengthened as the learner constructs and transfers knowledge about the visuals, text, and related writing. Making and creating connections during academic conversations stimulates the brain to continue to look for information in short-term and long-term memory (Sousa, 2011). In addition, as students monitor their own understanding throughout the lesson cycle, they further develop their metacognitive skills.

 AFFIRMATION: A Gallery of Understanding

Directions:

**T (Total Group), p (partner),
s (small group), I (Individual)**

At this time, the Linking Language posters support you in closing the lesson and bringing together the language and conceptual learning that has taken place. Your students are now ready to take their learning to writing. The Affirmation phase provides an opportunity for all learners, regardless of language proficiency or academic level, to produce evidence of what was understood and learned.

- Have students write a paragraph showing their understanding of the topic and key concepts. Remind them that the posters provide a compilation of ideas, vocabulary, and words that are their own and have been accumulated throughout the lesson.

- Depending on the age and language level of students, you can have them create paragraphs that explicitly answer the essential question or connect to the objectives, or you can have them create writing pieces that connect to outside-the-classroom situations that require them to apply their ideas to the real world.

- Encourage students to use words from the Linking Language posters as they write their paragraphs.

Instructional Tips:

- Students' writing will help you gauge how much learning and growth has taken place.

- If you would like to use these writing samples for evidence of growth over time, then you can use rubrics to evaluate them. Make sure to provide your students with the rubric in advance.

- As students write their paragraphs, remember that the transfer may not be automatic for all students. You might need to carefully attend to students who need additional modeling and support. Sometimes allowing students to first verbalize aloud what they want to say can support their ability to record their ideas on paper.

- Encourage students to share their final summaries with a partner to celebrate all that they have learned!

Affirming Student Ownership: *"I" Get It!*
How does this process celebrate CLD student learning?

- **Sociocultural:** Linking Language supplies students with a visual representation of their progression of learning. Posting students' completed posters at the end of the lesson or unit is a great way to affirm their culturally situated background knowledge as well as their new learning. The writing that occurs at the end represents each student's individual growth.
- **Linguistic:** The posters scaffold the culminating writing task for students by allowing them to refer to a visible collection of images, key vocabulary, concepts, and ideas. Additional opportunities to synthesize learning through discussion with a partner can further promote application of new academic language.
- **Academic:** This strategy supports differentiation of the final product to ensure that all students are challenged. Scaffolds are built in to support learners cognitively and

linguistically. With these resources, CLD students frequently exceed the expectations that we set for them. As they provide evidence of what they have learned through their writing and share their success with peers, students further develop their academic self-concept.
- **Cognitive:** Linking Language enhances CLD students' metacognitive awareness by making the learning process transparent. Nothing about learning is magic. We build new knowledge by using what we already know as a foundation. We often rely on collaboration with others to enrich our own understanding. The transition from visual connections, to the key concepts/vocabulary and sticky notes, to the written documentation of individual learning at the end of the lesson allows students to see learning as a multifaceted, manageable process.

SPOTLIGHT: Early Literacy Connection

As early childhood educators, we know that skills such as alphabetic knowledge (letter recognition), phonological awareness (e.g., rhyming, alliteration), and vocabulary are precursory skills for learning to read (Shonkoff & Phillips, 2000). We are challenged to teach young children the literacy skills that are essential for success in school and life, particularly for increasingly diverse learners.

Linking Language is a visual strategy that can help teachers incorporate critical early literacy skills in English by accessing students' background knowledge and existing vocabulary regarding a particular picture from a story. All children, regardless of their backgrounds, have strengths that we can build on. As teachers, we need to know precisely what skills each child controls and plan instruction accordingly.

To modify the Linking Language strategy for young CLD students, teachers can engage them in the following activity , built around the reading of a story:

Activation:

- Select one picture from the story that you can share with the whole class that previews key information from the story. Have this picture photocopied and taped to the center of a large piece of chart paper.

- Tell students to look at the picture and think of all the things they see in the picture.
- Then have the students share what they see with a partner.

Connection:

- Next, have the students orally share what they see with the teacher and the rest of their classmates. As the students are sharing, write their observations around the picture on the chart paper for the whole class to see. As you are writing, be sure to model the sounds and spelling of each word.
  - In this way, CLD students will begin to focus on and internalize the phonetic and structural patterns of the English words.
  - By highlighting common features in the words such as beginning consonants, rhyming words, and letter patterns, you are providing an introduction to basic phonics skills in English.
- After recording your students' observations and discussing them from a content perspective, have them find words that begin with the same sound.
  - In this step, CLD students are explicitly practicing phonemic awareness skills by attending to the sounds of the English language in context.

(Continued on the next page)

SPOTLIGHT: Early Literacy Connection *(continued)*

- To further connect this activity to visuals and the key vocabulary words in the story, you could have a picture for the word on one side of a 3 × 5 note card and the word on the other side. Give every student a card before reading the story and have them hold up their card when they hear the word read aloud.
  - To challenge students, have them listen for the words on the chart as you read the story aloud. Ask them to raise their hand if they hear one of the words.
- Make sure to stop periodically to discuss the story. Incorporate opportunities for student collaboration so that students can use their developing language skills to express their opinions, ask questions, and make personal connections to the story. Emphasize the meanings of the vocabulary words in context.

Affirmation:

- Have students discuss the takeaway lesson or key points to remember from the story. Make sure to revoice students' use of key vocabulary words.
- To assess students' phonics development, give them a copy of the book and have them work with a partner to find words that start with the same letter. As students locate these words, have them write them down in a list. At the end of the lesson, the lists can be turned in for you to review and revisit the next day.

Note: These purposeful, meaningful activities allow all of the students to hear and practice the sounds of the key vocabulary words that they will hear in the story and throughout the lesson. For some CLD students, they will be hearing these sounds for the first time.

It's the "*i*" Thing

Linking Language is a strategy that can help students connect with content at their own linguistic level. Because visuals can provide additional context for students, this strategy works well for making content comprehensible for *all* learners. When you plan your instruction, allow all of your students to connect with visuals as they negotiate the meaning of the academic vocabulary. As you proceed with the lesson, support students to self-monitor their comprehension. Use the resulting insights and your own observations of student learning to provide necessary adaptations and support.

One Classroom's Perspective

From the 3rd-grade class of Stacey Winkler

Activating:

Our essential question for this week was: *How can you use what you know to help others?* Considering that this is a very broad question, I decided to use the strategy of Linking Language with my students. I started the lesson by placing my students into six different groups. Each week we introduce eight new vocabulary words to students, and this week we did the same thing. However, today being Wednesday, I knew I had to take my students to the reading and connect the words to the reading of the week. With that in mind, I put two or three pictures on each of the posters. The visuals related to the vocabulary words for the week.

We started the lesson by having students write their thoughts about the pictures on the posters. I reminded them to do this individually because I wanted to see their

individual thoughts associated with the pictures first. All the posters were of different colors, so I could easily move them from poster to poster. As students finished the first poster, I just told them to move to a different-colored poster. As they moved, I reminded them to first scan the words that were already on the poster next to the picture and then formulate their own thoughts. They were also free to write the words/expressions in their native language. I know my Hmong student likes to do that.

One Classroom's Perspective (*continued*)

Connecting:

After students finished working on all six posters, they went back to their original poster. At this time, I asked them to look at all the new words that had been added on their posters. Some students were just in awe of the number of new words they had on the posters. After they were done looking for connections that existed between some of the words on the posters, I posted the Linking Language posters at the front of the room. Next, I shared the vocabulary words with the students and we connected the vocabulary words with the different posters. Once we had made connections between the new vocabulary and the words on the posters, we moved into the reading.

In our "Wonders" unit there are different kinds of readings included with different weeks. I chose one where students could really relate back to their Linking Language posters and focus on some of the vocabulary words. As we read the story, we stopped and talked about how the story events related to the posters. My questioning at this time was more about students focusing on text evidence and the details from the story. We also did quite a few small group discussions at this time in order to have students relate the details from the story to the many ideas they had on the posters. I found it quite helpful to have the posters at the front of our room so the students could see the many details they already had and connect them to the new ideas they were gathering from the reading.

Affirming:

Once we had finished the story, I had students discuss one more time the main idea from the story and how it had evolved. As a whole group, we talked about the ways the posters related to everything we had read. We went through some of our previously written ideas on the posters and discussed those as a whole class to summarize our own understandings of the story. Afterward, I had students go back to the essential question and write their own thoughts in response to it. At this time, their task was to use the details and ideas from the text to go back to the essential question and write their narrative. When some of the students finished their paragraphs,

I asked them to share their ideas with the class. I was quite impressed with some of their writing. My class was heavily involved in the activity through to the end. There was lots of discussion today and lots of writing that emerged through our lesson.

STRATEGY

Picture This

This strategy builds on the strengths and background experiences of my CLD students. Students were able to express their individual ideas of the meaning of the vocabulary word so they could correct or affirm their own knowledge. The strategy also encourages the acknowledgment and celebration of diversity among all students in the classroom. Each time, five different students were allowed to share with the entire class, putting them in the spotlight.

—*Kari Ritter, 2nd-Grade Teacher*

Where Theory Meets Practice

Making word meanings and relationships visible to the learner is a powerful way to actively guide the student in constructing knowledge. For CLD students, connecting to a word visually can be critical. However, it is important to remember that simply using a visual is not enough. Visuals are interpreted through the cultural lens of the learner. Discussion of the visual among peers helps students construct word meaning (Blachowicz & Fisher, 2014; Stahl & Vancil, 1986). Linking this discussion to text is essential because such contextualization further supports students as they work to define or bring meaning to the words and create links to content.

Picture This is a strategy that supports students to engage in the lesson and experience making connections between visuals, vocabulary, and content. The strategy fosters cognition by building pathways for students to understand how images guide them to conceptual understanding. Oxford's (1990) System of Learning Strategies would categorize Picture This as a cognitive learning strategy that deals with *analyzing and reasoning* because students are asked to reason inductively and analyze expressions to determine how a picture and its corresponding clues can be used to make connections to vocabulary and content.

In the Picture This strategy, students engage in a four-step process. First, they are introduced to visuals that represent critical concepts and vocabulary. Using the visuals, students apply their background knowledge to engage in an inductive task by determining *what they see* and *what they think*. After completing the task, students are introduced to the topic and the vocabulary words. The sequence and focus are determined by the objectives of the lesson. Teachers often use Picture This as a strategy for introducing vocabulary, others use it for introducing the topic, while some use it to embed the vocabulary within the core concepts to be taught. What is important is that the strategy is used to provide comprehensible input and challenge students to engage with the content inductively.

While engaged in the strategy, CLD students have opportunities to practice vocabulary, engage with the content, and discuss their connections with their peers at each step. By working through this process of analyzing and reasoning, students draw upon their own background knowledge, experiences, and inductive reasoning skills to determine what each word means in relation to the topic and concepts to be taught.

MATERIALS & RESOURCES

Materials Needed: Picture This Template (two per student) • three pictures (for K–3) or six pictures (for 4–8) from the text, the Internet, magazines, newspapers, library books, picture cards, etc. • sticky notes (enough for each student to have one per vocabulary word) • pencils/pens

Template: Picture This Template (see page 35); also available for free download and printing from tcpress.com/accelerating

---

ACTIVATION: A Canvas of Opportunity

Directions:

i (individual)

- Select three or six appropriate pictures to support students' learning.
  - You can project pictures for the whole class to see, make copies for small groups to share, or have a copy of each picture for each student. The pictures can be taken directly from the text or from other sources (e.g., the Internet, magazines, newspapers, library books, picture cards).
  - Digital media also can be used. (For the next steps, you would simply stop a video as the critical concepts are covered and have students record what they saw/ heard and what they connected to.)
- Show students the preselected images one at a time.
- Have students individually record on the Picture This template what comes to mind as they look at the picture. In the "What I see" column they will draw a picture of what they see, and in the "What I think" column they will write all the words they think of when they see the picture.
  - Encourage students to reach deep into their "permanent memory folder" to record as many words as possible.

- Remind students that they can use their native language, English, or drawings to capture their thoughts.
- Use questioning techniques as students work. Ask them to describe all the things they see in the picture as well as what they think of when they look at the picture.
- Repeat this process for each picture.
- You may choose to be building a story that moves the learner to predict what the topic will be or you may have already shared the topic and be pointing out what is to come.
- Use students' words and pictures to revoice what is shared.
- After students have finished documenting their individual responses on their templates, have them share what they have written with a partner.

Activating the "*i*"
How does this process activate CLD students' existing knowledge?

- **Sociocultural:** CLD students have the opportunity to individually brainstorm and document background knowledge and experiences based on their interpretation of the pictures. They also have the opportunity to engage in discussion with peers and hear their interpretations, which may spark additional connections.
- **Linguistic:** Students' use of nonlinguistic representations to demonstrate what they see reduces the stress associated with writing, particularly for CLD students in the initial stages of second language acquisition.

- **Academic:** Activities during this phase help the teacher create a low-risk academic environment and set the stage for all students to be active participants in the learning process as they make individual connections to content-based pictures.
- **Cognitive:** The peer discussions incorporated in this strategy create conditions that allow students to share multiple ways of knowing and thinking about each picture.

CONNECTION: The Broad & Narrow Strokes of Learning

Directions:

T (Total Group), p (partner), s (small group)

- Place students in small groups of four students.
- Share with the class the vocabulary for the lesson. Have students individually write the vocabulary words on their sticky notes, one word per sticky note.
- Next have students work with a partner to discuss their thoughts on each word. Ask students to place the sticky notes on their template beside the picture that best matches each word.
- As you proceed with the lesson, support students to make text connections. Have them stop periodically to consider ways that their new learning connects to the pictures and words they drew/wrote on their template.
- Have students document what they are understanding on the opposite side of their paper.
- Again, be sure to have students discuss in pairs or small groups as they are making connections. As the lesson progresses, you will continue to move back and forth among pair talk, small group conversations, and whole-group discussion.
- As students are constructing knowledge by making and discussing connections to the text and vocabulary, circulate around the room and observe what they are saying and doing.
  - Ask individual students to provide the rationale for specific connections.

  - Revoice key connections for the entire class.
  - Provide additional support to any students who might be struggling.
  - Note connections that you will use in the next phase of the lesson.
- As you finish working with the text, have students discuss their understanding of the vocabulary words as a small group. Have them come to consensus about which words are best aligned to each picture. Have students move their sticky notes accordingly.
- Have groups share out ideas as you facilitate whole-group discussion related to the relationships between the vocabulary words and the content of the lesson. If desired, have students remove their sticky notes and write the words beside the corresponding pictures to reflect the outcomes of the whole-class discussion.

Connecting to the "*i*+1"
How does this process move CLD students from the known to the unknown?

- **Sociocultural:** Students are actively engaged in discussions with peers to support meaningful content connections during the lesson as they share insights based on their own perspectives and understanding.
- **Linguistic:** Having CLD students engage in active discussion with their peers helps them process their thoughts as well as articulate their understanding of content and vocabulary.

- **Academic:** As students continue to connect new learning to the original pictures and words documented on the Picture This template, they are able to confirm/disconfirm their original ideas and are visually reminded of the academic foundation that their background knowledge provided for the lesson.
- **Cognitive:** This strategy creates conditions that allow students to express *multiple ways of knowing* during the course of the lesson.

AFFIRMATION: A Gallery of Understanding

Directions:

**T (Total Group), p (partner),
s (small group), I (Individual)**

- Pass out a new Picture This template to each student.
- Tell students you are going to show them the same pictures again and now they are to think about what they have learned.
- As each picture is shown, ask the students to use the left-hand column to write what they see and how it relates to the content, given what they have learned.
- Ask students to use the right-hand column to write about a new idea or understanding that they will take away from the lesson. These also can include applications to the world outside the classroom.

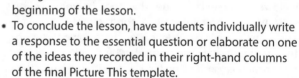

- Throughout this time, guide students toward your lesson objectives.
- Be sure to have students discuss in pairs or small groups how their thinking has changed from the beginning of the lesson.
- To conclude the lesson, have students individually write a response to the essential question or elaborate on one of the ideas they recorded in their right-hand columns of the final Picture This template.
- Have students share their writing with a partner.

Affirming Student Ownership: "*I*" Get It!
How does this process celebrate CLD student learning?

- **Sociocultural:** This strategy helps students synthesize multiple perspectives about the lesson's vocabulary and concepts into a personally meaningful statement about each picture that reflects their understanding.
- **Linguistic:** Students' use of academic vocabulary and language is stretched to the *i*+1 as they develop their own meaningful sentences to demonstrate their new understanding of the content.

- **Academic:** Students' individual sentences and final writing demonstrate the level of internalization and knowledge they have gained about the vocabulary and critical concepts.
- **Cognitive:** The completed Picture This template scaffolds CLD students' use of a variety of cognitive, academic, linguistic, and even sociocultural skills to synthesize in their own words what they have learned about the content.

Author Talk: Affirmation

Each CLD student brings a unique set of experiences and background knowledge to the classroom. However, depending on what stage of second language acquisition (SLA) they are in, students differ in their ability to share their knowledge in English. For example, a CLD student in the preproduction stage of SLA (the first stage) is able to provide only one- or two-word responses. On the other hand, a student in the early production stage of SLA (the second stage) is able to respond in short sentences. The more teachers know about the linguistic biographies of their CLD students, the better equipped they are to differentiate their instruction and support their students' academic achievement (Herrera, 2016). This strategy enables students at all levels of language proficiency to actively participate in the process of inductively determining the meanings of the vocabulary words and content.

Some teachers who implement this strategy admit to initially thinking that their CLD students would not be able to successfully complete the various tasks of the strategy because they require students to engage in higher-order thinking. Yet teachers have found that this strategy actually enables their students to better retain the meanings of the vocabulary terms because they are not told the definitions at the outset. Rather, students must work out the definitions by using their own background knowledge, clues provided in the text/lesson, and peer support. Consequently, Picture This has proven extremely effective in stretching students' thinking to the zone of proximal development (Vygotsky, 1978).

SPOTLIGHT: Early Literacy Connection

Research findings indicate that children's success in reading and writing is supported by solid development of oral language skills (McGee & Richgels, 2014). At the preschool level, oral language development not only contributes to children's literacy success but also plays a pivotal role in their academic and social development. Young children generate language when their beginning efforts are accepted and reinforced. According to the National Research Council (1998), language development during the preschool years—in particular the development of a rich vocabulary and some familiarity with the language forms used for communication and literacy—constitutes an important domain of preparation for formal reading instruction.

Providing meaningful opportunities for oral language interaction is one way teachers can foster vocabulary acquisition for young CLD students. To help these children catch up with their peers who are native English speakers, we need to provide comprehensive instruction that includes an emphasis on vocabulary. The Picture This strategy incorporates structured oral language activities that help students advance their development of oral English language skills.

To modify the Picture This strategy for young CLD students, teachers can implement the following directions.

Activation:

- Select two pictures that represent two of the key vocabulary words from a story you are going to read aloud.
- Rather than having the students individually try to draw or write what they see when they look at each picture, post each picture at the front of the room on a large piece of poster paper or on a white board.
- To keep the two pictures separate, we recommend displaying the pictures as a T-chart. Tell the students they are going to play a game called "I Spy!"
- Explain that it is their job to "spy" or name all the things they see in the picture. Give students a few minutes to look at each picture and then have them share all the things they spied with a partner.
  ◦ If possible, try to pair CLD students who speak the same native language (L1) so they can communicate in that language if they choose.
- Next, ask each pair to share one thing with the class that they spied in each picture until all partners have shared. Be sure to write students' comments below the corresponding picture on the board.
  ◦ If students choose to share in their L1, write their responses in the L1 (if possible) and in English.
  ◦ If needed, allow the student to come up and write in the L1 or draw an image to represent the response on the board for you.

SPOTLIGHT: Early Literacy Connection (continued)

Activation (continued):

- As you are writing, talk about the words and labels given by the students to promote their oral language development.
- After recording what the students see, ask them what they feel when they look at the picture.
- Have students share with a partner before recording whole-group responses on the T-chart.
- Once again, focus on highlighting the oral language used by the students to describe their feelings.

Connection:

- Finally, show the students the two vocabulary words and have them predict which word belongs with which picture and why. Explain to the students that they are making a guess based on the clues they have so far.
- Once the class has reached a group consensus, tape the vocabulary words under the corresponding pictures and tell the students that it is their job to listen for the words in the story.

- Begin reading the story. Tell the students that when they hear the words from the story, you will stop reading. Then the whole class will check to see if they matched the correct vocabulary word to each picture.

Affirmation:

- After you have read the story, revisit the two pictures and vocabulary words from the story.
- Place students in small groups of three or four students. Explain that each group will generate two sentences, one for each of the vocabulary words. Each sentence will be written on an individual sticky note.
  - Make sure to circulate to each of the groups to provide any needed support with the writing task.
- After each group has written their two sentences, bring the whole class back together. Ask each group to read their sentences and place the sticky notes on the appropriate pictures from the story.
- Revoice students' use of the vocabulary words and connections to the content.

It's the "i" Thing

Picture This supports students' connections to content by allowing them to use visuals as a way of constructing knowledge. Students activate their background knowledge as they record "What I see" and "What I think." Picture This supports students to work with the target words and concepts in multiple contexts, guiding them to enhance their understanding of how context clues work and utilizing discussions with peers to further develop their own individual understanding. The same visuals used at the beginning of the strategy are used again at the end of the lesson to provide a more visual demonstration of the learning that individual students have achieved as a result of their critical thinking and practice with the words and concepts of the lesson.

One Classroom's Perspective

From the 2nd-grade class of Amanda Donahey

Activating:

Our reading series has three vocabulary words each week that students focus on. Vocabulary is a crucial part of comprehension, and my students come to me with limited vocabulary. They are often able to draw a picture and describe a word but fail to know the word itself. Sitting at their desks in teams of three, students had to discover three new vocabulary words. They did this through the Picture This strategy. First, students were directed to turn over a picture and draw what they saw and write down any thoughts that came into their heads.

Connecting:

Second, students were given the dictionary definitions of the vocabulary words and had to match them to the correct picture. Third, students were given short paragraphs or sentences from the text we were going to read and were instructed to match them to the correct picture and definition. Then, students were given the vocabulary words and had to match them with the correct definition, picture, and text passages.

Students partnered to read the story with their new vocabulary words in context. Throughout this lesson students were able to communicate with their teammates and bounce ideas off each other. The implementation of this strategy provided me with the insight that many of my CLD students use the context to figure out the meaning of new vocabulary words. They also benefited from the use of pictures and dictionary definitions. I was impressed with their ideas and thoughts.

Affirming:

Students were asked to create new meaningful sentences with their partners using the vocabulary words. I felt that this lesson went well. I do believe my students benefited from the strategy. Students were able to successfully give definitions and use the vocabulary words correctly in context. All CLD students were able to use the text, pictures, and definitions to discover the correct vocabulary word. The students were excited and engaged throughout the activities.

TEMPLATE: Picture This

Name: _____

Date: _____

Picture This

	What I See . . .	What I Think . . .
Picture #1		
Picture #2		
Picture #3		

STRATEGY

Pictures and Words

I think this lesson really benefited each of the students because they were able to draw what they were thinking and then put words to their pictures. For many of the students, doing the drawing first really helped them to be able to come up with the words that matched their drawing. The students really reacted positively to the lesson because they were able to use their creativity. I also think that having the students come back together at the end and share what they drew and the order in which they drew it really helped to emphasize the point of retell.

—*Kristin Fisher, 4th-Grade Teacher*

Where Theory Meets Practice

Student motivation plays a large role in our facilitating their success. Lessons that are relevant and interesting keep students engaged in the learning process and increase student motivation (Routman, 2003). Herrera (2016) notes that it is easy for us as educators to "get stuck in what has been researched or prescribed within our own teaching cultures and pay little attention to the cultural context of the student or the role of individual motivation in the learning process" (p. 52). By building upon CLD students' existing knowledge, educators are more likely to motivate and engage their students in the lesson. As Jensen (2008) emphasized in his research, "in order to get learners to be creative and have greater subject interest, higher self-esteem, and the ability to be reflective, there must be intrinsic motivation" (p. 124).

It also is important to provide CLD students the opportunity to make meaningful connections between what they know and already bring to the lesson and the new concepts and skills they are going to learn. In high-performing schools, these connections are explicitly made throughout the lesson to enhance student understanding (Gunning, 2006; Langer, 2001). To promote and make effective use of these connections, a variety of factors need to be in place:

- All students need to be held accountable for participating in the activities.
- All students need to be provided true access to the activity, regardless of their language proficiency level. This requires scaffolding efforts on our part as teachers.
- Students' background knowledge and interests need to be captured at the onset of the lesson.
- Students' initial connections between their existing schemas and new content need to be documented.
- The activities used throughout the lesson need to reinforce (and further ignite) students' connections to the new material being held in working memory (Sousa, 2011).
- Students need to be able to use the text to make and articulate connections to the key concepts and the content-specific vocabulary.

• Students need opportunities to try out their ideas and benefit from alternative perspectives in the context of peer interaction in pairs and small groups.

The power of the Pictures and Words strategy is that—by meeting all of the conditions identified above—it provides CLD students with the opportunity to make meaningful connections to text and content throughout the lesson.

Students are immediately asked to make and document connections to the text based on their own background knowledge. As the lesson proceeds, students reconceptualize their initial connections to reflect key content vocabulary and new content presented in the text. The ongoing restructuring stretches students both academically and cognitively as they continually refine their understanding. By having students document their evolving understanding as the lesson progresses, the strategy helps students develop a concrete tool for demonstrating their learning.

MATERIALS & RESOURCES

Materials Needed: Pictures and Words Template (one per student) • sticky notes • books to share with the whole class • pencils/pens

Template: Pictures and Words Template (see page 43); also available for free download and printing from tcpress.com/accelerating

Checklist: Student Academic Behavior Checklist (see page 192); also available for free download and printing from tcpress.com/accelerating

---

ACTIVATION: A Canvas of Opportunity

Directions:

i (individual)

• Begin the strategy by first sharing with students the academic vocabulary and the topic of the lesson. When selecting the academic vocabulary, focus on the six to eight most important words that will communicate the essence of the story/topic. *Note:* If you are in the primary grades, you may want to choose words that will support students to retell the story.

• Next, focus on the vocabulary words, one by one, with students. Ask them to individually write the words on the reverse side of their Pictures and Words template along the left-hand side. After students have written the words:
  ◦ Have them individually draw what comes to mind when they hear, read, and say the word. Encourage students to think about the topic and how the word may be related to the topic or associations they make from their own background experiences.
  ◦ Remind students they can write in their native language and/or in English to document their connections.

• Have students discuss in pairs the connections they are making. Allow them to borrow ideas if needed.

• As students are making connections, circulate around the room and observe what they are writing and sharing.

◦ Ask students to provide the rationale for their connections.
◦ Note what the students have written and discussed so you can use the information as you bridge into the text/lesson.

• Next, ask students to think about what they have produced related to the academic vocabulary of the lesson as well as the title of the story/topic in order to predict what they think the story/lesson will be about.
  ◦ Provide each student with three sticky notes. Have students place one sticky note over each box on their template.
  ◦ Have students draw three pictures, one on each sticky note, to represent key ideas, events, or concepts that they predict will be included in the story/lesson.

• Have students do a quick turn-and-talk to share their predictions with a partner. As they do this, circulate around the room and listen to the ideas the students are sharing with each other. Revoice predictions that provide alternative possibilities.

Activating the "*i*"
How does this process activate CLD students' existing knowledge?

- **Sociocultural:** Engaging students in academic talk with their peers about the key vocabulary and overall topic promotes culturally relevant and biography-driven connections to the text.
- **Linguistic:** Discussions with partners provide all students the opportunity to check their understanding and discuss ideas one on one, which keeps the affective filter low. When students are strategically paired, they also have the opportunity to provide and receive L1 support as needed.

- **Academic:** Previewing key vocabulary words before the lesson and having students connect to them through pictures and their own words provides a springboard from which they can continue to make connections to the content throughout the lesson.
- **Cognitive:** Asking students to predict what they think the story is about based on the topic and academic vocabulary helps CLD students develop their ability to draw on their background knowledge when completing academic tasks.

 CONNECTION: The Broad & Narrow Strokes of Learning

Directions:

T (Total Group), p (partner), s (small group)

- Once students have finished discussing their predictions, bring them back together and share with them that they will be confirming/disconfirming their predictions as the class proceeds with the story/lesson.
- Begin reading the story/text and stop when you encounter any of the academic vocabulary words. Ask students to write a sentence (sentence starters are helpful) relating the word to the story/content.
  - Students can write the sentences on sticky notes or on the reverse side of their template near the respective words.
  - If the connections were written on sticky notes, have students place the sticky notes on the reverse side of the template near their initial thoughts about the respective words.
- At relevant points in the lesson, have students stop and record their own mental images/connections to that section of the story/content by drawing in the boxes

of the template. Students can move their prediction sticky notes to the side of the template.

- Model your own mental imagery/conceptual connections regarding the first section of material. You may choose to share a text–self connection, text–text connection, or text–world connection by saying, "This section reminds me of _____."
  - Remind students that they can illustrate text–self, text–text, and text–world connections.
- Have students to do a turn-and-talk with a partner regarding the specific section of the story/topic and have them share their mental images with each other.

Author Talk: Connection

Pictures and Words is ideal for supporting teachers in aligning their instruction with English Language Arts (ELA) standards, especially with regard to the type of text they have their students read. For example, many teachers have focused on using Pictures and Words with informational text, which is an emphasis of most ELA standards. This emphasis is due in large part to the disproportionate percentage of narrative text versus informational text taught at the elementary level. Narrative text is often easier for CLD students to visualize. Pictures and Words prompts CLD students to visualize what is occurring in informational text as well, and thereby supports teachers in providing scaffolding that allows all students to access and understand more challenging informational text. Initial implementation of this strategy with narrative text and subsequent use with informational text will promote CLD students' strategic use of visualization across text types.

The adaptability of this strategy has allowed highly successful implementation by classroom teachers. In fact, we are continually surprised by the ways in which teachers at multiple grade levels have adapted and used Pictures and Words. For example, teachers have used it as a strategy to get to know their students at the beginning of the school year, by having their students write about their lives in Pictures and Words. With younger students, teachers might use three boxes and ask the students to draw the following:

- *Picture 1:* Family and/or important people in the student's life
- *Picture 2:* Favorite activity or hobby
- *Picture 3:* Favorite thing about school or something that makes school challenging

For older students, teachers can use six boxes and have the students identify six things about their biography. Teachers who have used Pictures and Words in this way report that it has been one of the best ways for them to get to know about the lives of their learners.

Connecting to the "*i*+1"
How does this process move CLD students from the known to the unknown?

- **Sociocultural:** Explicit modeling by the teacher and opportunities for peer discussion during the lesson help CLD students continue to make schematic connections throughout the lesson. As students illustrate and formally articulate text–self, text–text, or text–world connections, the content becomes more culturally relevant.
- **Linguistic:** The balance of drawing, writing, speaking, and listening activities in this phase of Pictures and Words supports students to remain engaged in the lesson. The words and images that students produce serve as scaffolding for English learners to articulate their evolving understanding of the story/content.
- **Academic:** The Pictures and Words strategy promotes students' concrete connections to text and vocabulary as they confirm/disconfirm their initial vocabulary associations and content predictions.
- **Cognitive:** By sharing their own mental images/conceptual connections with peers, CLD students are exposed to multiple perspectives and are able to redefine their understanding as necessary.

AFFIRMATION: A Gallery of Understanding

Directions:

**T (Total Group), p (partner),
s (small group), I (Individual)**

- Have students in small groups retell what was learned.
  - Have students refer to their vocabulary sentence sticky notes and their illustrations on the template to support their discussion of their images/connections to the content.
  - Make sure students actually practice using the vocabulary words as they discuss their connections and new understandings.
- Now that students have had additional practice with using academic language to articulate their thoughts, have them return to the lines of the Pictures and Words template. Ask students to write the details to explain their ideas associated with the illustrations in each box. Encourage students to incorporate relevant vocabulary words in their writing.
- Next, ask the members of each group to work together to create a group statement that summarizes the essential aspects of the story/topic.
  - Remind students to use the academic vocabulary they have learned and connected to throughout the lesson within their summaries.

- Once the groups have finished their summaries, have them share the summaries with the whole class.
- Allow students to display their completed templates on the wall (if they wish) so that the class can see the various interpretations/connections of their peers.
- Students also can use another copy of the Pictures and Words template at the end of the lesson to summarize their learning. To do this, have students draw images related to the critical content in the boxes and incorporate the target vocabulary in their written descriptions on the lines. Students can then use their completed templates to write individual summary paragraphs.

Affirming Student Ownership: *"I" Get It!*
How does this process celebrate CLD student learning?

- **Sociocultural:** Students' completed Pictures and Words templates make evident for learners how they used both visual representations and words to document their learning process. Each product is unique and reflects the cultural interpretation of the learner.
- **Linguistic:** Sharing their mental images/connections with peers allows CLD students to articulate their cognitive understandings and biography-driven connections in their own words. Hearing peers' interpretations of the text also provides CLD students with the opportunity to learn from their peers.

- **Academic:** The completed Pictures and Words templates and group summaries provide concrete evidence of students' understanding of the content and vocabulary.
- **Cognitive:** Through peer discussion and collaboration, students are challenged to apply new learning and articulate knowledge gained at a much higher cognitive level than if asked only to complete the task independently.

SPOTLIGHT: Early Literacy Connection

Pictures are universal stimuli to aid learning that provide a starting point for language sharing in the classroom. As Curtis and Bailey (2001) have stated, "Pictures provide something to talk about. They take the focus off the language learner during oral practice and turn it to the picture" (p. 11). Teachers can use pictures containing familiar objects to elicit words from children's vocabularies. Because pictures can be used as a stimulus for reading, writing, and other literacy activities as well, they have much potential for use with young CLD students.

Early childhood teachers can use pictures to introduce and reinforce key vocabulary words that are relevant to the topic the class is learning. A picture can evoke mental images to help English learners recall a term or concept. Pictures can be used with any and all languages, are easily accessible, and can be used to reinforce literal, critical, and creative thinking.

To modify the Pictures and Words strategy for young CLD students, teachers can implement the following adaptation.

Activation:

- Select a book that has vivid pictures that students can readily connect to during a read-aloud.
- Begin the lesson by sharing three vocabulary words. Write the words on the board, pronounce them, and have students echo them back. Then have students briefly discuss the words with a partner.
- Have students share out ideas about the vocabulary words. Jot down ideas beside the words on the board.
- Next, have the students look at the cover of the book and talk to their partner in order to make a "partner prediction" about what they think the story will be about.
- Have partners work together to draw their prediction on a piece of paper that they can share with the whole

class before reading the story. As students share their pictures, post them at the front of the room and label the objects in the pictures.
  - Alternatively, if time is limited, have each set of partners orally share their predictions with the whole class and document these on a large piece of chart paper at the front of the room.

Connection:

- To ensure that students are actively involved in the reading of the story, tell them that they will be listening to the story to see if their predictions (guesses) are right.
- Explain to students that they also will be listening for the three vocabulary words. If they hear one of the words, their job is to raise their hand to let you know so that you can stop reading and everyone can talk about what each word means in the context of the story.
- After this discussion for each word, have students use the Pictures and Words template to draw a picture related to the meaning of the word in the box and use the lines provided to write the word.

Affirmation:

- After reading the story, ask the students to look at their "partner prediction" pictures again.
- Explain to the students that they can make any changes to their original prediction pictures to make their predictions correct. If needed (especially if they need to make lots of changes), partners can use the reverse side of the paper to draw a completely new picture.
- After the students have revisited their prediction pictures, have them share with the class some of the changes that they made to the pictures. Be sure to have students explain *why* they made the changes.

Author Talk: Parental Use of Pictures and Words

Parents also can use Pictures and Words as an activity with their children in their home environment. Employing the strategy in the home setting promotes language development in students' native language, with the parents sharing their own biography-driven perspectives. Provide parents with the overarching topic that you will be focusing on in an upcoming lesson. Then have parents work with their child to draw a picture that in some way connects to the topic. Parents can label various objects in the picture in their native language. Then the child can select three objects to

illustrate in the boxes on their Pictures and Words template. Next, the child can write the name of each object on the corresponding lines. This activity helps students build critical background knowledge as well as maintain their development of the native language. Encouraging parents to explore the topic through pictures and their native language also promotes students' English language acquisition, because abilities and knowledge developed in the first language often transfer to the second language.

One Classroom's Perspective

From the 2nd-grade class of Lara Evans

Activating:

I started the lesson by sharing with students the title of the story, *Ugly Vegetables.* The first thing we talked about was the genre of the story as being fiction, since I wanted students to consider that as they worked on their Pictures and Words templates. I shared with them that today they would be doing a lot of predictions and then sharing their ideas about the story. As I handed students the Pictures and Words template, I shared a model of the template that I had drawn on the board so they could see how the strategy would work. I had included their vocabulary words on the back of their templates and we did a quick review of the words to make sure they included thoughts about those in their predictions.

I discussed with students that they were going to write and draw their predictions about the story on sticky notes. Their task was to look through the pictures in the story and record their predictions on the three sticky notes I gave them. I shared with them that as I am making my predictions, I might think of the associations I have

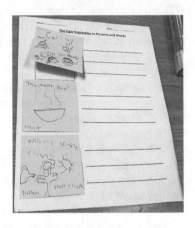

with the vocabulary words. Before they actually drew their predictions, I had students discuss their predictions with their partners, and then some of them shared their predictions with the rest of the class. As students completed their three predictions on the three sticky notes, I told them that throughout the story we would see if their predictions were right. If they were right, they would just place the sticky notes in the book where they found that particular idea. If their predictions weren't right, then they could place them on their nametags. After students finished their predictions, we moved on with the story.

Connecting:

We got into our book, and I had students read in their small groups. As they read, I had them stop at specific points—I wanted to make sure students would focus on important details from the story as they worked with their templates. When we stopped, the first thing I did was have them draw images in the boxes on their templates. They drew images of the events that were happening in the story. I gave them several opportunities to turn and talk to peers around them. As they did, I had them share what they heard their partner share and whether their predictions were correct. This step also helped students as they wrote sentences about the pictures on the lines beside each picture.

Students shared lots of interesting ideas at this time. Some students put their sticky notes in the book and

some I found were putting them on their nametags. I went to individual students and had them talk about whether they found the prediction to be true or not true. I also shared some of the ideas from students' Pictures and Words templates with the rest of the class. Throughout this phase, I also asked students to share the reasons why they wrote the sentences they did. We continued reading and stopping at different points so students could draw their images from the text and write about them on their template.

Affirming:

As we finished the story, students had three important details (visuals) and sentences to go along with them about what we had read. Next, I had students share all of their details from their Pictures and Words template with their peers at the table. This gave me a chance to listen to some of the details they had on their templates. Then I shared with them that at this point their task was to write a summary using the events from their Pictures and Words template. On the back of their templates underneath the vocabulary words, I had created a box for the summary. This is where they added their final summaries about the story. As students finished, I had some students share their stories with the rest of the class.

TEMPLATE: Pictures and Words

Name: _____

Date: _____

_____ in Pictures and Words

STRATEGY

Mind Map

This strategy gave my students a chance to organize their own thoughts before being taught new content. They were each allowed to enter the lesson on their own level. They had the choice of writing or drawing their thoughts on the page. Next, my students were able to meet their social needs by having role models in the classroom during partner and small-group discussion. Students of all abilities were able to participate in this lesson on their level while learning important grade-level content.

—*Kerry Wasylk, 4th-Grade Teacher*

Where Theory Meets Practice

Traditionally, mind maps consist of words and pictures that are linked and arranged around a central key concept. Instructionally, mind maps are generally used to aid students in generating, visualizing, structuring, and classifying thoughts (Buzan, 1989). For CLD students, mind maps are much more than just nonlinear representations of a key concept. They are tools that can be used to promote students' academic knowledge and linguistic proficiency in English by providing a concrete tool for: (1) identifying and elaborating on prior knowledge before the lesson, (2) guiding note taking and the organization of information presented during instruction, and (3) summarizing individual learning at the end of the lesson.

Mind maps can be used by educators to uncover each student's background knowledge by igniting their individual associations to the topic. According to Herrera (2016), when educators observe these associations, validate them, and elaborate on students' initial connections they make learning meaningful and culturally relevant. Research on the brain has also found that graphic organizers like mind maps "help students read to learn subject matter in all content areas because they capitalize on the brain's innate

aptitude for remembering patterns" (Sousa, 2014, p. 103). For English learners at the initial stages of second language acquisition, the opportunity to represent their knowledge nonlinguistically is particularly beneficial.

During the lesson, mind maps can help educators "tap into what students are thinking as they listen, interact, and work with the information that is shared during the lesson" (Herrera, 2016, p. 53). Through this BDI strategy, teachers explicitly model links between students' background knowledge and the new curricular information. Students negotiate visual representations of this new knowledge for the mind map through meaningful interaction with peers in their small groups. These visual representations help students further understand and explore the relationship between the information presented in the text/lesson and their own schemas (J. Hill & Flynn, 2013). Such opportunities for collaboration support overall comprehension of the lesson and students' development of content-specific vocabulary.

Ultimately, the Mind Map strategy makes students' ways of knowing and thinking public. The sharing that takes place among students as they work in small groups is particularly powerful, as the information shared among peers adds depth to their individual understanding of the topic and provides the teacher with insights that can be used to guide all members of the learning community to achieve the lesson's goals. The completed mind maps serve to document the entire learning process and provide a valuable scaffold for students as they individually summarize what they learned in writing.

MATERIALS & RESOURCES

Materials Needed: Blank sheet of paper (one per student) • poster paper • colored pencils/markers • pencils/pens • sticky notes (optional)

Rubric: Student Assessment Rubric (see page 193); also available for free download and printing from tcpress.com/accelerating

---

 ACTIVATION: A Canvas of Opportunity

Directions:

i (individual)

- Share with students the topic of the lesson and ask them to individually brainstorm about the topic for 1–2 minutes on a blank sheet of paper.
- Encourage students to write or draw whatever they think of, since the mind uses both linguistic (English and L1) and nonlinguistic representations. *Tip:* As students are brainstorming, make sure to emphasize that there are no right or wrong answers, so their affective filters remain low and ideas flow freely.
- Once the students are done with their individual brainstorming, have them share their ideas in small groups.
- Next, give each group a piece of poster paper on which to draw their mind map. Have students write the con-

cept in the middle of the poster paper and then ask all group members to add their individual ideas to their group's mind map using colored markers.

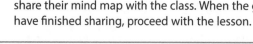

- Give students 3–5 minutes to individually illustrate or write something on the group's mind map.
- Bring the class back together and have each group share their mind map with the class. When the groups have finished sharing, proceed with the lesson.

Author Talk: Activation

One of the questions we are most frequently asked when working with teachers of CLD students is, *How can I make sure I am engaging all my CLD students in the lesson?* With the Mind Map strategy, teachers have an immediate tool for monitoring CLD student engagement in multiple ways. First, all students brainstorm and document what they know about the topic before meeting in small groups. Teachers can observe or gather these individual CLD students' responses to see what prior knowledge students brought to the lesson. Second, by allowing student responses to be linguistic and nonlinguistic in nature, CLD students at all levels of language proficiency are able to actively participate in the process and document their responses. Third, having students share their ideas in small

groups and once again document responses on the group's mind map gives the teacher another opportunity to actively engage CLD students in the learning process.

Teachers who have implemented the Mind Map strategy with CLD students have found that having students share responses in small groups also keeps their affective filters low because they are allowed to learn from one another as they discuss vocabulary words and lesson concepts. By providing the option to continue using linguistic as well as nonlinguistic representations, the teacher can ensure that all CLD students still have equal access to the activity. To help monitor student engagement and increase individual accountability, the teacher can have each student within each group use a different color of marker.

Activating the "*i*"
How does this process activate CLD students' existing knowledge?

- **Sociocultural:** Mind maps provide each student with a low-risk environment in which they feel safe to activate and document their background knowledge.
- **Linguistic:** Students at all stages of second language acquisition are able to record their background knowledge using linguistic or nonlinguistic cues. Allowing students to use whichever language(s) they choose for disclosure also promotes full participation.

- **Academic:** Students are set up to experience a sense of accomplishment from the onset of the lesson in relation to the content and language learning objectives.
- **Cognitive:** Mind maps allow students to see how their ways of thinking are similar to and different from those of their peers. Such representations of schematic connections set the stage for students to develop multifaceted, nuanced understandings of the topic.

CONNECTION: The Broad & Narrow Strokes of Learning

Directions:

T (Total Group), p (partner), s (small group)

- Begin reading the story/text. Stop at regular intervals and have students talk with one another in their small groups about the different concepts being encountered.
- After students have finished discussing their ideas, have them individually add new information to the group's mind map using sticky notes or a marker of a color different from the one they used to record their initial understandings. By doing this, you will be able to distinguish brainstormed associations from new learning throughout the lesson (which may span several days).
- You can further expand upon this task by asking students to work in their small groups to connect their new learning with their initial ideas on the mind map (as applicable).
- As students record and expand upon connections among the group concepts, informally monitor their work and listen to their conversations. During this time, note the following:

- Connections between students' existing knowledge and the topic that you can build upon within the lesson to make content more comprehensible to the students.
- Preexisting content vocabulary.
- Accuracy/clarity of relationships among concepts.
- Key concepts/ideas that students are struggling with.
- Have students individually continue to add words to clarify, elaborate, or incorporate content concepts on the mind maps throughout the lesson.

Connecting to the "*i*+1"
How does this process move CLD students from the known to the unknown?

- **Sociocultural:** More meaningful connections to the lesson are promoted among students when CLD students' experiences and knowledge, as shared in the Activation phase, are linked to the key content and vocabulary of the lesson.
- **Linguistic:** CLD students' connections are enhanced when they are allowed to engage in meaningful discussions with peers about the content/concepts on their mind maps.

- **Academic:** The Mind Map strategy facilitates students' learning of academic vocabulary throughout the lesson, as the activities provide learners with multiple, meaningful exposures to the words in the context of the topic.
- **Cognitive:** Students gain valuable cognitive learning strategies during the lesson to promote their comprehension, including note taking and organizing information.

 AFFIRMATION: A Gallery of Understanding

Directions:

**T (Total Group), p (partner),
s (small group), I (Individual)**

- At the end of the lesson, have students confirm/disconfirm their initial connections to their background knowledge, based on what they have now learned about the topic.
- Display each group's completed mind map and do a gallery walk as a class. Encourage students to discuss similarities and differences among the mind maps in their small groups and as a whole class to further reinforce students' comprehension.
- Allow students to use their mind maps as a scaffold as they complete curricular tasks, end-of-chapter tests, or cloze exercises individually.
- Throughout this phase of the strategy, encourage students to transfer their thoughts and connected ideas

into a piece of writing. For example, students can individually write a summary connecting the ideas recorded on the mind map. (**Note:** Transfer may not be automatic for all students; additional modeling and support may be needed to ensure that students are successful with the task.)
- Encourage students to share their final products with a partner to show all they have learned.

Affirming Student Ownership: "*I*" Get It!
How does this process celebrate CLD student learning?

- **Sociocultural:** The mind map is a visual representation of the progression of learning throughout the lesson for the students. Posting students' completed mind maps at the end of the lesson/unit is a great affirmation of both their background knowledge and their learning.
- **Linguistic:** Students are able to summarize their thoughts using experiential and academic language,

as they have the completed mind map to refer back to when discussing or writing about the topic.
- **Academic:** Seeing other groups' completed mind maps supports students to self-assess their own understandings of the content and language of the lesson.
- **Cognitive:** Students' revised schemas for the topic are reflected in their writing as they summarize what they learned.

SPOTLIGHT: Early Literacy Connection

Tabors, Roach, and Snow (2001) found that many factors impact the development of early literacy skills, including the amount of extended discourse at home, the density of rare or sophisticated words in home conversations, and parental support for literacy activities (e.g., book reading). To support parents in developing these early literacy skills with their children, it is important to provide them with concrete strategies they can use in the home with their children when engaged in literacy activities.

Families must be seen as an asset in the schooling process, and all families regardless of socioeconomic status, race, language, or culture can be important contributors to their children's success and to their children's school (Violand-Sanchez, Sutton, & Ware, 1991). Parents of CLD students may or may not be literate in English, but they can apply the Mind Map strategy immediately with their children regardless of the language in which the literacy activity is conducted.

To modify the Mind Map strategy for young English learners, teachers can do the following as a home–school connection.

Activation:

- To help parents of CLD students promote early literacy skills at home, you can send home bilingual books or books in the students' L1 before reading them in English in the classroom.
- Ask the parents to read the book to their child and then encourage them to do a mind map with their child about the book.
- Prepare directions on how to make a mind map for the parents.
  - In the directions for the parents, tell them to label the mind map images as their children draw them to help the children associate the word with the picture (Buzan, 2003).
  - The parents can write the labels in whichever language they are most comfortable writing.
  - By performing this strategy in the native language, parents are supporting their children's future transfer of knowledge from the native language to English because they are providing the foundation in the L1.
- Send the necessary materials, such as paper and pencils, for the children to complete the project at home.
- When the children return to school the next day,

encourage them to share their mind maps with you and/or the whole class. Even if the information is shared in the students' L1, you will have visual cues to the initial connections they made to the story.
- You can then work with the whole class to create a class mind map on the topic.
- To create the class mind map, have the students look at the cover of the book you will read and talk to their partner about what they see and the connections they make to the picture.

Connection:

- In creating the mind map for the whole class, use a large chart paper or the entire white board. This ensures that everyone can see the mind map and that there is room for everyone to add their connection.
- Ask students to share aloud with the rest of the class one of the connections they discussed with their partners. As students are sharing, have them come up one at a time and write or draw the related word or image on the class mind map.
- Have each student use a different-colored writing implement when marking on the mind map.
- Continue this process until all of the students have added their connection to the mind map.
- Revoice student connections to highlight similarities and differences.
- Read the story aloud to the students. As you read the story, stop at specific points and draw the students' attention to the connections they made on the class mind map. Allow them to discuss new thinking with their partners.

Affirmation:

- After reading the story, revisit the class mind map.
- Ask the students if there are any new connections they want to add.
- To support new connections:
  - Have students talk to each other about the new links they have made and about some of the old ones that are already on the mind map.
  - Add students' new connections by putting the connections on sticky notes and adding them to the class mind map. Alternatively, add them to the mind map using a different color of marker.

One Classroom's Perspective

From the 2nd-grade class of Stephanie Wilhite

Activating:

Our essential question of the week is, *How are kids different around the world?* So today we did the Mind Map strategy so students could explore the essential question. The first thing I did to start the strategy was focus on the vocabulary words. Some of the vocabulary words were pertinent to students' creation of mind maps, so I shared the word cards with visuals on them with my students.

Next, I had each group write the essential question on a big poster paper. I had students discuss the essential question in their small groups. I had strategically grouped students for this activity so that each group would have an opportunity for rich conversation as they shared and discussed their initial ideas with each other. Then I had

students individually splash some of the words around the essential question. This was the start of their mind map.

I did explain to students that their mind map would essentially be a map of their minds and that they would be using the poster paper to connect all the ideas that they gathered from the story. After they were done splashing their initial thoughts, I had them share out ideas they wrote on their mind maps.

Connecting:

Next we moved into the book. I read the shorter introductory reading activity with students today to help them understand the essential question and also give them enough time and practice with their mind maps. As I read the story first, we stopped at specific points and students discussed what they had learned from the story about differences that kids exhibit. Some of the ideas they talked about were the ways kids celebrated different things and the foods they ate. As they discussed, I had students add those ideas to their mind maps and circle the new ideas they were adding. We took turns reading the story so students could keep adding more ideas to their mind maps. We continued adding new ideas until we had finished the story.

Affirming:

As we finished the story and our mind maps, I had students share out one more time the differences they saw with the kids around the world. Students used their mind maps to support them in this process. Once they were done with this part of the strategy, I had them respond to the essential question using a five-sentence summary. To do this, I gave them a topic sentence and, using that topic sentence, their task was to tell me five things they learned from the story that kids do differently around the world. I had students put their books away and just use the mind maps for writing their five-sentence paragraph. As students did this, I went around and gathered some of their summary statements and shared those with the rest of the class. I feel like this was a very nonthreatening strategy that went quite well for my learners.

STRATEGY

Listen Sketch Label

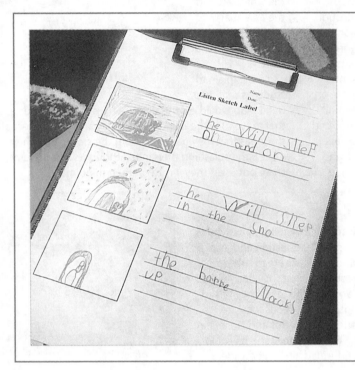

I used the strategy of Listen Sketch Label to work on the skill of visualization for my students. They did great. Students worked with each other and answered each other's questions as we worked on the strategy. The best part was to look and see if the pictures from the story matched their pictures in the boxes. They were so excited to share their sketches and their written statements throughout the lesson. Lots of big words were used today to explain their ideas.

—*Madison Nicholson, Kindergarten Teacher*

Where Theory Meets Practice

When students encounter words and phrases in text, it is important for them to be able to understand their meaning. Many phrases and words have both literal and figurative meanings. According to Tompkins, Campbell, Green, and Smith (2015), "literal meanings are the explicit dictionary meanings, and figurative meanings can be metaphorical or can use other figures of speech" (p. 160). For the most part, children who are native speakers of a language are very adept at inferring the meaning of phrases within a text based on the context of conversations. However, the meaning of language is not always clear for CLD students, for both cultural and linguistic reasons. Figurative language in particular poses a significant challenge, in that English learners translate the new phrases/words they encounter literally, which tends to cause confusion. Our students need in-depth opportunities to explore the text/content in order to analyze linguistic clues and references that can support their understanding, both now and in the future.

Often the way we make meaning of words, phrases, and larger passages of text is through creating mental imagery/ visualizing. Boerma, Mol, and Jolles (2016) note that pictures facilitate students' creation of a mental representation that can support them in their comprehension of text. Listen Sketch Label is a BDI strategy that relies heavily on students' creation of visuals as they make connections between what they hear and what they bring to the text as learners.

Listen Sketch Label takes CLD students through a step-by-step process of listening attentively to the text, connecting to it on a personal level, and documenting their mental imagery/visualization throughout the life cycle of the strategy. As students listen for language cues and references, context clues, and explicit details about the concept/story, they develop mental images that they then transfer to paper via sketches. This process supports them in creating a personalized learning scaffold to support their in-depth understanding of the text and their engagement in group tasks.

Through this strategy, students are encouraged to combine their illustrations and the written language of the text as they determine the overall meaning or idea behind the various concepts of the text/story. Essentially, this strategy supports dual coding of the concept—students' brains use both words and pictures to create multiple representations of the concept (Boerma, Mol, & Jolles, 2016; Paivio, 2006). The deeper processing that results supports learners in attaining higher levels of comprehension (Bartholomé & Bromme, 2009; Schüler, Arndt, & Scheiter, 2015). The artistic and interactive process of this strategy is sure to pique students' interest and keep them engaged throughout the lesson.

MATERIALS & RESOURCES
Materials Needed: Listen Sketch Label Template (one per student) • sets of index cards on which the vocabulary words are written (one set per group) • pencils/pens
Template: Listen Sketch Label Template (see page 57); also available for free download and printing from tcpress.com/accelerating
Checklist: Student Academic Behavior Checklist (see page 194); also available for free download and printing from tcpress.com/accelerating

 ACTIVATION: A Canvas of Opportunity

Directions:

i (individual)

- Create sets of index cards on which you have written the target vocabulary (one vocabulary word per card).
- Place students in groups of three or four students and give each student a Listen Sketch Label template. Provide each group a set of index cards. Note: The template can be copied on both sides to double the number of boxes for student responses, if desired.
- Share the essential question/outcomes of the day with your students. Explain to the students that they are going to do a strategy that will help them create mental images/visualize the story/text from their perspective.
- Share the vocabulary of the lesson with the students. As you share the words, have students write the words on the side of their individual strategy templates.
- Next, have students use their group's set of index cards to individually write words (in their native language or in English) or draw images that come to mind when they read the vocabulary word on each card. Have stu-

dents pass the index cards around until all students have documented their initial connections to each of the words.
- Have students discuss in their small groups the things they wrote about the words on the index cards. Ask students to share their examples and their related meanings with their group.
- As your students share, remember to circulate around the room to gather examples you can revoice for the rest of the class.

Activating the "*i*"
How does this process activate CLD students' existing knowledge?

- **Sociocultural:** When students are allowed to first write and then discuss with peers what they think each word might mean, they are provided with a low-risk opportunity to articulate their initial connections.
- **Linguistic:** As students record their initial understanding of the vocabulary words, they are able to draw upon their native language as a resource as well as practice new English language skills.

- **Academic:** When students share their ideas with one another, they are able to hear numerous examples of how individuals might interpret words and make meaning in different ways.
- **Cognitive:** Students' sharing of their initial interpretations of the words promotes curiosity and subsequent engagement in the lesson.

CONNECTION: The Broad & Narrow Strokes of Learning

Directions:

T (Total Group), p (partner), s (small group)

- Now is the time for students to dig deep into the idea of visualization through the text that they are working with. Remind them to leave the index cards with vocabulary associations on the table.
- Explain to students that their next task will be to listen to the text and then sketch their mental images in the boxes provided. Then they will write about (label) their visual associations on the lines provided.
- Since listening is a skill that is tied to comprehension, the first part of this strategy can be where you read aloud a small chunk of the text and have your students listen alongside.
- Stop after a few minutes and have students discuss with a partner what they heard. Remind students to talk about what they visualized/created in their minds as they heard the passage.
  - Visualization can be a harder skill for some students to connect to. Having the opportunity to talk it out with a peer can help facilitate this cognitive task.
  - During the first few implementations of this strategy with students, you may need to model the skill of visualizing when trying to infer the meaning of a phrase within the context of a text.
- After students have finished discussing, have them sketch their mental image for the first portion of text in the first box.
  - These mental images might represent specific details from the story, or they might relate to ideas such as cause and effect or sequencing.
  - You can tailor your progression of this strategy based on the skill you want your students to attain.
  - To help students move toward the intent of the story/text while they create their mental images, ask them to keep the following in mind: the context of the text,

individual words within the phrase, and any information from their own background knowledge that can help them infer the meaning.

- After students have finished sketching their mental image in the box, have them share and explain their image to the rest of their small group.
- Next, have students use the lines beside the box to write about/label their visualization of the text.
- After students have finished writing, share with them the visual from the text itself (if one is included). This way, students can see how their visualization compares to that of the text.
- Repeat the process of having students listen to the reading, discuss thoughts, sketch mental images, share with their group, and write about their mental representations as you proceed with the text.
  - You also can have students read the text as partners or small groups and then follow the sequence with creation of mental images and labeling them on the template.
  - The whole purpose is for students to listen closely and connect to the details from the story/text either being read aloud or as they read. When students connect with details, they are able to visualize better. Asking students to sketch their mental imagery ensures individual accountability for this process and promotes their selective listening.

Author Talk: Connection

Visual thinking and literacy is increasingly highlighted in schools today. We know that a combination of pictorial and nonpictorial representations can provide students with multiple ways to meaningfully comprehend text. Students are able to develop enhanced mental representations that support their more in-depth comprehension. Listen Sketch Label is a wonderful strategy for teachers to use to provide CLD students with explicit instruction for developing their visualization skills.

Teachers have commented that Listen Sketch Label as a strategy supports their students in getting involved in the text and in the process of understanding the meaning behind it. As one 3rd-grade teacher shared, "My students love this strategy! They are always asking when they will get to draw the meanings of the sentences again and talk about them with their friends!" When asked why she thought her students enjoyed the strategy so much, this teacher commented that she felt that her students took ownership of the activity. They were the ones deciding what to draw and how to explain their mental images to their friends; she was not giving them the answers.

By turning over the responsibility to the students, this strategy enables them to be in charge of their own learning. More and more, students' (and teachers') engagement with the curriculum can tend to feel restricted. As this strategy clearly illustrates, the more we give our students ownership of their learning, the more they get out of the process.

Connecting to the "*i*+1"
How does this process move CLD students from the known to the unknown?

- **Sociocultural:** As students share and discuss individual interpretations and sketches of their mental images, they build valuable cooperation skills and develop capacities to think about a concept from multiple perspectives.
- **Linguistic:** The Connection phase integrates a balanced ebb and flow of listening/reading, visual thinking, speaking, and writing, which supports English learners' continuous engagement in the lesson.
- **Academic:** The Listen Sketch Label strategy helps students analyze text to find clues that provide context

and/or that relate to their background knowledge. This process facilitates the development of mental representations to support comprehension of grade-level content.
- **Cognitive:** Having to justify their interpretations of the text within their small group engages CLD students in the application of key cognitive skills, including elaborating on prior knowledge, using imagery, and making inferences.

 AFFIRMATION: A Gallery of Understanding

Directions:

**T (Total Group), p (partner),
s (small group), I (Individual)**

- Have students look at their finished templates and use their sketches and labels to orally summarize their learning/understanding of the text as a group. Encourage them to discuss any major differences in understanding, and refer to the text for clarification.
- Now students are ready to turn their finished Listen Sketch Label templates into a piece of writing to provide evidence of their understanding of, or engagement with, the text.
  - Have students use their templates as a resource to write a succinct summary of the text.
  - Have students create an alternate ending for the text (you can allow them to use additional boxes and lines to capture their thinking first in a Think Sketch Label format).
  - Provide students with a cloze passage that relates to the text and have them complete the passage using their descriptions from the finished strategy template as a reference.
  - Have students use the Listen Sketch Label template to answer comprehension questions at the end of the story/text or respond to the essential question.
- Provide students with the opportunity to share their finished summaries with a partner or with their small groups.

Affirming Student Ownership: *"I" Get It!*
How does this process celebrate CLD student learning?

- **Sociocultural:** Having students discuss as a group how they would summarize their learning, taking into consideration the multiple perspectives of their peers, provides a shared learning experience that supports them in seeing one another as valuable members of the learning community.
- **Linguistic:** The ongoing practice of articulating their thoughts about the images and labels on their templates provides CLD students with valuable practice in using English for authentic communication and expression.

- **Academic:** By the end of the Affirmation phase of the lesson, students have had many opportunities to solidify and demonstrate their understanding of the story/text and related academic concepts.
- **Cognitive:** Students are challenged to think critically about the text and evaluate their own understanding as they discuss and listen to their peers' interpretations of the different sections of the text and consider their final written pieces.

SPOTLIGHT: Early Literacy Connection

Gentry (1987) identified six developmental stages for spelling: precommunicative, semiphonetic, phonetic, transitional, conventional, and morphemic/syntactic. When approaching the instruction of spelling with young children, it is important to be aware of these stages as they influence how students spell words. For example,

- The spelling of a student at the precommunicative stage looks like a bunch of scribbles and drawings of caricatures (Boyd-Batstone, 2006).
- Students at the semiphonetic stage of spelling are able to write letters (mostly consonants) that indicate the dominant sounds at the beginning or the end of a word.
- Phonetic spellers include all the sounds featured in a word, but their spelling is typically inventive in nature (Boyd-Batstone, 2006).

Research by Schickedanz and Casbergue (2004) found that "it is rare for preschool children to move beyond the beginning stages of semiphonetic spelling, and most will not progress to fully phonetic spelling until kindergarten" (p. 40).

For young CLD students, spelling can be especially difficult because they are working with sounds that may not be present in their native language, or that exist in their native language but in a different position. CLD students need opportunities to engage in lots of conversations to build their vocabulary and understanding of the English language. To support CLD students in their movement from semiphonetic spelling to phonetic spelling, the teacher can use a modified version of the Listen Sketch Label strategy.

To modify the Listen Sketch Label strategy for young CLD students, teachers can do the following variation. Note: For this variant of the strategy, you can use consonant–vowel–consonant (CVC) pattern words that are critical for young CLD students to understand. The CVC pattern is when a single vowel occurs between two consonants, and the vowel is pronounced as a short vowel sound.

Activation:

- Write three CVC words (e.g., cat, dog, pig) on the board and include a picture for each.
- Ask the students to think about the words on the board and share any thoughts about them.
- After the students have shared their thoughts about the CVC words, explain to them that these are CVC words.
- Model how to say each word and pronounce each sound.
- Ask the students the following questions: *What is the first sound? What letter makes that sound?* As you do this, have students think of any words in their own language that start with that sound. Circle the first letter of each word in green.
- Then ask the students about the middle sound, with the following questions: *What is the next sound? What letter makes that sound?* Again, make connections to the same sounds in the students' native language. Circle the second letter of each word in yellow.

SPOTLIGHT: Early Literacy Connection (*continued*)

Activation (*continued*):

- Finally, ask the students about the last sound in the word, with the following questions: *What is the last sound? What letter makes that sound?* Make additional connections to the same sounds in the students' native language. Circle the last letter of each word in red.
- Review each of the words in the following format: Read the word, say each sound in the word individually, and read the word again. Point to each word as you say it.
- Have the students read the words with you.

Connection:

- Read a book that has many words that follow the CVC word pattern.
- Give each student a Listen Sketch Label template.
- Choose two words from the story that follow the CVC pattern. Have students listen as you say each word and then have them echo the words back to you.
- Now read the first word again. This time after saying the word, have each student draw a picture in one of the boxes to represent what they think the word means.
- Have students discuss their ideas with a partner.

- Listen to students as they discuss so you can formatively assess their understanding. Revoice connections for the class.
- Come to consensus on the meaning of the word as a class. Allow students to revise their drawing as needed.
- Next to the box, have the students spell the word by writing down the sounds they hear as you sound out the word for them.
- Repeat this process for the second word.
- If time allows and/or students are able, encourage them to write the words in their native language as well. By doing this, you are promoting your CLD students' transfer of knowledge from the L1 to the L2.

Affirmation:

- After the students have completed the Listen Sketch Label template, place students into pairs. Give each pair a blank sheet of paper.
- Have students work together to illustrate an original "story" that incorporates both of the words from their template.
- When they have finished, have each pair combine with another pair to form a small group of four students.
- Have pairs read their stories in their small groups.
- You can ask each group to select one of the stories to share with the class.

It's the "*i*" Thing

Listen Sketch Label is a strategy grounded in the belief that, with appropriate support, students can self-regulate their own learning. All students are exposed to the same input as they listen to the content information; however, the output expected from individual students is varied and differentiated, depending upon their sociocultural, linguistic, cognitive, and academic biographies. Students use sketches throughout the lesson to capture their mental imagery/visualization. This strategy makes clear for students that each individual's connections to a text will be unique and highly dependent upon the links they make to their own schemas. With the aid of multiple opportunities for interaction with peers, students support one another to comprehend the text and achieve the lesson's goals.

One Classroom's Perspective

From the kindergarten class of Madison Nicholson

Activating:

I started the lesson by having students think of how visualization works. Our story of the week is *Bear Snores On,* and since visualization is one of the skills that I am working on, the Listen Sketch Label strategy worked best for this. To get students on the path of visualization, I first had them visualize an event from the story. I orally shared a piece from the story and had students individually create mental images to form their ideas about that piece. We have done metal images before so this was an easy step for my students. I had students share their associations with each other before sharing them with the rest of the class.

Next, I shared the front page of the text with students and just had them look at the visual of the page. I had my students discuss with each other what mental images they were creating about the book. What events did

they think might be in the book? After they were done creating their mental images, I had them discuss this with their shoulder partners. Then I had them individually draw their initial visual image in the top box of the template and write on the lines beside it. As they did this, I gathered some of their initial associations and their labels. Some of the students wrote words like *hibernation.* I was happy to see this, since my students have been studying the word in their science unit.

Connecting:

Then we got into the story and actually read it. I had already marked specific places in the text for me to stop and have students visualize the text and draw their mental images in the boxes. As I read the book, I didn't show them the visuals from the book since I really wanted my students to create their own mental images. As I read, I stopped at specific points and had students discuss what they thought the image would be for that part of the story. We also made sure to discuss certain vocabulary words that would help them in creating their pictures. As they did that, I had them draw in the next two boxes their own visualizations. As they finished their visuals, I also had them label the visuals on the lines next to them. When we finished the book, I showed students the visuals and they were able to see how their pictures were different from the book.

Affirming:

Next I had students look at their templates one more time to share with each other how they visualized and the labels they wrote. Then I had them work with a partner on sharing three events from the story using their Listen Sketch Label template. While they did this, I also had them sequence the events to show the progression of the story.

Name: _____

Date: _____

Listen Sketch Label

STRATEGY

Story Bag

The Story Bag strategy was a perfect way to get the class motivated and excited about learning new words. The implementation of this strategy gave me the chance to see that the working vocabulary my students had been building throughout this unit was becoming established and comfortable. Students replied to questions and offered their thoughts about the story. I was pleased to see their level of participation high and their motivation strong.

—*Shilo Burnham, Kindergarten Teacher*

Where Theory Meets Practice

Good readers use pictures, titles, headings, text, and background knowledge and experiences to make predictions before they begin to read. Predicting involves thinking ahead and anticipating information and events in the text. After making predictions, students can read through the text and refine, revise, and verify their predictions (Duke & Pearson, 2001). Predictions encourage active reading and keep children interested in the story/text.

Making predictions activates students' background knowledge about the text and helps them make connections between the new, unknown information and the known information they already possess. By making predictions about the text before reading, students use their existing knowledge and what they think might happen to connect to the text.

Story Bag is a strategy adapted from the work of Lado (2004) that helps CLD students establish a purpose for reading as they make predictions about pictures and objects that will and will not appear in the text. The strategy begins as a teacher-directed activity and evolves into a student learning strategy through repetition and meaningful contact with vocabulary words and academic concepts.

Story Bag is a strategy that can help teachers capitalize on student differences, and at the same time it provides a single tool that supports predictions, word building, and meaning making. Strategies such as this that convey respect for student differences become the basis for meaningful relationships and favorable academic results (Gay, 2010; Irvine, 1990; Ladson-Billings, 2009).

MATERIALS & RESOURCES

Materials Needed: Story Bag • pictures/objects that are and are not in the story • poster paper or white board to post T chart • blank sheet of paper or Story Bag Template (one per student) • brown paper bags (one per student)

Template: Story Bag Template (see page 64); also available for free download and printing from tcpress.com/accelerating

Rubric: Student Assessment Rubric (see page 195); also available for free download and printing from tcpress.com/accelerating

ACTIVATION: A Canvas of Opportunity

Directions:

i (individual)

- Place students in small groups of three or four students.
- Have the students examine the front cover of the book, and explain that they will make predictions about the objects that will or will not be in the story.
- To support students in making their predictions, write the following on a white board or a large piece of poster paper. Have students individually draw the same T chart on a piece of blank paper or use the template provided.

In the Story	Not in the Story

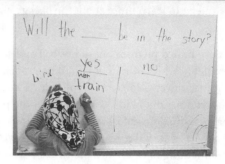

- One by one, pull objects/pictures out of the Story Bag and ask the students to predict whether the item will be in the story or won't be in the story. Have students first record their individual predictions and then discuss their predictions in their small groups.
  - As students are predicting, have them explain why they think the item will or will not be in the story.
  - Circulate around the room to listen to student conversations about their predictions and related rationales.
- After students have had a chance to discuss their predictions in their small groups, bring the discussion to a class vote for the first item. Then tape/place the item under the appropriate column. Alternatively, you can also have students write the name of the item in the correct column.
  - If students are not sure whether an item will or will not be in the story, you can place the item on the line between the two columns. Alternatively, you can add a "Maybe" column and have students place the items there.
- Repeat the voting and posting process for each object/picture.

Activating the "i"
How does this process activate CLD students' existing knowledge?

- **Sociocultural:** By asking students to provide a rationale for their predictions, the Story Bag strategy allows students to make their background knowledge public.
- **Linguistic:** Children learn not only the language the teacher addresses but also the language they overhear around them (Au, 2002). The Activation phase promotes awareness of academic language connected to the topic as CLD students hear peers' articulation of rationales for their predictions.

- **Academic:** Story Bag promotes comprehension from the very outset, as students have exposure to visuals that connect to the text prior to their reading the material.
- **Cognitive:** The CLD student uses his or her background knowledge and clues from the cover of the text to make logical predictions.

Author Talk: Activation

As teachers, we know that our students come to us with varied experiences. Consider how Ms. Amy Berg used the Story Bag strategy to learn more about the backgrounds of her students:

> As Ms. Berg pulled pictures out of her bag and students predicted which would or would not appear in the story, the conversations were typical for a 2nd-grade classroom. Often kids would laugh at the pictures that would come out of the bag. Occasionally, a student would make a deeper connection to a picture and say something like "That's a picture of a war. . . . Where I come from, there was a lot of fighting and wars. It was really scary and not safe for our family. That's why we moved here." As soon as Ms. Berg heard comments such as this, she opened up the discussion to the class. As students later discussed their ideas in groups, Ms. Berg walked around the room to listen to the students talk. Later on, when she started reading the story, she made a point to revoice some of the ideas the students had shared, thereby creating

a true community of learners where everyone's ideas were being valued and brought to life.

As you use this strategy, consider ways you can create conditions and situations in the classroom that will allow students to share their many culturally bound understandings. A few tips that teachers have shared with us include:

- As you pull a picture from the bag, have students talk in pairs first about why they think the picture is critical for the book and second about how the picture relates to them as individuals.
- Have students in pairs or small groups use the pictures that were shared at the beginning of the lesson to create their own stories revolving around the topic. As appropriate, this can be used as a summative assessment for comprehension.
- Have students individually or in pairs use computers to search the Internet as an added resource after you have finished reading the story. They can look for pictures and objects that could be added to the story.

 CONNECTION: The Broad & Narrow Strokes of Learning

Directions:

T (Total Group), p (partner), s (small group)

- As the text/story is read, call on students to verify the objects/pictures as they appear in the text. This can by done by having students come to the front of the room and determine whether the objects/pictures are in the correct column. If they are not, have the students move the objects/pictures to the appropriate column.
- As a student verifies or moves an object/picture, have the class members talk to each other about the way the object/picture is used within the context of the story to help them understand the notion of context clues. Guiding questions you might ask your students include:
  ○ Were our initial predictions correct? Why or why not?
  ○ What does this mean for us as readers?
- As you continue reading the text, stop at key points and have students discuss the text/story in their small groups.
- As an extension, have students write in their notebooks the names of the objects/pictures as they appear in the text. When the reading has been completed, students can retell the story using these words.

Connecting to the "*i* +1"
How does this process move CLD students from the known to the unknown?

- **Sociocultural:** The visual nature of the activity allows students to use their personal schemas to connect to the text and make meaning for themselves.
- **Linguistic:** Students are able to practice their selective listening skills as they listen for the mention of specific objects while the text is being read aloud.

- **Academic:** Students are able to broaden their understanding of contexts in which given objects/pictures might be relevant.
- **Cognitive:** Students are able to become "constructively responsive" readers (Pressley & Afflerbach, 1995) as they think about the initial placement of the pictures/objects in the columns and then finally place each item in the correct column based on the text.

 AFFIRMATION: A Gallery of Understanding

Directions:

**T (Total Group), p (partner),
s (small group), I (Individual)**

- After the story has been read, place students in pairs and pass out the objects/pictures, giving one object/picture to each pair of students.
- Have the students work with their partner to find the page in the story in which the object/picture appears, or be prepared to tell the class that the object/picture did not appear in the book.
  - For the objects that did not appear in the story, stretch your students cognitively by asking them to explain why they initially thought they might appear in the story.
- Next, pass out story bags to each student. Inside each

story bag, have the individual pictures reflective of the story for students to manipulate.
- Have students individually sequence the pictures in the order in which they appeared in the story.
- Finally, have students individually write a summary of what they remember about the story on the outside of their story bag.

Affirming Student Ownership: "*I*" Get It!
How does this process celebrate CLD student learning?

- **Sociocultural:** As students interact with their partner and report to the class, they have an additional opportunity to develop their collaboration skills and share their background knowledge (if their object/picture was not in the text).
- **Linguistic:** The visuals in the story bag provide non-linguistic support for students' writing process.

- **Academic:** As students work to explain which objects/pictures are and are not in the text, they solidify their understanding of the text.
- **Cognitive:** Students are able to gain ownership over their learning as they employ sequencing and summarizing skills.

SPOTLIGHT: Early Literacy Connection

Story Bag is an effective strategy that allows students to predict whether or not various objects or pictures are going to appear in a text that is read aloud by the teacher. Because predictions vary based on the background knowledge and experiences of the student, this strategy is ideal for highlighting sociocultural elements of students' biographies. Story Bag provides the frame for the following activity that students can do at home with their parents and then replicate for their peers in the classroom.

As young CLD students enter our classrooms, each one brings a unique set of experiences and skills. Some students may have strong academic backgrounds and know how to read in their native language. CLD students' home language and previous cultural and educational experiences give them a sense of belonging and support their ability to learn a new language and so should not be subtracted from the learning of English (Wong Fillmore, 2000).

To modify the Story Bag strategy for young CLD students, teachers can set it up as a home–school connection. When students are familiar with the routine of the Story Bag strategy and have used the strategy multiple times, they should be encouraged to create their own Story Bag activity for their peers with help from their parents, as described below.

- The students can choose a book from their home library or a book from the classroom that they can check out to take home.
  - The selected book should be one the student is familiar with or one that is at the individual's independent reading level.
- Explain to the students that they will be creating a Story Bag activity with their parents at home, and that they will then bring back their story bag and conduct the activity with their classmates.
- The teacher will need to provide each student with a Story Bag Template (see page 64) to take home.
- The students will use the Story Bag Template to classify objects that are in or not in their story.
- With their parents, the students will select objects from the story that will be used, as well as some other objects that do not belong in the story.
- Students can draw or cut pictures out of magazines to represent objects that will be included in their story bag. The pictures need to be small enough to fit on the Story Bag Template
- After the students and their parents have completed preparing the story bag, have the students share their book and story bag with their classmates in small groups.

Activation:

- Have the students separate into small groups of three or four. Provide each group with a T chart or Story Bag Template.
- Each student will have a chance to be the leader in the group. The leader will share the story bag he or she created at home with the other students.
- Have the leader show the cover of the book to the group and ask the group members what they think the story will be about.
- Each group will discuss what they think the story will be about. After a brief discussion, have the leader start to show one object at a time from the story bag.
- As the leader pulls out each object, have the group members do the following:
  - Take turns in saying the beginning and the ending sounds of the name of the object/picture.
  - Take turns in sharing any other words associated with the object/picture. Students can also share the words in their native languages.
  - The leader will ask if the object will be "in" or "not in" the story. After the group comes up with consensus on where to place the object, the leader will list that object on the T chart or template the teacher provided.
- This process will continue until all of the objects have been placed on the two-column chart.

Connection:

- If the leader can read the story, have him or her read it aloud to the other students in the small group.
  - If the student is not able to read the story aloud, have an adult (older book buddies, office staff, paraprofessionals) read the story for him or her.
- As the story is read, the students can change the objects to the proper category ("in" or "not in") if necessary.

Affirmation:

- After the story has been read, have the leader check to see if the objects from the story are in the correct category.
- Then have the leader ask the other students what their favorite part of the story was and explain why it was their favorite part.
- Lastly, have the leader share his or her favorite part of the story and tell why it was the favorite.
  - As an extension, you can also have the groups write a few sentences retelling the story in their own words.

One Classroom's Perspective

From the kindergarten class of Shilo Burnham

Activating:

As I was preparing for this lesson, I thought carefully about my students' experiences with the Latin music and dancing that is known as Salsa. I knew that I could use the experiences of my para-educator, Mrs. Oliver, with Salsa dancing to help my students see and learn what this kind of dancing was like. I chose vocabulary that I knew would need clarification and extra practice. I also chose some vocabulary with dual meanings to provide extra practice with homophones. I wanted the activity to be engaging and relevant. The only English language learner (ELL) child that I have is Vietnamese. I knew that this language and information would possibly be very new to him. All of the students were excited when they found out they would

get to help decide what pictures would be in the story, and they eagerly volunteered to help tape them up on the white board.

Connecting:

The grouping for this activity was whole group; however, I feel I did a responsible job of asking the children to think/pair/share and have alternate ways of responding and thinking. At one point in my lesson, I asked students to try the Salsa dance with our para-educator. I knew that the Story Bag strategy would provide an exciting and motivating experience for my students to practice and potentially learn new vocabulary. They were invested and highly curious about the vocabulary words that I pulled out of the bag at the beginning of the lesson. I asked the students to put their finger on their nose, or their hand on their head each time they heard the word(s) in context as I read. As we encountered these words, I had students come up and put a star on the picture to show it was in the story. For the pictures

that we had originally placed in the "Not in the Story" column, we moved them to the "In the Story" column before putting a star on them. I was very pleased with the group participation and their responses.

Affirming:

After the lesson, I engaged the students in a brief discussion about the story so I could do a quick check of concepts and vocabulary. These conversations are extremely powerful for me, as I am able to do some basic assessment and observation about the students' comprehension and learning. Because I teach

kindergarten, this is one of the most important ways I am able to gather authentic information about my learners. I asked the students to engage in further thinking by doing a short writing activity in response to the story. I wanted to see what further evidence I could gather about their understanding from the book and the new vocabulary practiced and learned. Overall, I was very pleased with their learning and the results of my observations.

Story Bag

In the Story ☺	Not in the Story ☹

CHAPTER 2

Rigor: Leveraging Words Toward Academic Achievement

> We do not learn in a straightforward way—it is more staccato—we listen, we try, we concentrate, we try again, we make mistakes, we correct, and we learn together.
>
> —*Hattie & Yates (2014), p. 113*

ONE of the questions we as educators are asked most frequently is, "How do you know what vocabulary is most important for your CLD students to learn?" Before addressing this question, let us look carefully at what is being asked. What *vocabulary* is being referred to in this question? For teachers across the country, the objective of developing academic language (i.e., the decontextualized language of schools; the language of academic discourse, of texts, and of formal argument) is at the heart of vocabulary instruction (August & Hakuta, 1997; Beck, McKeown, & Kucan, 2013; Gersten, Dimino, Jayanthi, Kim, & Santoro, 2007; Tompkins & Blanchfield, 2004; Vaughn & Linan-Thompson, 2004).

The strategies presented in this chapter focus on teaching students how to interpret and internalize academic language, including academic vocabulary, so that it becomes personally meaningful to them and can be used in meaningful ways. Personalized contextualization of the vocabulary, according to research by Blachowicz and Fisher (2000) and as acknowledged by Fisher and Frey (2015), not only helps to increase students' understanding but also promotes their retention of the new words. Recent research has further solidified the documented link between students' vocabulary and their ability to comprehend what they read (National Center for Education Statistics, 2012). Vocabulary knowledge has been said to be the "great predictor" of school success when it comes to reading (Reutzel & Cooter, 2010). In fact, vocabulary knowledge has been shown to account for 80% of the variance in students' reading comprehension scores on standardized measures of achievement (Reutzel & Cooter, 2012). Given such statistics, it is not surprising that the education literature offers multiple frameworks and models for helping teachers identify key vocabulary to teach and providing them with systematic procedures to follow in teaching that vocabulary (see Beck et al., 2013, Calderón, 2007, and Marzano, 2004, for examples).

Selection and Instruction of Vocabulary Words

Students need to learn an enormous number of vocabulary words, and it is impossible to teach all of these words directly. However, not all words need the same attention. Beck et al. (2013) recommend choosing vocabulary words by determining their usefulness, their frequency, and the ease with which a student can restate their meaning in his or her own words. Researchers distinguish among three different tiers of vocabulary words.

Tier 1 words are basic vocabulary words—such as *cat, dog, clock,* and *jump*—that are heard frequently in social conversation and are seen in numerous contexts. These words rarely require direct vocabulary instruction in the school setting.

Tier 2 words represent more sophisticated vocabulary. These are words such as *consistent* and *assume* that mature language users employ in conversation and that are seen frequently in written text and standardized assessments. Tier 2 words also are encountered frequently in multiple content areas. Beck et al. (2013) feel that teachers need to target their direct vocabulary instruction on Tier 2 words because of the impact these words have on reading comprehension and because of their prevalence throughout a student's schooling.

Tier 3 words are content-specific words that appear in isolated situations and are rarely used in daily conversation.

Tier 3 words are often regarded as the vocabulary of the academic knowledge domain, and they are learned in highly specialized contexts such as chemistry, geometry, and physics. These are the words that students are least likely to be familiar with from daily life because they are so domain specific. As such, they are most frequently the focus of explicit instruction.

Selecting vocabulary words for CLD students requires a different approach from what is needed for native English speakers. Kinsella (2005) asserts that because vocabulary knowledge plays such a pivotal role in the overall school success and mobility of CLD students, all grade-level teachers must devote more time and attention to selecting vocabulary words. Teachers must explicitly teach the vocabulary that will enable CLD students to meet the demands of today's standards-based curricula.

Calderón et al. (2005) modified the three-tier system of Beck et al. (2013) for use in vocabulary instruction with CLD students. According to Calderón and colleagues, Tier 1 words for second language learners are words that represent concepts typically already known by CLD students in their native language. The students may simply need the correct English label to make the connection with their background knowledge. Teachers can also make connections with cognates in the students' native language.

Tier 2 words for CLD students include many words with multiple meanings, which can be especially difficult for English learners (August, Carlo, Dressler, & Snow, 2005). Unless CLD students are taught a word's multiple meanings, their limited background knowledge of the word might lead them away from a full and accurate understanding of its meaning in a particular context. Because Tier 3 words are, by definition, low-frequency words, these terms often can be translated to CLD students in their native language.

Biography-Driven Vocabulary Instruction

According to Herrera (2016), we as educators need to approach instruction from a biography-driven perspective in which we use information about students' sociocultural, linguistic, cognitive, and academic dimensions as a guide for creating the most effective learning conditions in our classrooms. Each student has learned specific vocabulary and other background knowledge within the home, community, and school contexts he or she has experienced. A student's background knowledge is constantly changing in response to facts, social customs, experiences, and emotions that are encountered and/or learned (Marzano, 2004). To support CLD students in making connections between their existing knowledge and the academic vocabulary of a lesson, we first need to identify the assets—especially the linguistic assets—that our students bring to the classroom and use those assets as the starting point for instruction.

In our work to support students' vocabulary development, we must continually remind ourselves that the major effort of a child's life leading up to schooling is building a "repository of social and interpersonal skills"; thus, most learning for students has come from watching others and imitating what they produce (Hattie & Yates, 2014, p. 6). When we ask students to move beyond and think for themselves, we are asking them to think in ways they generally are not accustomed to. By providing students with the scaffolding they need in order to make this level of thinking happen, we increase the likelihood that students will add words and concepts to their schemas. How we teach vocabulary and explicitly link it to text is critical to accelerating learning for CLD populations. If the links are not personally meaningful and co-constructed with others, there is less chance learners will acquire the vocabulary for use in the future (Fisher & Frey, 2015).

Research has shown that a critical element for students in their acquisition and retention of vocabulary knowledge is their ability to make connections between their existing background knowledge and the new material being presented in a lesson (Gunning, 2006; Langer, 2001; Nagy, 2003). For CLD students, who face extra challenges linguistically and culturally, support in making these connections is essential. Effective vocabulary instruction must go beyond applying a "formula" for selecting key vocabulary words. Rather, the task must be approached from a biography-driven perspective in which our knowledge of individual students drives our selection of vocabulary words and guides our instructional efforts throughout the lesson.

Reutzel and Cooter's (2010) meta-analysis of the most successful methods of vocabulary instruction produced the following list of principles for effective vocabulary instruction, based on the research of Coyne, McCoach, Loftus, Zipoli, and Kapp (2009), Rasinski (1998), and Stahl (1999):

- *Principle 1.* Vocabulary should be taught both explicitly and incidentally.
- *Principle 2.* Learning how to construct vocabulary from rich contexts is valuable.
- *Principle 3.* Effective vocabulary instruction must include depth of learning as well as breadth of word knowledge.
- *Principle 4.* Multiple meaningful exposures are important for learning new vocabulary. (Reutzel & Cooter, 2010, pp. 226–227)

Building on Principle 1, the strategies described in this chapter provide a structure in which vocabulary is taught both explicitly and incidentally. The strategies begin by explicitly providing students with a stimulus or introduction to the new vocabulary in a way that actively involves each student in the learning process through listening, speaking, reading, or writing. Students are directed to attend to the topic, concepts, and vocabulary of the lesson and make immediate personal connections to them. As the lesson proceeds, students are engaged in the incidental use and application of the lesson vocabulary and other academic words.

Principle 2 emphasizes the importance of the student learning how to construct vocabulary from rich contexts. In our work with CLD students, we have seen that vocabulary knowledge expands when students have numerous opportunities to encounter new words in rich and varying contexts. The key issue in extending students' background knowledge is making specific connections between what they already know and the new material (Wessels, 2008). Without such connections to vocabulary words, the new information will not make it into storage in students' permanent memory (Swinney & Velasco, 2006). Working memory has the ability to activate information from both the sensory and the permanent memory. If students have sufficient meaningful exposures to the vocabulary while it is in working memory, the information will move into permanent memory. The strategies introduced in this chapter are designed with this goal of retention in mind.

Building on Principle 3, the strategies of this chapter have been designed to address depth of learning as well as breadth of word knowledge. The Activation phase of the strategies provides students with avenues for developing a "conceptual hook" (Young & Hadaway, 2006) to the information already in their permanent memory, which gives them access to all of their previous connections to that specific information (Svinicki, 1991). During the Connection phase, students engage with texts, hands-on materials, and peers in order to make connections between their background knowledge and the new vocabulary. Because students activated their schemas in the Activation phase, the previously established connections allow them to think more deeply about the meaning of the vocabulary words, which increases their metacognition (Wessels, 2008). A continual focus on students' use of academic language throughout the lesson ensures their exposure to (and practice with) a wide variety of words. Finally, during the Affirmation phase, students are provided with structured opportunities to use academic language, especially the key vocabulary, to demonstrate their learning.

Principle 4 highlights the need for students to have multiple meaningful exposures as they learn new vocabulary. A foundational component of each strategy is collaboration among students. By employing strategic grouping configurations that reflect consideration for students' individual biographies, teachers are better able to ensure that when students discuss academic vocabulary in pairs and in small groups, they will be able to gain new and deeper contextual understanding of the words and concepts. The structured opportunities for student collaboration and sharing of ideas yield innumerable opportunities for learners to hear and practice a wide range of words in authentic communicative tasks. As students use the vocabulary to make predictions, confirm/disconfirm initial associations, express ideas, and summarize learning, they become more likely to store the meanings of vocabulary words in their permanent memory, where they can be accessed, consciously or unconsciously, whenever needed (Stahl, 1999).

Strategies in Practice

In this chapter you will find descriptions of the following seven strategies, which explicitly create conditions that encourage learners to value and expand upon their preexisting vocabulary knowledge and linguistic abilities:

- DOTS
- Foldable
- Pic-Tac-Tell
- Vocabulary Quilt
- Thumb Challenge
- Magic Book
- IDEA

STRATEGY

DOTS

D etermine what I know
O bserve
T alk to peers as we elaborate
S ummarize what we learned

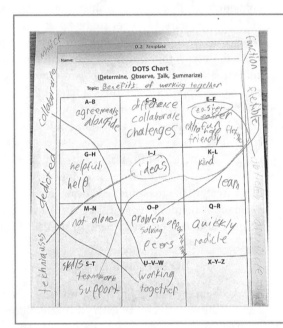

I love the DOTS chart because it is such a great advanced graphic organizer. The strategy starts by having students share their initial thoughts and connections to the topic. As they move more deeply into the topic, they are able to relate to the essential question and keep track of their own thoughts through the DOTS chart. Through discussions and by relating their ideas on the chart to their readings, they are able to pull out more of their connections, take their learning back to the essential question, and tie together everything they are learning. DOTS takes learning beyond teacher-led discussions. Having the DOTS chart in their hand helps lots of students that are not confident in their own abilities, since they have a tool in their hand throughout the lesson.

—*JoAnna Euston, 5th-Grade Teacher*

Where Theory Meets Practice

In culturally and linguistically diverse settings, teachers are often required to test the limits of what is possible as they try to provide a balance between the science and the art of teaching. On a daily basis we strive to create conditions and situations for making learning an expectation and a reality for our students. These expectations are grounded in the multiple teaching and learning processes and actions that we conduct daily with the learners in our classrooms. One highly discussed and researched topic of instruction has been vocabulary development.

For far too long, vocabulary development among students has been viewed as an isolated process. To this effect, we often implement strategies or activities at the beginning of the lesson but then fail to take them into the work time of the lesson. Vocabulary instruction of this kind becomes an isolated sequence within the delivery of a lesson, with little attention paid to the ways everything fits together in relation to the identified grade-level skill and overall meaning of the lesson. Due to this isolated nature of many vocabulary development activities, the important associations that exist between vocabulary and comprehension often are lost.

DOTS is a strategy that helps educators push the boundaries and "connect the dots" linguistically and academically for CLD students. The processes involved within the scope of the strategy allow teachers to base their instruction in practices that are proven effective for all learners. Throughout the lesson, vocabulary is seen as integral to learning, and students are guided to build upon their collective ideas and knowledge base.

Learning theories and research have long demonstrated that determining and using student knowledge as core to our instructional delivery ensures that connections are made for advancing language and content learning (e.g., Ambrose, Bridges, DiPietro, Lovett, & Norman, 2010; Dewey, 1938; Lent, 2012; Marzano, 2004). If in fact this is true, the first question that bears to be asked by the teacher is: *What experiences and knowledge does the student bring that would support learning?* Subsequent questions include: *What will need to happen at the beginning of the lesson in order for me to determine and document what each learner in the community brings and what associations will need to be made to help connect what is collected to the standard(s), essential question, language, and content objectives of the lesson? What kinds of tools do my students have access to during the lesson to take ownership over their own learning?* The DOTS strategy and the tool itself supports teachers in gaining insight into students' knowledge resources and provides learners with support they need in taking ownership over their own learning.

The "**D**" in DOTS relates to ***determining*** and documenting what the learner brings, which allows the teacher to move theories such as Vygotsky's *zone of proximal development* (ZPD) and Krashen's *i+1* toward the reality of the classroom (Krashen, 1985; Vygotsky, 1978).

An ecology is created where the teacher provides opportunities for learners to share what they bring with themselves, and takes explicit, recurrent actions to connect that information to the essential question/objectives/outcomes of the day. This step often involves moving beyond the science of classroom practice to be aware of the learner and begin implementing processes that help create a classroom community. The tool on which students record both their initial and their evolving connections to the vocabulary and content throughout the lesson serves as part of a cognitive learning strategy that supports reading comprehension and manipulation of ideas (Herrera et al., 2014). The recurrent and repetitive (systematic) nature of the strategy implementation allows students to continually monitor their understanding of the content, thereby leading to metacognition that enables them to recall, self-plan, and reflect on their own learning progress.

Observing for and cognitively interacting with the most important information and vocabulary throughout the lesson provides the learner with opportunities to focus on the core information needed to grow both linguistically and academically. Unfortunately, students often are not aware of the flow of the lesson and the association between vocabulary and comprehension. Content is presented in abstract ways that leave hidden the manner in which interlocking blocks of language (vocabulary) fit together to create a whole (content). Students' tools are limited to worksheets where they fill in the blanks or otherwise respond without cognitively monitoring their own processes. Teachers are left unaware of what is being learned and the ways the student is processing language and learning, from both a cultural and a linguistic perspective.

The DOTS strategy prepares learners with a tool for becoming aware of what is most important. By using the DOTS chart as a cognitive tool in their hands, learners document connections they make throughout the work time phase of the lesson. The knowledge development and language gains that take place throughout the class time are incrementally added to the chart so that the cumulative collection can be accessed by the learner for future use.

Talk is essential to developing language and supporting the learner throughout all stages of the lesson. The DOTS learning tool provides students with the opportunity to use the language they have available to weave and reweave their academic learning using both the social and the academic language they documented at the beginning of the lesson, as well as the language (vocabulary) they have collected from text, teacher, and peers. The teacher utilizes the tool to provide the learner with a scaffold for working with, reviewing, and rehearsing what has been learned. Talk structures are intentionally selected as the lesson unfolds (situationally), and the teacher conducts periodic formative assessment at checkpoints that are the result of allowing learners to make public what they understand. It is from this vantage point that the teacher can navigate the ZPD and ensure *i+1* using both the academic language of the content area and the native language and English that the learner has available given the level of language proficiency.

The "**S**" in DOTS, ***summarizing***, supports students to bring to closure their meaning-making experience, which has taken shape through a connected series of learning actions throughout the lesson. At this stage of the lesson, learners are left with a tool that reflects their unique learning processes and supports their summarization, synthesis, and paragraph generation. Students can highlight and showcase what they have learned; teachers can take the documented evidence of student understanding toward assessment. As students summarize what they learned, the DOTS chart can be used to reinforce their understanding and application of the information. Moreover, the DOTS chart provides English learners with a necessary scaffold to ensure their full participation. Research has concluded that such reinforcement and application of learnings in practice increases comprehension for all students (Cooper, 1986; Cunningham, Moore, Cunningham, & Moore, 1999; Peregoy & Boyle, 2017; Rasinski & Padak, 2009; J. L. Vacca, Vacca, & Gove, 2014).

MATERIALS & RESOURCES

Materials Needed: DOTS Template appropriate to grade level of students (one per student) • paper • colored pencils/markers • pencils/pens

Template: DOTS Template, two versions, one with 6 boxes (which might be more appropriate for K–1 students) and one with 12 boxes (for older students) (see pages 77, 78); also available for free download and printing from tcpress.com/accelerating

Checklist: Student Academic Behavior Checklist (see page 196); also available for free download and printing from tcpress.com/accelerating

Video: A video clip illustrating implementation of this strategy is available for viewing online at coe.k-state.edu/cima/biographycrt

---

 ACTIVATION: A Canvas of Opportunity

Note: Two versions of the DOTS chart have been included as templates for your use at the end of this strategy. The first version might be more appropriate for K–1 students, as there are fewer boxes (6 versus 12) to complete.

Directions:

i (individual)

- To begin the "**D**" (*determine*) portion of DOTS, ask students to think about their past experiences or knowledge. Remind them that they have to determine what it is that they may know about the topic that is going to be the focus of the day or the week.
- Once they have created a mental image or thought of words and pictures, ask them to determine their most important and relevant ideas for the topic. Have them use the alphabetical system to individually document these in the specific boxes of the DOTS chart. Remind them that their ideas on the chart will be used as a means to connect to new ideas as they get into the text.
- Allow 3–5 minutes for students to complete this part.

Instructional Tips:

- During this time, the teacher has the opportunity to attend to CLD students (as needed), reluctant learners, or students who might need assistance. By asking strategic questions, we can help prompt student thinking and attend to their biographies.

- Encourage learners to write in English and/or the native language and draw as many ideas and words as they can think of on their charts. The DOTS chart is their resource from the very beginning, so allow for any opportunity through which students can use the resources they come equipped with to document their knowledge.
- The teacher's role as primarily a silent observer during this time can lead to creation of a classroom ecology where students feel comfortable to take risks and share what they know without being overly influenced by teacher talk.
- To spark students' thought and imagination, you can also orally revoice some of the students' ideas from the DOTS chart as way to add to the class's collective understanding of the topic.
- As you circulate around the room, *gather students' words and document the words* from students' individual DOTS charts onto a master chart for later use.

Activating the "*i*"
How does this process activate CLD students' existing knowledge?

- **Sociocultural:** By explicitly connecting to the words and skills of students' background knowledge, learners are able to bring their own critical understandings that are rooted in their prior knowledge (community) and funds of knowledge (home). These initial connections to their knowledge systems set learners on a personal path to learning that often leads to *i* +1.
- **Linguistic:** When every child is given the opportunity to share the knowledge and skills they have available, teachers are able to gather the information needed to move learning forward. Allowing students to respond in their L1 ensures that all students can actively participate

in this lesson regardless of what stage of SLA they are in at the time. When explicit links are made between the L1 and L2, the transfer of knowledge and skills across languages also is promoted.
- **Academic:** This strategy provides teachers with ways of capitalizing on students' assets that are academic in nature. By weaving in language support through the DOTS chart, they set the stage for enhanced academic learning.
- **Cognitive:** Because every student is afforded a manageable entry point to engage in the lesson, learners begin to develop a sense of themselves as successful contributors to the learning process.

 CONNECTION: The Broad & Narrow Strokes of Learning

Directions:

T (Total Group), p (partner), s (small group)

 Bridging to the Content— Drawing the *i* into the Lesson

At this stage of the lesson, the DOTS chart has become a tool for learners that both scaffolds their language development and prepares them to gather information, ask questions, formulate their own ideas, and articulate their views, thereby constantly promoting academic development.

- After the students have finished recording their initial connections, pair students and provide them with time to share their ideas with each other. Circulate around the room to listen to/solidify student connections.

Instructional Tips:

- At this time, remind students how much they already know about the topic that is evident from the words and images they have on their DOTS charts.
- Allow students to "borrow" words from their peers during this time by writing down borrowed words with a colored pencil. This step can become an intentional act for students as they consistently share ideas with each other and add to their own knowledge base.

 Digging into Text

- Introduce the target vocabulary by having students individually write 8–12 key vocabulary words for the lesson around their DOTS chart. (Remember, the purpose of the tool is not to teach isolated vocabulary but to reinforce the words and ideas that relate to the identified skill of the day or week and the learning outcomes.)

(Continued on the next page)

CONNECTION: The Broad & Narrow Strokes of Learning (continued)

- The "**O**" portion of DOTS lets students make their own *observations* on how they connect to the content.
  - Have students individually *connect the dots* by drawing lines between their words and the target vocabulary they wrote around the edges of their charts. This step during the lesson is critical because it helps students identify the already established connections between their own schema and the vocabulary. The vocabulary and the students' related words provide a foundation for what is being learned. Drawing on this foundation promotes comprehension and sets the stage for writing.
  - Read the text/proceed with the content and have students add to their charts additional related words/concepts in colored pencil.
- As you orchestrate instruction, make sure to connect to the identified skill/standard. (For example, if the skill for the week is using contextual clues or finding text evidence, then have students add related ideas/concepts so that by the end of the lesson, students will have a compilation of ideas related to the targeted skill.)
- Stop at different points in the lesson to discuss the curricular words in context. Throughout this time, encourage students to have meaningful conversations using their DOTS charts as guides. The more you encourage

use of the DOTS chart during the lesson, the more it will become a personalized learning tool for students. Keep encouraging students to add words to their charts.
- As the lesson continues, the "**T**" portion of the strategy calls for teachers to provide students with multiple opportunities to *talk* within pairs, small groups, and the whole group about their associations between the words they individually (and as a community) generated and the target vocabulary words and key concepts.
- Listen to students' conversations and provide constructive revoicing of their thinking and ideas in order to confirm, clarify, elaborate, extend upon, or review.

Instructional Tips:

- Encourage students to add the page number in the text where they find associations to a specific skill or vocabulary word.
- Ask students to add the curriculum definitions of the vocabulary words to the backs of their charts.
- Focus on reinforcements of concepts and skills rather than just isolated words.
- Remind students that the DOTS chart is their personal note-taking tool. No two DOTS charts will look the same.

Connecting to the "*i*+1"

How does this process move CLD students from the known to the unknown?

- **Sociocultural:** Both teachers and students realize that language is bound by the sociocultural dimension of the individual. Opportunities for talk allow all members of the learning community to benefit from others' experiences and perspectives.
- **Linguistic:** Schematic connections are strengthened as students gain new words and practice using academic language to engage in authentic conversations about the content.
- **Academic:** The consistent ebb and flow of meaningful interactions supports more rigorous and relevant learn-

ing; students use their charts to question, formulate ideas, and consistently articulate their views.
- **Cognitive:** Cognitive processing of information is influenced by one's culture-bound lens for perceiving and interpreting the world. The DOTS chart supports learners to document their unique ways of processing the lesson's content. Having a tool in their hands to capture their progression of thought and understanding provides students with evidence of learning that has taken place.

AFFIRMATION: A Gallery of Understanding

Directions:

**T (Total Group), p (partner),
s (small group), I (Individual)**

At this point in the lesson, the DOTS chart has evolved into a tool for students that helps them stay connected to the essential question, plan their own outcomes, and celebrate their learning. It gives them hope about understanding the content and about their own achievement as they see a collection of words, phrases, and visuals on their own respective DOTS charts.

- The **"S"** (*summarize*) portion of DOTS helps learners move beyond understanding isolated pieces of the lesson and toward seeing the content, vocabulary, and academic language as integrated and useful for understanding and solving problems in today's world. They see that their own ways of thinking and learning along the way have supported the community to reach a greater depth of understanding. The content is meaningful and personal to all students; this relevance supports them to complete *challenging activities* that reflect high academic expectations for all.
- The tool helps the teacher and students take a more summative look at learning by having students *summarize* what they have learned. For individual accountability, have students do one or both of the following:
  - Use the vocabulary and ideas on their DOTS chart to create persuasive paragraphs that articulate their arguments in support of some aspect of the topic or identified skill.

  - Tie their learnings back to the identified skills of the lesson and write a paragraph that summarizes the key ideas and details from the lesson.
- Have students share their paragraphs with peers and/or their small group.

Instructional Tips:

- Prior to using the DOTS chart for individual accountability, teachers may wish to review by:
  - Having students, in pairs, write a paragraph discussing a connection between their own words and the academic vocabulary of the text. This activity provides students with one more opportunity to connect the dots and extend their learning. It also provides scaffolding for the subsequent task of individual writing.
- As students share their paragraphs with the class or each other, have them also share out the process of learning that took place through the DOTS strategy. When students articulate ways in which the DOTS chart supported their understandings and allowed them to add to their own linguistics, academic, and cognitive repertoires, they further develop their metacognitive abilities.

Author Talk: Affirmation

As we come to the conclusion of the directions involved within the sequence of DOTS, one thing becomes very clear: this strategy is not just about teaching vocabulary. Yes, vocabulary is at the heart of the teaching and learning processes, but these processes are standard actions that should be a part of every lesson and every dialogue that occurs in classrooms. We can no longer afford to look at vocabulary as an isolated skill. It simply doesn't exist! Rather, we need to look at vocabulary as a building block that leads to comprehension, fluency, and writing.

Throughout the presentation of the DOTS strategy, we have emphasized the importance of validating and build-

ing upon CLD students' ways of processing and learning. The DOTS strategy provides educators with the perfect vehicle for such validation by encouraging students to provide information in their native language whenever possible, allowing them to share their ideas through pictures, and embedding instructional conversations throughout the life cycle of the strategy. By allowing students a range of ways to express themselves, educators can more accurately determine what each individual student knows and brings to the lesson. To maximize this knowledge gathering, we recommend that teachers carefully observe students as they are completing their DOTS chart and ask them questions about what they are writing. The students' answers, combined with your observations, will help you make decisions about which students to partner together (e.g., which students might benefit most from hearing a particular peer's thoughts) during the lesson.

An added layer of this strategy can be sending a blank DOTS chart home with students. This step can be a way of capitalizing upon the funds of knowledge that parents and families have. Encourage your students to have "instructional conversations" about the topic at home with their family members in much the same way that they use the tool in the classroom. As they engage in conversations, have students record their family-based connections on the DOTS chart. As we incorporate this step, we find out more about the sociocultural dimension of the student's family. We learn about the traditions, patterns, and unique ways of that particular family.

Continually revisiting the DOTS chart throughout the lesson helps CLD students make critical links between the words they brainstormed (the known) and the words they hear when the teacher is presenting the lesson (the unknown). One of the most effective techniques we have seen for employing the DOTS chart is for teachers to display a poster-sized version of the chart at the front of the class. As the lesson begins, the teacher adds words that the students wrote on their individual charts. During the lesson, new words are added to reinforce students' comprehension of the preselected vocabulary. Whenever possible,

we encourage teachers to explicitly model for the students how connections can be made between the words students shared on the group chart and the key vocabulary as it is encountered throughout the lesson. Teachers who have implemented the DOTS strategy in this way have reported that this approach has indeed promoted the most powerful connections for both their CLD and monolingual English-speaking students.

During the summative portion of the lesson, educators must make multiple decisions related to their own use of the DOTS chart. Of course, there are endless opportunities for informal assessment of students' learning throughout this teaching and learning process. However, for summative assessment, think of these options:

- Use the "S" portion of DOTS to review and solidify the content with the students, and then return to your curriculum-required assessment tools.
- Create a checklist or a rubric that sets clear expectations for students' understanding of the vocabulary words or the paragraphs they create. As you develop the checklist or rubric, consider the variations that students will exhibit due to their individual stages of language acquisition. (An example of a DOTS-based checklist is provided in the Appendix.)

As you implement this strategy, remember that it is about *connecting the dots* between what the individual student knows and his or her new learnings related to the topic.

Affirming Student Ownership: *"I"* Get It!
How does this process celebrate CLD student learning?

- **Sociocultural:** Teachers and students gain insights into ways the cultural perspectives of the learning community may have shifted as a result of perspectives shared and new learnings.
- **Linguistic:** When teachers revoice words, phrases, and links students made, they showcase for the class examples of their individual and collective growth in linguistic and conceptual understanding.
- **Academic:** This phase ensures individual accountability for learning as students incorporate their own voice in

their writing or the predetermined outcome of the lesson.
- **Cognitive:** As the strategy culminates, emphasis is placed on the meaningful processes that promote learning. Students develop an awareness that these processes originate with their own ways of knowing, evolve to reflect their unique ways of thinking, and finally support their individual application of the lesson's content and language within their own means of understanding.

SPOTLIGHT: Early Literacy Connection

Children come to school with very different literacy and language skills in their first language, which impact their ability in the second language (August, 2004). While native English speakers have been hearing the sounds (e.g., phonemes, intonation) of the English language on a daily basis since birth, many CLD learners are hearing these sounds for the first time. As such, learning to read can be challenging for young CLD students; it is often difficult for them to hear the sounds of the English language. The DOTS chart can be used to demonstrate how sound matches to print in the students' native languages and in the English language. When children understand that there are relationships between the letters of written language and the individual sounds of oral language, their literacy skills are greatly enhanced (Herrera et al., 2014).

The Power of Native Languages

To highlight connections between sounds and written symbols using DOTS, choose a topic students will work with as they complete the DOTS chart—first at school, and then in their homes. As mentioned in the Author Talk section, you can send a blank DOTS chart home and ask parents to write meaningful words from the native language on the chart for that particular topic. Alternatively, parents can simply add words from the native language onto the already completed English version. This activity (1) exposes students to ways in which the sounds of different languages match to print and (2) helps students create conceptual links between their native language and the newly learned information from the classroom. When students return to school, allow time for them to discuss with a partner or small group their comparisons between the English version and the native language version. If there happen to be cognates (i.e., words that are similarly spelled and have similar meanings) between the words in the student's native language and English, the students can locate the similarities and differences in the word's spelling and pronunciation in the two languages.

It's the "*i*" Thing

DOTS is a strategy that provides students with structured opportunities to practice language. Teachers can employ the strategy to help differentiate their instruction, because it can be used to practice vocabulary with partners or small groups. At the same time, other students can use the DOTS chart to write sentences with the same vocabulary words. The same processes can be used during core instruction and tiered instruction. Thus, this strategy can be readily used with any subject material to help students add more and more words to their vocabulary.

One Classroom's Perspective

From the 5th-grade class of JoAnna Euston

Activating:

This lesson was a follow-up lesson to their "Wonders" unit. The essential question was: *What are the benefits of working together?* We started the lesson by having students talk with a partner about at least one benefit of working together. As students shared, I rephrased some of their ideas with the whole class. This became an initial opportunity for them to discuss what they knew about the topic already. Next, each student received a DOTS chart. The topic of the lesson was *Benefits of Working Together.* I had all students individually write their ideas on the DOTS chart.

(Continued on the next page)

One Classroom's Perspective (*continued*)

Activating (*continued*):

We began by reviewing how the DOTS chart worked. Even though we had done this strategy a few times, they need periodic reminders on the alphabetical system of the DOTS chart. We completed one box on the chart together as an example so the students better understood how to add ideas to their own charts. Students did a great job filling in their DOTS chart with their initial ideas. I also reminded them to think of their vocabulary words in order to add more ideas. I gave them about 3 minutes to write their initial ideas on the DOTS chart. As the students finished adding their ideas, I had them share their ideas with their table groups. Their task during this time was to listen to their peers as they shared ideas and gather more information on their DOTS charts. I wanted them to see how much information they had on their DOTS charts already.

Connecting:

To get students into the lesson, I had them write all the words connected to the lesson on the outside of the DOTS chart. Next, I had students work with their shoulder partner to find a connection between the words they had on the inside of their DOTS chart and the words on the outside. I asked them to just find connections with a couple of words that synthesized their thoughts. As students worked on the connections, I went around and listened. When they had finished, they shared their ideas with the class. As they were sharing, I made sure to ask them for the rationale behind their connections. Wherever connections needed to be expanded, I made sure to expand upon those thoughts so that the whole class might benefit.

Then we moved into the article. I chose the article carefully, knowing that this group included students with disabilities and also students who needed help with their language skills. I used this knowledge to pair them up with a different partner for the reading portion. As students read, I reminded them to add more ideas to the DOTS chart about words and also details from the article that helped answer the essential question. Lots of students exchanged information with each other. I brought students back together after a couple of minutes of reading and had them share what they had gathered from the article. I used lots of questioning at this time to elicit students' connections to the topic and to the ideas that they were adding to the DOTS chart. I have a few students in this class who have had issues with understanding the reading process, so I made sure to have instructional conversations with them during this whole process. I wanted students to connect with the reading at a personal level as well. I knew that I needed to stop and check with students during this time, because although I knew that some of the students would be fine, others would need some help.

Affirming:

For me, affirming was about going back to the essential question and yet also helping the students in the class understand that when it comes to working with others, the more we understand ourselves and others, the better we are. To move students into affirmation, I re-read the last portion of the article to get them to understand the main idea behind it and to help them begin to visualize ideas for their own narratives that they were going to write. After the reading, I had them individually visualize their idea for a bit. It wasn't my intention for them to share their ideas with the class, but I was surprised that students were eager to share. I proceeded by having them

write a narrative paragraph about a time when they helped a classmate or the classmates helped them. It was amazing to see that some students wrote about their siblings and some wrote about themselves. We are continuing to add to our paragraphs even two days later. Overall, I was quite pleased with the way the lesson unfolded.

TEMPLATE: DOTS

Name: _____

DOTS Chart
(Determine, Observe, Talk, Summarize)

Topic: _____

A–B–C–D	E–F–G–H
I–J–K–L	**M–N–O–P**
Q–R–S–T–U	**V–W–X–Y–Z**

Note: This version of the template might be more appropriate for K–1 students. Some teachers consider the lesson topic and key vocabulary and then select a total of only six letters to focus on, with one letter per box. This can make the task more manageable and guide students to consider words most relevant to the topic. However, it can also restrict students' thinking and make connections to the native language more difficult. Teachers therefore are encouraged to consider the needs of their student population as they make decisions about the format of the chart. A 12-box template (suitable for older students) is also provided.

TEMPLATE: DOTS

Name: _____

DOTS Chart
(Determine, Observe, Talk, Summarize)

Topic: _____

A–B	C–D	E–F
G–H	**I–J**	**K–L**
M–N	**O–P**	**Q–R**
S–T	**U–V–W**	**X–Y–Z**

Note: A simpler version of the DOTS template with only 6 boxes (three rows of 2 boxes, or two rows of 3 boxes), each covering more letters of the alphabet, might be more appropriate for K–1 students. A 6-box template is also provided.

STRATEGY

Foldable

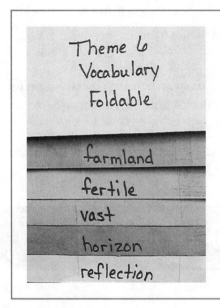

Foldables are an engaging activity that provides children the opportunity to demonstrate the knowledge they have previously held or gained through instructional teaching. The method of breaking down the assignment helps lower my CLD students' anxieties and sets all students up for success. My class this year tends to rush through assignments and not apply their previous knowledge to assignments or assessments. The information in the foldable is made comprehensible in manageable and meaningful units of information put in a very tactile and hands-on format. Through the use of foldables students were able to apply their learning in a format that demonstrated knowledge and understanding while lowering the anxiety that assessments oftentimes generate.

—*Cheryl Werth, 3rd-Grade Teacher*

Where Theory Meets Practice

Although we would like to think of learning as a linear process, it is instead a process that often becomes messy as it unfolds in the classroom. Throughout the teaching and learning cycle, students often become emotionally and cognitively involved as learning starts to evolve and multiple viewpoints begin to take shape. As students collaborate with peers to engage in multiple types of activities, and as they participate in conversations that teachers facilitate through questioning, revoicing, and prompting, they have innumerable opportunities to reinforce their understanding of the target words and concepts. At the same time, students need tools to support their efforts to make sense of all the bits and pieces of information and layered conversations.

When teachers use strategies that provide the learner with a systematic way to organize words, concepts, or information, they help strengthen the networks in the learner's brain that in turn support his or her recall of the information learned. It is easy for all students, and especially English learners, to become overwhelmed with new information. In order to sustain high levels of engagement throughout the lesson, we need to guide students to see how the information/content being presented in the text/ lesson aligns with the objectives, essential question, or goal of the lesson. We also need to continually support students to make personally relevant connections to the content and language they are learning.

When we teach material using contextually isolated worksheets or separate a task from its authentic context, these actions are unlikely to lead to meaningful processing by the learner. The basic principles for effective instruction have long been documented. According to Ausabel (1968), if we were to target only one principle for teaching, we would focus on figuring out what the student knows, and teach him or her with that piece of information as our guide. Hattie and Yates (2014) state: "It's far easier to build and coherently organize existing knowledge than to learn new material de novo" (p. 114). Remember, comprehended input (rather than merely comprehensible input) is the goal (Krashen, 2009). Learners must be provided with tools that support them to systematically and coherently organize the most important information to be learned and taken to permanent memory.

BDI strategies like Foldable provide students with advanced organizers that allow them to make and record their ideas and connections using both words and images. As teachers implement these organizers, they are able to provide space for students to document what is personally relevant as well as the essential takeaways of the lesson. We as educators are aware of the need to move beyond passive learning and toward learning that is more active, relevant, and meaningful for the learner. Using tools like foldables throughout the lesson not only sets conditions for active engagement but also helps students continually consider the language and content of the lesson in relevant, authentic contexts.

The Foldable strategy is ideal for ensuring that students have multiple, meaningful opportunities to interact with vocabulary. Because this strategy provides learners with a "tool in their hands," it promotes their mental processing of the content and scaffolds their communication with peers. In this way, the tool/graphic organizer of this strat-

egy lowers both the linguistic and the academic load of the lesson, especially for English learners. With continual opportunities to build from the known (before and during the lesson) to the unknown from text and teacher, the learner is able to keep up with what is important and become a more autonomous learner.

MATERIALS & RESOURCES

Materials Needed: Paper (four or five pieces per student; multicolored paper optional) • markers/colored pencils • pencils/pens

Instructions: Creating Your Foldable (see page 86)

Video: A video clip illustrating implementation of this strategy is available for viewing online at coe.k-state.edu/cima/biographycrt

---

ACTIVATION: A Canvas of Opportunity

Directions:

i (individual)

- Share the overarching topic of the lesson with the whole class.
- Before you share the critical vocabulary/concepts, have the students individually create a foldable according to the instructions at the end of this strategy description (page 86).
- Once the students have finished assembling the foldable, have them individually write the vocabulary words/concepts on the top of each flap (one word/concept per flap).
- Next, have students create a three-column grid on each flap, as shown below.
- Ask students to individually write or draw what they know regarding each word/concept in the "My prediction" column. Encourage students to use the native language (L1) and/or English (L2).

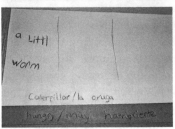

Instructional Tips:

- To help students brainstorm in order to make predictions, remind them to think of places/situations where they might have heard about the topic.
- This strategy is great for teaching concepts that together comprise a whole (e.g., steps of a process, categorization of subcomponents, timeline of events). Make sure to help students make the connection from one tab to the next as you proceed with the lesson.
- Leave an extra flap at the bottom of the foldable for additional information.

My prediction	What I learned from teacher, text, peers	Why it is important

Activating the "*i*"
How does this process activate CLD students' existing knowledge?

- **Sociocultural:** CLD students are able to make predictions that are based on the background knowledge (funds of knowledge, prior knowledge, and academic knowledge) they bring to the lesson.
- **Linguistic:** Students at all levels of English proficiency have access to the vocabulary words. They are able to use linguistic or nonlinguistic representations to express their predictions about the words/concepts.

- **Academic:** The information is made more comprehensible because it is divided into manageable and meaningful units.
- **Cognitive:** The Foldable strategy enables CLD students to record information about concepts and vocabulary in the form of a usable visual that is a hands-on representation of their understanding.

 CONNECTION: The Broad & Narrow Strokes of Learning

Directions:

T (Total Group), p (partner), s (small group)

 Bridging to the Content—Drawing the *i* into the Lesson

In this phase of the lesson, the foldable becomes a tool that provides a linear guide on how the information will build throughout the lesson. It gives the student permission to document his or her own thoughts in a way that allows the foldable to become a cognitive note-taking tool. This tool can then be used to ask questions, provide rationales/evidence, serve as a springboard for discussion, and build in opportunities to check for understanding.

- Have students share with a partner what they already know about each word/concept based on what they have written.
- As the students share, walk around the room and listen to the discussions they are having. Remember to revoice some of the students' ideas. These will help the class make further connections with the content.
- Allow students to add to their individual predictions based on what is shared during the partner and whole-group discussion. Have students circle or underline any new information that is added so you will know it resulted from discussions.
- Pose questions that arise from the discussions.

Instructional Tips:

- At this time, the foldable is a tool for students to record additional connections to their knowledge systems.

Encourage your community of learners to help each other in achieving this goal.
- Your documentation of students' ideas and your revoicing of those ideas for the rest of the class further supports the creation of a community of learners that helps one another throughout the learning process.

 Digging into Text

- Prepare students by pointing out generally where in the text they will come across the key vocabulary and concepts.
- Remind them that they must be ready to write down/take notes as the lesson progresses and think about what will help them remember what they are learning.
- Proceed with the lesson, and as you come across a vocabulary word or key concept during the lesson, have students individually record their new understandings in the column "What I learned from teacher, text, peers." If applicable, have students record the textbook page numbers on which they found examples/ideas related to the word. Students can also choose to use drawings to record the examples they found.

(Continued on the next page)

CONNECTION: The Broad & Narrow Strokes of Learning (*continued*)

- As students work on their foldables, at various points throughout the lesson allow them to do a turn-and-talk to discuss their new learnings about the vocabulary words/concepts with each other in their small groups.
- When students have finished working on their foldables, allow them to discuss one more time with each other all the words as they relate to the content/concepts. This rehearsal promotes their English language acquisition and overall retention of the words/concepts.
  - Placing the students in a variety of small-group settings during the lesson is highly encouraged, as this regrouping allows them to benefit from hearing other students' perspectives and understandings related to the content being covered.
- While information is being shared, encourage students to add new insights to their foldables.

- For the intermediate grades, move back and forth between the foldable and other paper/pencil activities you use during the lesson. What is important is that the students see the relationship/connection across all activities, with the foldable serving as the anchor.

Instructional Tips:

- Use the back of the foldable in strategic ways to have students summarize, write in relation to their learning, or go to other sources to look for information.
- During this phase of the lesson, strategic questions are critical, as they help direct students toward key content understandings.
- As you ask questions, remind students to use their foldables as the source of information for their responses.

Author Talk: Connection

Highly effective teachers adapt the Foldable strategy to reflect the needs of their individual students. For example, they take into consideration their students' developmental level and need for native language support. For some students, teachers might require only a picture or a one-word description of the concept. Other students might be asked to provide a meaningful sentence for each term. Still others might also incorporate a full paragraph with supporting details. In each case, the student is held accountable to demonstrate his or her understanding of what is learned.

What is most important for teachers is the ability to listen and learn from what is being expressed by the learner. As teachers, we need to reflect upon the seeds of knowledge that are being produced/processed in the moment as we move toward abstract concepts. This step helps us better support students to make meaning of something that might not immediately connect to their frames of reference.

Beyond the academic, as we observe lessons unfold we are continually struck by the social/emotional component of teaching and learning. This strategy lends itself to facilitating connections to the personal dimension of the learner, as there are many opportunities for students to share about their funds of knowledge or emotional responses to what is being learned. We often speak of relationships and relevance in education, followed by the importance of making sure our lessons are rigorous. Yet, we commonly fail to follow through with providing the learner with a tool that can serve multiple purposes. The Foldable strategy allows students to document their personally meaningful responses to new language and concepts in an organized way that transcends the limitations of many other tools. Making connections throughout the lesson is the first step—from there the opportunities are endless.

Connecting to the "*i*+1"
How does this process move CLD students from the known to the unknown?

- **Sociocultural:** When using foldables in the Connection phase, CLD students are encouraged to work with peers to support their learning. In this environment, students are able to continue to build upon their existing schemas as they learn the target words/concepts in context and through small-group and class discussions.
- **Linguistic:** Through the multiple exposures to the vocabulary/concepts, English learners are able to expand their conceptual connections and understanding of key vocabulary. Documenting the information related to the words as they are encountered in the lesson/text also promotes acquisition of the terms in English.

- **Academic:** Foldables allow the students to continually record and organize details as well as process the contextually appropriate use and meaning of vocabulary/concepts covered in the lesson.
- **Cognitive:** CLD students are actively engaged in monitoring their learning throughout the lesson. This type of engagement leads to a higher level of understanding, promotes development of metacognitive skills, and supports greater retention of the vocabulary and conceptual understanding.

AFFIRMATION: A Gallery of Understanding

Directions:

**T (Total Group), p (partner),
s (small group), I (Individual)**

In science, math, and English language arts, we often teach and then move to asking students to create a model, solve an equation, or write for a specific purpose. The foldable provides the student with the steps, sequence, or terms to use when they go on to construct, evaluate, or write in response. As such, the foldable is a powerful tool that supports learners to create *as they meet the expectations set before them and demonstrate their learning.*

- Spiraling back and forth between the words/concepts on the foldable and the larger lesson will support the learner in fully comprehending the material. Have students return to the "Why it is important" column and write why each concept/word is important.
- Allow students to discuss their ideas with a partner or their small group. Make sure to listen to students' conversations and revoice critical connections.
- As desired, provide additional opportunities for students to review and rehearse what they have learned. Remind them to refer to their foldables for ideas and support.
- Next, have students use the back of the foldable to individually write a paragraph or a summary using the target words/concepts. Students might focus on one or more of the following areas in their writing:
  - Setting, plot, and overall theme of the story.
  - Language conventions of transitions, sentence structure, mechanics, and so forth.

- Persuasive or expository paragraph development, depending on the topic.
- Sequence of a process and key considerations at each step.
- You can also have students use the foldable to quiz a partner on the words/concepts.

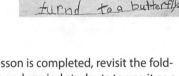

- When the unit or lesson is completed, revisit the foldable one more time and remind students to use it as a study tool.

Instructional Tips:

- As students summarize their learning, have a peer provide feedback.
- Create a rubric that aligns with expected outcomes for the written product.
- Hold each student accountable for producing something individually; this will serve as evidence of his or her own learning and provide a source for affirmation of linguistic and academic growth.
- There are no limits on uses for the tool at the end of the lesson. Be creative in deciding where to go next!

Affirming Student Ownership: *"I" Get It!*
How does this process celebrate CLD student learning?

- **Sociocultural:** Students develop self-confidence in themselves as learners as they gain deeper levels of understanding, as demonstrated through their completed foldables.
- **Linguistic:** CLD students can continually revisit their foldable to solidify the grade-level vocabulary words and concepts they are learning in English.
- **Academic:** The final phase of the Foldable strategy holds students accountable for documenting what they learned. Students apply reading, writing, and reasoning skills as they articulate new understandings and incorporate the target words/concepts.
- **Cognitive:** The completed foldable captures the progression of students' thinking related to each word/concept. Students can use their foldables as a scaffold as they demonstrate their learning in written and oral forms.

SPOTLIGHT: Early Literacy Connection

"For children to learn to write, they must write" (Beaty & Pratt, 2007, p. 231). However, it is important to remember that young children's writing initially consists of drawing and scribbling. Foldables are a great way to support the evolution of young children's writing at home, as parents and children work together to combine drawings and sentences of more structured writing. To guide parents in the use of foldables at home, you can suggest using the following activity.

Let's Write!

Teachers can send blank foldables home with students and encourage parents to write culturally relevant "stories" with their children. To create these story foldables, parents can dictate the story to their children and have the children first draw a picture on each page. Then the children can listen as parents, sounding out the words in their native language, record one sentence for each page of the story. After the pictures and sentences have been completed, the parents can read the story again with their children, talking about the pictures and sentences together. The parents should be encouraged to conduct this activity over several days so that their children will not be overwhelmed by having to do all of the pictures on the same day (unless, of course, the children want to).

For parents who might question the validity of creating the story in their native language rather than in English, emphasize the importance of the native language and cross-language transfer (Cummins, 2001). In addition, tell the parents that this helps their children build a solid literacy foundation that sets the stage for them to become proficient readers and writers in English.

One Classroom's Perspective

From the 4th-grade class of Cathy Hayes

Activating:

Foldables are a tool that I use in my classroom regularly. My students enjoy constructing the foldables, and it has been proven to be effective for allowing my students to organize their thoughts in words. For this lesson, I was introducing a new story (*The Great Kapok Tree*) and I wanted to make sure my students understood the academic vocabulary associated with the rainforest (i.e., *rainforest, canopy, understory, underbrush,* and *ancestors*). So I had the students each make a foldable and label each flap using the vocabulary terms I had identified before the lesson. Then I had students individually predict what they thought each word meant. After making their predictions, I had the students share them with each other.

Connecting:

We then began to read the story as a whole group. To help students focus on the key vocabulary, I asked them to listen for each word on their foldable; when they heard one, they were to raise their hands to stop me. Each time we encountered a vocabulary word in the text, we discussed its meaning as a whole group. After agreeing as a class on the meaning of the word, students individually wrote the definitions into their foldable. Students also added a sentence or definition in their own words that would help them remember the meaning of the word.

Affirming:

At the end of the lesson, students used the information from their foldable to write a summary of what they had learned about the rainforest. Students were encouraged to use specific vocabulary words from their foldable in their summaries. I noticed that the Foldable activity [strategy] not only helped my students have a better understanding of the story but it also increased their confidence. What I have learned about foldables is that a student at any level is capable of completing one, and students take ownership of their work when constructing a foldable.

INSTRUCTIONS: Creating Your Foldable

Materials: A single foldable will require four or five pieces of construction paper in different colors and a stapler.

Step 1:	Depending on the number of vocabulary words/objectives for the lesson, have students use four or five pieces of paper in different colors.	
Step 2:	Layer the sheets of paper on top of each other with an inch of space between each color.	
Step 3:	Fold the paper stack in half, stopping an inch below where the same color meets itself, so that there are two layers of the same color in the middle. Make a crisp crease.	
Step 4:	Staple at the crease.	
Step 5:	When finished, students should be able to flip and view both sides of each colored page.	

STRATEGY

Pic-Tac-Tell

The strategy provided me with a new way to teach my students key vocabulary. As a 2nd-grade teacher, I am always looking for interactive ways to teach vocabulary. Pic-Tac-Tell kept my students engaged from the beginning to the end of the lesson! The individual sentences they came up with at the end of the lesson were also a great way to assess each student's understanding.

—*Nikki Snyder, 2nd-Grade Teacher*

Where Theory Meets Practice

Too often, vocabulary instruction is approached as an artificial process in which isolated words are identified and tested. Approaching vocabulary instruction in this manner does not allow teachers to adequately explore the breadth of students' understanding (Fisher & Frey, 2008). When implementing BDI, teachers need to reflect on their overall goals for vocabulary acquisition. According to research by Díaz-Rico (2013), two important goals of vocabulary acquisition are to "expand the breadth and depth of existing word knowledge and to build habits of independent word acquisition" (p. 180). The key to meeting these goals is for teachers to implement strategies for literacy development that guide students first to identify and then to build upon their existing word knowledge throughout the lesson.

Pic-Tac-Tell is a strategy that supports educators in preassessing students' existing word knowledge at the onset of the lesson. Teachers can then use resulting insights to help contextualize vocabulary, guiding students to make meaningful links between what they already know and the meaning of the word in the context of the lesson. Such links to students' existing schemas help ensure that language and

content connections are not quickly forgotten (Sousa, 2011). The incorporation of visuals, cooperative learning, and individual student assessment allows students to build upon their initial understanding, discuss their learning with peers, and individually demonstrate their word knowledge gains.

The **Pic** portion of the strategy emphasizes mental imagery. In this step, students are asked to activate their knowledge by "picturing" what they see or think of when they read the word. Research by Sousa (2014) also indicates that readers who form mental pictures are more likely to understand and remember than readers who do not visualize. By having students individually visualize and record what the word means to them, teachers are able to assess their students' existing word knowledge. The fact that students are able to make their connections on individualized index cards that they can manipulate in this phase, as well as later in the lesson, also benefits CLD student's comprehension (Fisher & Frey, 2008).

After documenting their individual connections, students' **Tac** onto their existing word knowledge by using it as a foundation for learning in the Connection phase of the lesson. Explicit instruction followed by repeated practice with the vocabulary terms in context and in collaboration with others helps students gain:

- Declarative knowledge (knowing what the word means),
- Conditional knowledge (knowing when to use the word), and
- Procedural knowledge (knowing how to use the word in context) (Díaz-Rico, 2013).

Throughout the process, students make meaningful connections between their existing knowledge and the new knowledge they are constructing. They also work with peers to confirm/disconfirm their initial connections.

The **Tell** portion of the strategy provides students with the opportunity to summarize and share their learning with the classroom community. To effectively summarize, students must decide on information to keep, delete, and substitute (J. Hill & Flynn, 2013). To facilitate this process, CLD students are challenged to individually construct meaningful sentences using the key vocabulary they have learned throughout the lesson. Using a takeoff of the popular children's game Tic-Tac-Toe, students place the key vocabulary in a Tic-Tac-Toe pattern (three across, three down). Each student then selects three words "in a row" using a Tic-Tac-Toe approach. Once students have selected their words, they write meaningful sentences about the topic in which all three words are used appropriately.

MATERIALS & RESOURCES

Materials Needed: Pic-Tac-Tell Template (one per student) • nine key vocabulary words (preselected) • 3 × 5 index cards (nine cards per group) • four different-colored markers or pencils (per group of four) • a book to share with the whole class • pencils/pens

Template: Pic-Tac-Tell Template (see page 94); also available for free download and printing from tcpress.com/accelerating

Rubric: Student Assessment Rubric (see page 197); also available for free download and printing from tcpress.com/accelerating

---

 ## ACTIVATION: A Canvas of Opportunity

Directions:

i (individual)

- Identify nine key vocabulary words and write each word on the front of nine different 3 × 5 index cards to make a set of cards. Make additional sets of vocabulary cards to ensure that every group of four students has a set.
- Divide students into groups of four and give each student a different color of pencil or marker.
- For the **Pic** portion of Pic-Tac-Tell, ask students to ignite, or activate, their background knowledge for each of the nine vocabulary terms by "picturing" and/or writing what they know in their L1 or L2. As they begin working on each card, have students simply draw a line using their colored utensil to portion off their corner of the card. *Tip:* To support students' understanding of the task, model what students need to do as a whole group.

- Have each group of four students rotate their index cards clockwise among group members until every corner has something drawn/written on it.
- Allow approximately 5 minutes for students to complete this part. During this time, circulate around the room and make note of connections that students are making. *Tip:* You can revoice connections to help all students brainstorm ideas about the words.

Activating the "*i*"
How does this process activate CLD students' existing knowledge?

- **Sociocultural:** When vocabulary instruction is situated within the lived experiences and frames of reference of our students, it is more personally meaningful. According to Gay (2010), these connections to students' experiences promote higher interest and facilitate the ease with which students learn the vocabulary.
- **Linguistic:** Encouraging CLD students to express their existing knowledge of key vocabulary terms/concepts using visuals provides students at all stages of second language acquisition with opportunities to demonstrate what they know. For students who feel more comfortable documenting their knowledge in writing, allowing the option to use the L1 enables all students to fully engage in the task.
- **Academic:** Providing the opportunity for all students to document their existing knowledge before the lesson "enables teachers to move away from abstract ways of using students' background knowledge toward specific ways of linking students' culture, language, and experience to content and vocabulary" (Herrera, 2016, p. 97).
- **Cognitive:** The hands-on format of the first step of this BDI strategy increases the likelihood that students will invest in the process of linking to their background knowledge systems.

CONNECTION: The Broad & Narrow Strokes of Learning

Directions:

T (Total Group), p (partner), s (small group)

- After students have finished recording their initial connections on all the cards, have them share their ideas with each other in a small group.
- Circulate around the room to listen to student connections. Make sure to have students elaborate if the connection initially is unclear. Affirm students' existing background knowledge by revoicing images and words they have documented on their cards. *Tip:* Encourage students to look for similarities among the pictures and/or words on the cards.
- Document connections between the target vocabulary and students' existing knowledge by writing each vocabulary term on the board in a Tic-Tac-Toe pattern (three across, three down). Have students share out examples of the pictures and/or words they placed on their 3 × 5 index cards and write some of these around the words on the board.
- The **Tac** portion of Pic-Tac-Tell supports students' connections between the key vocabulary and the content of the lesson. Share the topic of the lesson and the target skill/learning objectives.
- As students engage with the text or lesson content, have them write context-based definitions as vocabulary words are encountered.
  - Divide the vocabulary terms among the members of each small group. As the lesson proceeds, challenge

students to write content-based definitions on the back of each card for the terms they have been assigned as they encounter the words in context.
  - Remind students to paraphrase in their own words the context-based definitions they encounter in the text/lesson. *Tip:* Have students include the page number of the text with relevant information, as appropriate.
- To solidify students' connections and comprehension, provide them with multiple opportunities to *talk* within pairs, small groups, and as a whole group throughout the lesson. As part of this process, have students confirm with peers the accuracy of their written definitions.
- As students collaborate in various grouping structures, revoice their thinking and ideas to lead them to a greater depth of understanding about the topic, key concepts and vocabulary, and target skill/learning objectives.
- Have students confirm/disconfirm their initial connections made on the front of the 3 × 5 cards in their small group.

Connecting to the "*i*+1"
How does this process move CLD students from the known to the unknown?

- **Sociocultural:** Providing students with the opportunity to discuss peers' personal connections to the target vocabulary helps them make additional connections to their own background knowledge and see the words from new angles.
- **Linguistic:** When students are strategically paired and/or placed in small groups based on their biographies, they can support one another to develop their language skills. As CLD students observe and listen to more proficient language models, they are provided with *i*+1 input (Krashen, 2009).

- **Academic:** Using a variety of interaction patterns during the lesson helps CLD students build consensus with peers and determine when they need to return to the text to check for understanding.
- **Cognitive:** CLD students' thinking and learning are stretched to the zone of proximal development (Vygotsky, 1978) as they generate and share definitions for the identified vocabulary terms. Through interactions with peers and teacher revoicing, CLD students more fully see themselves as part of the learning community, accountable for analyzing text, expressing opinions, and making and evaluating predictions.

 AFFIRMATION: A Gallery of Understanding

Directions:

T (Total Group), p (partner), s (small group), I (Individual)

- The **Tell** phase of the lesson provides students with a way to apply their learning and authentically demonstrate their knowledge in written form.
- First, review the meaning of all vocabulary terms as a whole group.
- Next, to support students' synthesis of new language and concepts as well as ensure individual accountability:
  - Provide each student with a Pic-Tac-Tell Template.
  - Allow students to write the nine vocabulary words in any order on their template.
  - Explain to students that they will write sentences on the template using three of the vocabulary words in each sentence. They should select the vocabulary terms in Tic-Tac-Toe fashion by choosing three words in a row (diagonally, vertically, or horizontally).
  Tip: Model this process for the students as a whole group. Then allow students to practice the process

with a partner before releasing students to individual work.
- Observe students as they work to make sure their sentences demonstrate understanding of the vocabulary terms in the context of the lesson.
- Provide students with the opportunity to share their completed sentence(s) with a peer, a small group, and/or the whole class.
- If desired, use a rubric to assess and provide feedback on the students' final products. *Note:* See the sample Pic-Tac-Tell rubric provided in the Appendix.

Author Talk: Affirmation

Pic-Tac-Tell is a wonderful strategy for promoting explicit and systematic instruction of key vocabulary. Not only does it support students' active construction of meaning but it also helps them make meaningful links between existing knowledge and new learning in a fun and interactive way. To truly understand the potential of this strategy, consider it through the eyes of Mrs. Kathy Clark, a 6th-grade reading teacher:

> This strategy tied closely to my CLD students' background. They used their three chosen words that made the most sense to them. Building on their prior knowledge and background, it was easy for them to write their sentence. It is evident when CLD students struggle with meaning by the way they write, and it usually goes back to their upbringing in another language. One of my CLD students described a family celebration in her sentence. I was amazed at the ability she had to tie her three chosen words into a complete sentence that was perfectly written. It was very interesting reading their sentences and trying to clarify the picture in my mind of their family and home. The more insight I have into my students' biographies, the better I can provide proper education for them. This was a fabulous way of continuing my own education about my students and their histories. I used this information to help them build/clarify their vocabulary and make it part of their permanent memory for future use.

As shared by Mrs. Clark, this strategy promotes individualized instruction. By allowing CLD students to select the vocabulary they are most comfortable with and use it to create meaningful sentences, you give them the autonomy to show what they know while still keeping their affective filters low.

Additional tips for promoting your CLD students' success with this strategy include the following:

- Strategically pair CLD students so that they continually have the support of a peer with whom they can construct the meaning of the new words and make and share connections to what they already know.
- As students become proficient with this strategy, you can leave some squares on the grid blank and have students select words themselves.
- As you provide students with the vocabulary words, you can have them substitute antonyms or synonyms for words to demonstrate higher-level understandings.

Affirming Student Ownership: "I" Get It!
How does this process celebrate CLD student learning?

- **Sociocultural:** Allowing students to interact with peers before writing their individual sentences helps to build confidence that they will be successful with the task.
- **Linguistic:** Students practice using the vocabulary in meaningful ways (i.e., talking, reading, and writing) to demonstrate their understanding of the content.
- **Academic:** The Pic-Tac-Tell strategy empowers CLD students to actively transform text from isolated words on a page to words laden with meaning. They authentically demonstrate their learning by writing sentences that summarize their new understandings.
- **Cognitive:** The structure of the Pic-Tac-Tell summative task breaks from more traditional forms of summarization. The novelty of the strategy thus increases students' motivation to engage in the difficult cognitive process.

One Classroom's Perspective

From the 3rd-grade class of Jenny Wilk

Activating:

For our economics unit on "Wants and Needs," we did the strategy of Pic-Tac-Tell. The essential question we were trying to answer was: *What is the impact of an economic system on the needs and wants of all people?* In the last few days, we had talked about examples of needs and wants and how they relate to us. Today as I explained the topic, I reminded students of all the connections they have already made. However, I also told them that with the new words they would really have to dig deep. As I shared the objectives, I told them that their task was to work on words but also to pay attention to context clues, which would be our focus during the reading portion.

As I shared the cards for Pic-Tac-Tell with the students, I told them that their first step was to focus on their initial reaction to the vocabulary words. I asked them to think about whether they had ever seen or heard the words before. I asked them to consider whether they had heard their parents talking about the words or whether they had seen them on TV. I wanted students to create their own understanding of the words individually and then talk to their partners. As they began to document their first interpretation of the words on the Pic-Tac-Tell cards, I encouraged them to write in their native language as well.

As they worked, I went around and observed and listened to the students. I found them helping each other

quite a bit during this time by breaking the words apart and truly helping each other by explaining their interpretations to each other. As I walked around, I spent a little bit more time with my ELL students, since content-specific vocabulary words are sometimes hard for them to interpret. However, we used Google Translate on my phone and we kept working with the vocabulary words with my newcomer students as well.

As students finished, I had them share their initial interpretation with the whole class. Since I already had gone around and listened to their ideas, it helped me be able to point to certain students and have them share. I knew that with these specific students sharing, other kids in the class would be able to solidify their own ideas. I did remind students that our interpretations might look different since we had not read the book yet and context can influence the meaning of words.

Connecting:

After we finished with the nine word cards, I told students that at this point we would talk more about the words as we came across them in our books. This was also the time for them to look for context clues related to the specific vocabulary words. I had them partner read the text and encouraged them to create their visual together and also come to consensus about the meanings and the way the words related within the context. We kept bringing the focus back to the reading. As we came across the concepts, we stopped and added the visuals in the middle of the cards.

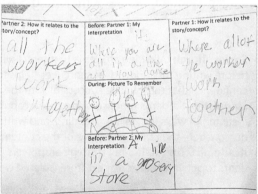

We also conducted lots of discussion about how these words were related to our economics unit overall. I am fortunate that I have students from different parts of the world, so I was really able to have my students talk about how they see these concepts in their home countries and how we also see the same things in the United States. One girl from India shared how there is a Lay's potato chip

factory in her hometown in India. Students were able to make an instant connection with export and import with this one, since so many students see the same potato chips in the United States, even though they are made in India. Overall, we had great conversations and I felt like our partners were able to have wonderful discussions about the words and use them in context. We stopped at regular intervals to keep adding to our Pic-Tac-Tell cards in order to record our during-the-lesson learnings.

One Classroom's Perspective (*continued*)

Affirming:

As we finished our reading, I had students work on their Pic-Tac-Tell grid. We actually made the grids with rulers, and students were able to place their cards in that format. It was a tangible visual for 3rd-graders and it also helped them see how they were supposed to create definitions using the Tic-Tac-Toe system. Students worked on creating the sentences with their partners. As I rotated around to make sure that students were able to create sentences, I reminded them to use words in a diagonal, vertical, or horizontal fashion. As students created the sentences, they used lots of transition words without my reminding them. Some of these words came directly from their economics unit. As students finished their sentences using the word cards, we shared out a few of them. Once we were finished, I had them go back and use their sentences to create a summary paragraph that shared their understanding of the economics unit and the essential question.

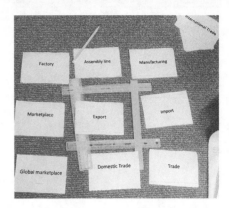

TEMPLATE: Pic-Tac-Tell

Name: _____   Date: _____

Pic-Tac-Tell

_____

_____

_____

_____

_____

_____

_____

STRATEGY

Vocabulary Quilt

The first time we did the Vocabulary Quilt was in our science class. Students loved the way they were able to refer to words and add their own ideas to the different vocabulary words on the quilt. I like the fact that this strategy starts with words but then moves toward the content, and the students are able to add to their own understanding. So, today we decided to use Vocabulary Quilt with our "Wonders" lesson. Even though the strategy starts with words we were quickly able to move into the book and add lots of ideas on the quilt. Students loved working with each other and we enjoyed the discussions and the additions to our quilt. At the end of the lesson, the students wrote their own paragraphs about the topic of weather. All in all, it stayed a well-connected lesson.

—*Stephanie Wilhite, 2nd-Grade Teacher*

Where Theory Meets Practice

A quilt, across many cultures, often is a tapestry that tells a story of the many fabrics that have been used and sewn together. In much the same way, the BDI strategy Vocabulary Quilt serves to move vocabulary from words taught and defined in isolation toward the key, Tier 3, content vocabulary that prepares students to have access to the concepts that are most critical to learning. The way we choose to teach vocabulary is the first step toward providing comprehensible input that may lead to conceptual understanding. Using the Vocabulary Quilt, vocabulary is introduced in ways that immediately create a pathway to relevance for the learner. This relevance supports learners in making connections to their own background knowledge and language and quickly creating the cognitive connections in order to "quilt" together the pieces/vocabulary that lead to comprehension.

A good vocabulary system is indeed an asset to a child. Students who possess knowledge of word meanings and are able to access that knowledge effectively are able to read and comprehend text more easily (Sidek & Rahim, 2015). In CLD settings, recognition of a student's literacy in the native language is the first step toward utilizing this knowledge in order to support his or her English acquisition. ELL students may have knowledge of the words in their native language, yet they might not know the label in English. When students are provided opportunities to engage in activities with peers and are encouraged to make use of both languages, they are able to practice their language skills at a much deeper level. The resulting academic conversations foster knowledge transfer, and rich written dialogues result.

Within the context of everyday teaching and learning, vocabulary is not about how many words we can say in a minute but rather how we can use the words to express what we know, debate what we disagree with, and question what we don't understand. Beyond that, vocabulary is essential to our writing as we explain our thoughts and ideas and demonstrate our understanding of the content.

When we provide opportunities throughout the lesson for students to piece together what they are learning, and give them a safe context in which they can discuss and reflect on the relationship between the words that have been generated and the core concepts, we provide students with enough access to language to ensure that a strong scaffold exists for rigor to occur. Learning is thus not left to chance. Students use the vocabulary, as well as connections between lesson content and their own background knowledge, to deepen their understanding and learning. This often leads to a cognitive belief that learning is possible.

By using strategic and intentional vocabulary development strategies, teachers can help students to bridge the gap between the language of the content and the language and background knowledge that they bring to the class. As teachers, we need to continually ask ourselves questions such as these:

- How can I ensure that my students, regardless of their language backgrounds and their abilities, have equitable access to strategies that will deepen their word knowledge?
- What impact does cultural schema and personal or prior knowledge have on the learning process for my English learners? Where does socioculturally rooted word knowledge fit into the picture?
- What kinds of scaffolds do my students need? What can I provide them during this particular lesson?

Often the answers to such questions rest in the ways that we support learners to make connections to the known information (background knowledge in their permanent memory) as they strive to make sense of the new information (language, concepts, and ideas of the lesson). When students make personally relevant schematic connections to the lesson, they are more likely to retain and be able access the new language and content at a later time (Sousa, 2011).

The Vocabulary Quilt strategy extends from literature and research indicating that the brain continually strives to create connections between preexisting, known informa-tion and new, unknown information (Donovan & Brans-ford, 2005; Sousa, 2011; Wessels, 2008; Wolfe & Brandt, 1998). In this BDI strategy, students first record thoughts and images that they immediately associate with the target vocabulary words in a process that prompts them to draw from their background knowledge. For CLD students, this strategy is particularly effective because it allows them to document what they know by using nonlinguistic representations (illustrations), their native language, and/or individual words or phrases in English. Because CLD students cannot always rely on their existing English language skills to learn and retain knowledge in English, the nonlinguistic supports have been found to be particularly important (Gregory & Burkman, 2012; J. Hill & Flynn, 2006).

Students' ongoing use of the vocabulary quilts throughout the lesson enables the teacher to continually encourage and guide students to make connections from the known to the unknown. Because students' initial understandings are documented and then revisited, teachers are able to clarify any misconceptions. Students are able to add to their understanding of the academic vocabulary as the lesson progresses, working together with peers as equal members of the learning community.

MATERIALS & RESOURCES

Materials Needed: Chart paper • sticky notes • textbook or other books • markers/colored pencils • pencils/pens • paper

Template: Vocabulary Quilt Template (see page 104); also available for free download and printing from tcpress.com/accelerating

Checklist: Student Academic Behavior Checklist (see page 198); also available for free download and printing from tcpress.com/accelerating

Video: A video clip illustrating implementation of this strategy is available for viewing online at coe.k-state.edu/cima/biographycrt

ACTIVATION: A Canvas of Opportunity

Directions:

i (individual)

- Choose eight vocabulary words (fewer for primary grades) based on their relevance to the lesson. Sometimes the words are predetermined from a curriculum; however, when you are trying to determine which words to choose, select those that can help your students articulate what has been learned both orally and in writing. At the end of the lesson, these words are the building blocks necessary to share conceptual understanding.
- To make the vocabulary quilt, create eight boxes on chart paper (or any other kind of paper) by folding it vertically twice and horizontally once. A Vocabulary Quilt Template is provided on page 104 as a model.
- Write the preselected vocabulary words in the squares (one word per square). Alternatively, depending on their age, have students write the words.
- Share the topic of the lesson with the class.
- Divide students into groups of four and give each group a vocabulary quilt.
- Explain to the students that they are going to write (in English or their native language) and/or draw whatever comes to mind (their associations) when they read each of the vocabulary words in the boxes. If they cannot think of anything, they can rewrite the word in the box and move to the next one.
- Often prior to students recording their associations to the words, the teacher says each of the words and

has the students repeat them. The teacher reminds students that they have seen the words, written the words, and spoken the words. Now they must draw or write what their brain has connected to the word.
- Give students 3–5 minutes to individually write something in the box for each word.
To enhance your ability to determine what individual students know, have each student in a group use a marker of a different color.

Instructional Tip:

- At this time, the quilt is a tool for students to activate their knowledge systems. Encourage your community of learners to help each other in achieving this goal. Your documentation of students' ideas and your revoicing of those ideas for the rest of the class further supports the creation of a community of learners that helps one another throughout the learning process.

Author Talk: Activation

As we observed a Vocabulary Quilt lesson in one classroom and saw kids work with their quilts to focus on the meanings of their words and finally take them to writing, we couldn't help but think of the many processes that the teacher had used to get her students not only to dig deep into their schemas but also to take their learning to the next level. Through the life cycle of the strategy in this class, the students manipulated their own understanding of vocabulary words. The teacher kept reminding her students that this is a skill that they need in order to be able to create their own understanding.

Keeping in mind her community of learners, which included many newly arrived English learners, the teacher

moved around the room in a supportive, encouraging way. She had placed the students in groups in such a way that they were not afraid of reaching out to their peers if they needed help. Students didn't feel intimidated by the new words that were on the quilt. By the end of the lesson, most of their talk revolved around how smart they were, since they had so many words on their quilts. Nothing brings joy to a teacher's heart more than the chatter of confident 2nd-graders celebrating their new learning.

The success of a strategy depends upon the actions within the classroom. This classroom observation reinforced for us the notion that it is the *reciprocal* exchange between the teacher and students as their academic and linguistic responses and actions build on each other that makes a strategy truly powerful. These behaviors unfold with the teacher's careful consideration of the unique needs and strengths of the individual students in the community of learners.

A learner-centered strategy like Vocabulary Quilt involves students in the creation of networks of ideas, from their initial responses to the words to the evolving ideas they continue to share with their peers. We need to watch our students' behavior consistently and be intentional at each step along the way in ensuring that our students are using the vocabulary words to begin to thread together the language they have available to them from the onset of the lesson. Through repeated practice, and with our guidance, students develop an understanding of how words are used to think, talk, and write about the content. Students ultimately own the words and make them a part of their linguistic repertoire. This is a goal for every English learner who walks through the doors of our schools and classrooms.

Activating the "*i*"
How does this process activate CLD students' existing knowledge?

- **Sociocultural:** Since making sense of information is so culturally and linguistically rooted, students can truly benefit from recording their own associations to the key vocabulary words. Student-centered inferencing occurs when students relate to the words through their own cultural lens.
- **Linguistic:** Language is learned by making sense of how words are associated. Creating opportunities from the beginning of the lesson for students to begin making these connections increases the chances that they will acquire the language and be able to engage fully in the lesson.
- **Academic:** Students need opportunities to think about the academic knowledge they bring to the classroom from other content areas. Academic words/cognates already known by a learner can unlock academic potential that we may not be aware of unless we open the door to students documenting and sharing their background knowledge. This strategy allows *each* student to show what academic knowledge he or she brings to the lesson before formal instruction by the teacher.
- **Cognitive:** Providing students with opportunities to depict their schematic associations to the vocabulary words allows the teacher to follow up by asking what certain words, phrases, or pictures mean. Such prompting enables the teacher to gain access into students' thought processes. With this knowledge, the teacher can better scaffold students' development of linguistic and conceptual understanding.

CONNECTION: The Broad & Narrow Strokes of Learning

Directions:

T (Total Group), p (partner), s (small group)

 Bridging to the Content—Drawing the *i* into the Lesson

In this phase of the lesson, the vocabulary quilt becomes a tool that creates a natural bridge between students' own associations to the words, using their own schemas, and the meanings of the words in the context of the larger lesson. This tool serves as a linguistic and academic scaffold that aids students in building language, lowering the affective filter, and supporting instructional conversations that have the potential to increase comprehension.

- After the students have written/drawn their associations, provide them with the opportunity to discuss in their group the rationales behind their connections. As students discuss, listen to their conversations and continue to document their already established associations so that you can use them as you bridge into the lesson and facilitate initial connections to text.
- When the students have finished sharing about the words, have students refer to the quilts throughout their learning process by either posting them in front of the room or leaving them on the tables. Proximity matters, since the goal is to have students continue interacting with the words as they listen to the teacher and get into text.

Instructional Tips:

- For many teachers, the transition into text begins with using what students have produced on the quilts to introduce the vocabulary. What students have shared becomes the source for providing student-friendly explanations of the words.
- The words and pictures that students have produced can also serve as a source for making predictions about the topic or for simply introducing the topic.
- Words can be categorized for different purposes (parts of speech, word parts, root words, cognates, etc.).

 Digging into Text

- As you get into the text or content during the Connection phase, the quilt transforms into a tool for questioning and comprehension. Make sure to refer back to the vocabulary, as well as the essential question/skills/outcomes for the day or lesson. Facilitate student connections and disconfirm misconceptions about the words and concepts.

- It is important to move the quilt from a words-based activity (completed in the Activation phase) to a strategy that aids students' understanding of the identified skill, text, and larger lesson. To do this, have your students add more information directly onto the quilt as they read the text, or give them sticky notes that they can use to write down additional information about the key vocabulary/content.
- When a vocabulary word is found in context, have students individually write the meaning of the word on a sticky note. Have students add their sticky notes to their vocabulary quilts.
- Students also can add sentences to the quilt that share the main idea or provide evidence to support the claims they are making. Encourage students to use the academic vocabulary they started with as well as the words they have added during the work-time phase of the lesson.
- As students add more ideas to the quilt, your revoicing of students' newly added ideas supports them in extending upon their understanding of the information documented on the quilts.

Instructional Tips:

- Stop at several places as you read the text to provide opportunities for small-group discussion and to help students identify connections between their new learning and the quilt.
- Focus on using the quilt as a way of providing comprehensible input to your students. By constantly reminding them of the words on the quilt and the skills that they can target by going to the quilt, you can help them move toward overall comprehension of the topic.
- Have students use the quilt to generate questions about the content of the lesson.
- As you move toward bringing the lesson to closure, have students use the quilt to review *what* has been learned and *where* it was learned.

Connecting to the "*i*+1"
How does this process move CLD students from the known to the unknown?

- **Sociocultural:** Students learning to accept themselves begins with creating spaces where each student's language, work, and knowledge becomes part of the shared learning process of the classroom community. No greater benefit exists for students than having their words and ideas become part of the language the teacher and their peers use to elaborate, reroute, or ask questions. Valuing the words spoken by another shows the highest level of respect and supports empathy and understanding at a different level. The vocabulary quilt allows students to work together to socially construct knowledge.
- **Linguistic:** Every time students refer back to the vocabulary quilt, they are provided with repetition and opportunities to use the vocabulary in authentic ways. The goal is to increase the complexity of the task and the use of language throughout the course of the les-

son. Through multiple opportunities to practice, students become more fluent in their articulation of what they know academically.
- **Academic:** As students use their vocabulary quilts throughout the lesson to scaffold their own engagement and success with various tasks, they begin to take ownership of the Vocabulary Quilt as a *student learning strategy*. A teacher's routine use of this BDI strategy supports students' use of the strategy for future independent learning.
- **Cognitive:** The ability to express ideas via different pathways and using different words is important as students begin to move toward more cognitively demanding tasks. Hearing multiple perspectives on the words and concepts during this phase allows students to broaden both their use of the academic language and their understanding of the overall topic.

 AFFIRMATION: A Gallery of Understanding

Directions:

**T (Total Group), p (partner),
s (small group), I (Individual)**

Often teachers move into writing and expect students to abstractly recreate what they have learned without the benefit of having documentation of the words and pictures that reflect their learning readily available for reference. As students prepare to write, take a test, or complete other end-of-lesson tasks, the vocabulary quilt serves as a useful scaffold. Such scaffolds are especially important for addressing the linguistic needs of English learners so that they can focus on demonstrating their content understanding.

- In order to provide students with an opportunity to share how much they have learned, you can do the following:
  - Have students individually or in pairs write a paragraph summarizing what was learned. Remind students that while they must include the academic vocabulary in their writing, they can also use any of the other words on the quilt.

- Have students use what has been generated by referring back to the quilt to answer the essential question.
- Have students create an expository or a narrative paragraph using a topic sentence generated from the ideas on the quilt.
- Use the quilt as a rehearsal tool prior to taking the test.
- Use the quilt to support students in completing the curriculum-dictated worksheets.

AFFIRMATION: A Gallery of Understanding (*continued*)

- For students with limited abilities in English, the following adaptations can be made in the writing activity:
  - Have students dictate the sentences to a teacher, paraprofessional, or peer who can write them.
  - Have students voice record sentences to share what they have learned.
  - Allow students to write in their native language.
  - Pair the students with more proficient peers who can help them write a paragraph/journal entry in English.
- Share with students the outcomes that have been achieved as a result of working together toward a common goal.

Instructional Tips:

- As students summarize their learning, have a peer provide feedback and refer back to the quilt to support the student in making connections.
- Create a rubric or checklist that aligns with expected outcomes for the written product.
- Hold each student accountable for producing something individually that will serve as evidence of their own learning and thus provide a source of affirmation for the linguistic and academic growth they have made.

Affirming Student Ownership: *"I" Get It!*
How does this process celebrate CLD student learning?

- **Sociocultural:** Students benefit from recognizing that they have more to gain by collaborating within a community of learners than trying to learn in isolation. Students' states of mind are influenced by how they have engaged and what they have produced in the classroom. The vocabulary quilt confirms for the community that each student contributed to the learning process.
- **Linguistic:** Students gain confidence by using new words and language to document their learning. Their language development is strengthened by the reciprocal nature of the conversation/dialogue that takes place throughout the lesson and becomes evident as the lesson closes.
- **Academic:** A great way to assess individual learning using this BDI strategy is via the student-generated writing, which incorporates the academic vocabulary while still emphasizing conceptual understanding.
- **Cognitive:** Revisiting the original vocabulary quilt to write their summary allows students to evaluate their deepened level of understanding of the key vocabulary words.

SPOTLIGHT: Early Literacy Connection

Because vocabulary development is a key ingredient in the learning-to-read process and is a predictor of success with future reading skills, children must be given more opportunities in the early grades to increase their vocabulary (Bortnem, 2008). The Vocabulary Quilt strategy allows students to interact with vocabulary words before hearing them in a story or upcoming lesson in order to make concrete connections between their existing knowledge and the newly introduced vocabulary. This foundational knowledge can then be used to build new understandings of the vocabulary.

Post What We Know

When implementing the Vocabulary Quilt strategy with young learners, consider the following adaptation:

- Start with a poster-sized vocabulary quilt with six to eight folded rectangles (depending on the number of vocabulary words). One vocabulary word should be written in the center of each rectangle. In addition to the poster-sized quilt, write each vocabulary word on a blank sheet of paper.

(Continued on the next page)

SPOTLIGHT: Early Literacy Connection (*continued*)

- Gather the students in a whole-group area and explain the class vocabulary quilt. Read and point to each word to make sure all of the students can see and hear the word being read aloud.
- Model how to activate your background knowledge with one of the words from the quilt. Write words and draw your associations with the vocabulary word.
- Next, ask students to volunteer their associations with the word you chose. Add those to the quilt.
- Place the students in small groups; there should be enough groups for each to take one of the remaining vocabulary words. Make sure that every student in the group has a writing utensil of a different color. This allows you to make a quick assessment of the students' background knowledge and engagement in the task.
- Explain that students are to write or draw whatever comes to mind when they hear or read their group's vocabulary word. Remind students that if they have no associations with a word, they can simply rewrite that word on the paper.
- After the small groups have finished, bring the students back together as a whole group.
- Revisit the whole-class vocabulary quilt. As you read each word, have the group with that particular word share their associations.
- As the group is sharing, rewrite their thoughts on the whole-class quilt. Then ask the whole group if they have additional associations with the word that need to be added. Continue this process until all of the vocabulary words have been discussed.
- Throughout the story or lesson, continually refer back to the whole-class quilt and make necessary changes to capture the accurate meanings of the vocabulary words.

One Classroom's Perspective

From the 2nd-grade class of Stephanie Wilhite

Activating:

I used Vocabulary Quilt with our "Wonders" series for Language Arts. As we started, I reminded students that the strategy is to help us to expand our vocabulary and to answer our essential question: *How does weather affect us?* I went over the quilt and the way it works with students. Everyone was divided into groups of four. As I divided them I strategically placed them in groups so some students could help my ELL students, especially the ones who are new to the country. I gave them pre-made quilts with the eight vocabulary words on them already written. I went over all of the eight vocabulary words with students and we did one of the boxes of the quilts together to see how we would add our initial ideas to the quilt. I asked them to think about the words that are on the quilt and the ways they are tied to weather. At this time, the students were to dig into what they already know about the word and then add their ideas to the quilt. I had students give me their ideas on the first word, which was *damage*. I asked them to share their ideas associated with the word with me. As they did, I wrote their ideas in the first box to show them how it is done. I also did a think-aloud for them at this point to show them the visual that I associated with the word. After this, I let my

students work on the quilt by themselves. They attended to the remaining seven words in their small groups.

This Activation stage of the lesson lasted about 10 minutes; however, what I found was that my students knew so much about the content already. Students who speak Spanish as their native language and are fairly new to the country were participating right alongside others. I went around and asked students for some of the associations they were making on the quilt and rephrased some of the students' ideas. However, the best part of this stage was allowing students to be able to share with the whole group what they wrote on their quilts. I made sure to ask specific questions from students when I saw them struggle to make their own connections.

One Classroom's Perspective

Connecting:

After we completed all eight of the words, I had the students leave the quilts on their tables. At this time, we got into our workshop books. I explained to them that we would be reading the text; however, at the same time as we read, I would ask them specific questions to help them add more ideas to the quilt. My students were so excited about the reading on weather, but more than that they were excited about making more connections to the quilt.

We did some choral reading at the beginning, which allowed me to show them how we were going to stop at different parts of the reading to discuss and then add more to the quilt. Then we moved into some partner and triad readings. As we did that, students didn't even need my help—they knew the process exactly. It did help that students had been placed in the groups in a way that they could do this on their own. They had peers to help guide them in each of the groups. I did have to scaffold partner reading for them a little, because at this time I realized that my students need a little bit more help in understanding how partner reading works. However, we were able to add more ideas to our quilt as we moved through this part of the lesson. As we finished, I had my students scan their quilts for a few minutes to think about what they saw that would answer the question: *How does weather affect us?* I liked that my students interacted with each other on the topic and kept focusing on the essential question at this time.

Affirming:

To move my students into this phase, before having them write about the topic of weather, I first had them create a web collaboratively on the back of their quilts. I wanted them to first summarize the lesson and the story before they moved into writing. I told them that this was the time for them to work collectively on summarizing all the effects of weather in a web format. So they wrote "Weather" in the middle and created a web that shared how weather affects us. After they drew their webs, I moved them into the writing piece.

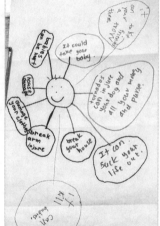

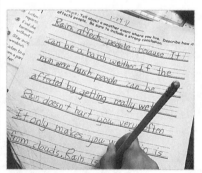

Their prompt was: "Tell about a weather event where you live." My students easily moved into responding to the writing prompt. As they wrote, I shared with them that they could use the quilt as a reference. I did tell them that I expected to see at least four of the words from the quilt in their writing pieces. Students used their quilts to create their paragraphs and as they did that I was able to go around and look for the kinds of associations my kids were making between the quilts and their writing pieces. Overall, this was a successful lesson!

TEMPLATE: Vocabulary Quilt

Vocabulary Quilt

Write a vocabulary word in the center of each box.

STRATEGY

Thumb Challenge

I loved to see them interact with each other on a personal level and try out their English. Students interacted by listening, speaking, and responding to a partner while giving the definition and an example word. The background knowledge came into play with the example they were to come up with. I could see them open up to each other, and it was a nice way to see them try out their listening and speaking skills in a safe environment. Because of the way it is set up, I walk around the room and can listen to the discussions and questions my students ask each other. Students were very excited to use something new to help them learn.

—*Anne Abell, 1st-Grade Teacher*

Where Theory Meets Practice

Research has found that learning is best when focused, diffused, and then focused again (Jensen, 2000a, 2000b; Sousa, 2011). The Thumb Challenge strategy provides students with this opportunity for learning that is focused, diffused through conversation, and then focused again as it is connected back to the text. "Brain breaks" help students develop the social/emotional skills needed to master rigorous academics in the social context of school (Bobe, Perera, Frei, & Frei, 2014). By allowing students to engage in student talk, where they are able to practice and apply their language/vocabulary in a safe environment, we provide them with the brain break they need to absorb the vocabulary.

Student talk is further enhanced when learners have opportunities to practice language with peers who have more advanced language skills. The more opportunities we provide for students to work together to negotiate meanings of academic terms, the more chances they have to extend upon their own learning. Opportunities for authentic communication such as this do much more to foster engagement and learning than skill-and-drill activities. Because students are both orally and physically involved

in the activity, this strategy also speaks to the multiple learning styles present in our classrooms.

Finally, repeated, meaningful exposure to vocabulary terms throughout the lesson is essential for CLD students to internalize new words and make them part of their permanent vocabulary. Thumb Challenge allows learners to practice their vocabulary repeatedly during interaction with peers. Through this strategy, students summarize the most salient information about each word in order to define it for their partner in a concrete way. Such summarization, according to research by Marzano, Pickering, and Pollock (2001), is a learned process and is a critical skill for all students.

> **MATERIALS & RESOURCES**
>
> **Materials Needed:** Six to eight key vocabulary terms • Thumb Challenge strips • sticky notes • textbook/story • pencils/pens
>
> **Checklist:** Student Academic Behavior Checklist (see page 199); also available for free download and printing from tcpress.com/accelerating

ACTIVATION: A Canvas of Opportunity

Directions:

i (individual)

- Explain the activity to the whole class, and introduce the six to eight vocabulary words for the lesson.
- Place students in pairs. Consider pairing students who share the same native language and are at slightly different levels of English language proficiency.
- Give each pair a Thumb Challenge strip with the vocabulary words already written on it. Make sure the same words appear in the same order on both sides of the strip (see example below).
- Tell students that they will be using the strips throughout the lesson.
- Have students discuss the words on the strip. They can use both English and their native language if they wish.
- As students discuss the words, give each student a sticky note for each word on the strip.
- Have students individually record on a sticky note what they know about each word based on the conversation

they had with their partner. They may choose to draw what they know or write in the language of their choice. Then have them put their sticky notes below the words on the Thumb Challenge strip. (*Note:* You may choose to have both students in each pair do all the words, or you can divide the words equally among students.)

- Circulate around the room to silently observe students as they are working and note connections that you can revoice for the whole group.
- Have partners work together to make a prediction about what the lesson/text will be about.
- Have each pair share their prediction with another pair.

Front of the Sentence Strip

plantation	wharf	customs	suspiciously	confronted	detain

Activating the "*i*"
How does this process activate CLD students' existing knowledge?

- **Sociocultural:** By accessing the personal memories and experiences each student brings to each word, the Activation phase provides a great opportunity to create a community of learners in which each member's prior knowledge is valued.
- **Linguistic:** Initially placing students in pairs provides them with a safe environment to orally share their ideas with a partner. The pairings are further enhanced when native language support is provided and stu-

dents are allowed to discuss key vocabulary terms in the L1.

- **Academic:** The connections discussed and recorded by students in this phase of the lesson allow teachers to tap into students' prior academic experiences with the vocabulary words.
- **Cognitive:** Students are more likely to take ownership over learning when they know a given strategy will be used through the entire lesson.

CONNECTION: The Broad & Narrow Strokes of Learning

Directions:

T (Total Group), p (partner), s (small group)

- After students have finished sharing, bring the class together and proceed with the lesson.
- As you come across the vocabulary words in the content portions of the lesson, make sure to allow partners to discuss the words again to build their contextual understanding of the words. Encourage them to

compare their new understandings with their original thoughts about the words.

- Once students have discussed a specific word, have each student in the pair write the definition of the word on the back of the strip, along with the textbook page number on which the definition was found.
- Have students remove their sticky notes from the front of the sentence strip.

Plantation	wharf	customs	suspiciously	confrunted	detain
A large farm used to grow cotton, tabacco, or sugar can worked. p. 31	a dock used to let passengers board on a steamboat a ship. p. 33	People that check the passengers or luggage for safety or illegal items. p.34	behavior causing another to mistrust. p. 37	to come face to face with in aggression. p. 38	to keep from going on "to delay" p. 40

Author Talk: Connection

As students work together to discuss and define the vocabulary terms, the teacher is able to circulate around the classroom and informally assess student comprehension and language use. One teacher noted that she found this aspect of the Thumb Challenge strategy particularly beneficial:

> I liked to listen to the CLD students' groups in the Thumb Challenge. This gave me an opportunity to discover the CLD students' ability to use their CALP [cognitive academic language proficiency] language in a social, less stressful setting. This really helped me know the starting point of one of my newer CLD students' CALP language development.

Promoting the use of the CALP language is a natural outcome of the Thumb Challenge as students are using the academic vocabulary to complete the strategy. However, what makes this strategy meaningful for the CLD student is the explicit activation of existing background knowledge and its connection to new learning in context. One teacher noted that it was during these discussions that he could see the connections students were making between the L1 and the L2 via cognates. For example, he overheard one student tell his partner, "You know, it's like *musica*, music." The student talk promoted throughout the phases of this strategy provides the teacher with ample opportunities to observe and document learning and gather information that can be used to make the lesson more meaningful and comprehensible to all students.

Connecting to the "*i*+1"
How does this process move CLD students from the known to the unknown?

- **Sociocultural:** Making links between what they initially thought about the vocabulary words and the actual meaning of the terms in context allows students to revise their schemas about each word.
- **Linguistic:** Students' repeated articulation and refinement of the meaning of the words supports their acquisition of the academic language.

- **Academic:** The larger a child's vocabulary becomes, the stronger his or her reading comprehension (Duke & Carlisle, 2011). Constant reinforcement and use of the vocabulary words allows learners to take ownership of the vocabulary terms and solidifies the transfer of the words into their permanent memory.
- **Cognitive:** Encountering the key terms in context and discussing them in a meaningful way supports students in examining their understanding of the words.

AFFIRMATION: A Gallery of Understanding

Directions:

T (Total Group), p (partner),
s (small group), I (Individual)

- Have each pair engage in a Thumb Challenge. To begin, have the students in each pair sit facing each other, with the Thumb Challenge strip between them.
- Ask both students to hold the strip by putting a thumb on the first word on the side facing them.
- Have one student start by reading the first word and then stating its definition.
- If the student who began first struggles or does not know a word, the other student starts sharing from the very first word. As this student shares his or her definition, the first student's comprehension is stretched to the next level.
- Be sure to tell students that if at any point they are both unable to figure out a word, they can flip the strip over to find the correct answer.

- As students are sharing, circulate around the room and listen to them to check for understanding.
- To move toward individual accountability for students:
  - Have students choose words from the strip and write sentences that summarize their understanding of the words.
  - Have students use words from the strip to write a summary of the main topic/concept of the story/lesson.

Affirming Student Ownership: *"I"* Get It!
How does this process celebrate CLD student learning?

- **Sociocultural:** The Affirmation phase allows the CLD student to articulate his or her complete understanding of the vocabulary term. This understanding reflects not only what was learned in the text but also the wealth of background knowledge he or she brought to the term, along with that which was learned from peers.
- **Linguistic:** CLD students are able to demonstrate their learning both orally and in writing.

- **Academic:** The Thumb Challenge strategy allows students to participate in a process-oriented activity for practice and application of the key vocabulary that also allows for authentic assessment of learning.
- **Cognitive:** Students can challenge each other at any point during the Thumb Challenge. When responding, they are stretched to a higher cognitive level as they justify their responses. The Thumb Challenge involves movement, which stimulates brain cells in ways that further promote learning (Sousa, 2011).

SPOTLIGHT: Early Literacy Connection

The Thumb Challenge can be used to promote language development in young children by using visual cues such as those modeled on the strip below. As in the word challenge, pictures should be mirrored on both sides of the strip.

What Do You See?

This is a great activity for the classroom or home. Create a Thumb Challenge strip with visual cues, such as the one pictured here, and have two students or a parent and child play together. Select one person to begin by point-

ing to the first clue on his or her side of the strip. Instruct this person to identify the object and/or describe it (e.g., *What shape is it? What color is it?*). If the person gets it right, he or she continues until he or she gets one incorrect. Then it is the next person's turn. The game is over when someone gets to the end of the strip without stopping!

It's the *"i"* Thing

The Thumb Challenge strategy helps students focus on the cognitively challenging skills of explaining, comparing, and finally synthesizing their understanding of the vocabulary words. The nonthreatening nature of the activities helps students express their level of word knowledge and use their language skills to agree or disagree with peers. This BDI strategy also can be used to determine which areas of word understanding and pronunciation students might struggle with.

One Classroom's Perspective

From the 2nd-grade class of Stacey Bowman

Activating:

I considered the biographies of my CLD/ELL students by looking at the prism model as I planned and introduced the strategy. I paired the students with partners that created positive relationships. This is important in the first dimension of the prism model (sociocultural) to help the students not feel anxious. Their partners also help in guiding their learning, making sure they understand so that frustration does not occur. Before the lesson, the students were assessed with play-based assessment (using the Thumb Challenge) on knowing the definitions of the six terms (*make connections, mental images, infer, question, schema,* and *big idea*). I noted the students who struggled.

Make connections | Mental Images | Infer | Question | Schema | Big Idea

Connecting:

I used the strategy to reinforce key content and/or academic vocabulary development *throughout* the lesson and used multiple grouping configurations (Tpsl). The total class listened to the story. Students wrote their thinking in their reading journals as I read the story. At the end of the lesson, they reflected on their learning and shared this with the entire class. The Thumb Challenge is a partner game played with their "thinking partners." Students have the same partner for the entire year. This allows a positive relationship to form, and partners are used to working with one another. The students then worked in small groups. They were asked to discuss what they had learned about the six terms we had been studying. Last, individually, the students were asked to read their books and place sticky notes in their book with examples of the six terms.

Affirming:

I used the strategy to support me in authentically assessing my students' understanding of the lesson, as evidenced by my anecdotal notes. Students were then assessed again with the Thumb Challenge at the end of the lesson to see if they could apply the terms. This allowed me to see if they had mastered the terms. Applying the knowledge requires a much higher level of thinking. Again, as students did this, I walked around talking to each group and noting areas of struggle.

STRATEGY

Magic Book

I enjoyed doing the strategy of Magic Book with my students. They remained engaged throughout the class and kept the focus on the vocabulary words. I heard extremely in-depth conversations and dialogues regarding the concept that we were working on. The groupings also helped my students move the strategy forward, and the best part was my students were able to use their magic books throughout the lesson regardless of their language levels.

—*Lindsay Blanchard, 2nd-Grade Teacher*

Where Theory Meets Practice

Exploring promising practices for English learners and the link between literacy instruction and language development, researchers such as Wong Fillmore and Valadez (1986), V. Anderson and Roit (1993), and the members of The Education Alliance (Coady et al., 2003) emphasize an approach that is rooted within the realm of cognitive strategies. Research has also shown that learning is more effective when students give input into the vocabulary they need to learn (Echevarría, Vogt, & Short, 2013). Drawing on both areas of research, Magic Book is a cognitive strategy that allows students to take control over their own vocabulary learning and use that knowledge to bridge into understanding the content of the lesson.

Magic Book provides CLD students with an interactive tool that supports them throughout the lesson and actively involves them in the learning process. In addition to the serving as a concrete note-taking tool, the Magic Book provides a fun and interactive way to encourage cognition and metacognition surrounding the vocabulary and concepts. According to research by Willis (2006), there is a direct correlation between increased student attention/engagement and the retention of information taught during the lesson. This is due in large part to the fact that engagement differs from participation in the level of thinking that is taking place on the part of the student.

The Magic Book strategy asks students to be more involved in the learning process. According to Hattie and Yates (2014), "The more the self is involved, the deeper the processing. So if we can induce students to uncover or deduce knowledge for themselves, then the experience is made meaningful, memorable, and enjoyable" (p. 77). As a note-taking tool, the Magic Book enables students to record what has been learned; they then can use the tool at the end of the lesson to share with or quiz a partner based on this information. Magic Books can also support learners in writing an essay focused on the most important information. Magic Books provide a perfect support for students' review of material both at the end of the lesson and before summative or high-stakes assessments. This strategy helps educators ensure that all students are cognitively engaged as they manipulate the content, and the hands-on tool allows learners to make "magic" happen throughout the lesson!

MATERIALS & RESOURCES

Materials Needed: Colored construction paper (two pieces per student) • scissors • curricular materials • pencils/pens

Instructions: Creating Your Magic Book (see pages 116–117)

ACTIVATION: A Canvas of Opportunity

Directions:

i (individual)

- Following the instructions at the end of this strategy description (pages 116–117), either make the magic books for the class ahead of time or provide students with the materials and guide them through the process of constructing their own magic books. (From our experience in schools, students in grades 3–8 have little trouble making their own magic books.)
- Begin the activity by sharing with students the academic vocabulary of the lesson. When selecting the vocabulary, think of the six to eight most important words that will illustrate/provide the learner with the essence of the topic. *Tip:* For primary students, the strategy can also be used to teach phonics rules. Simply choose six to eight words based on blends, ending sounds, prefixes, and so forth.
- Have the students individually write the words in the boxes on the checkered mat of the magic book (see, e.g., the second image for Step 9 on page 117).
- Next, have students repeat the words. Ask them to think of what words they associate with the terms after they have read, written, and said each one.
- Have students write some of their own words and ideas

associated with the vocabulary around each of the words (or, in the case of primary students, have them discuss the words with each other). Encourage students to draw visuals related to the words or write in their native language. *Tip:* Often teachers ask students to put a checkmark or their initials next to any of the words they have never seen or heard. This holds all students accountable.

- Have students briefly share their ideas with a partner. Encourage them to add their "partner words" to the boxes as desired. They can circle their borrowed words so you can identify what they added through collaboration with a friend.
- As students share with their partners, circulate around the room to gather/document ideas that you can revoice for the class and have available as you teach the lesson and get into text.

Activating the *"i"*
How does this process activate CLD students' existing knowledge?

- **Sociocultural:** Drawing visuals and writing in their native language helps students reflect upon their own personal experiences and look for meaningful associations with the words.
- **Linguistic:** When students write and discuss the words, they gain valuable practice with the academic vocabulary of the lesson.

- **Academic:** Students' initial encounter with the vocabulary words is at their individual baseline (*i*) level. Subsequent exposures promote exploration of the vocabulary at the *i* +1 level.
- **Cognitive:** The Activation phase allows students to compare their own associations with the target words to those of a peer. This stretches students cognitively as they consider alternative perspectives.

CONNECTION: The Broad & Narrow Strokes of Learning

Directions:

T (Total Group), p (partner), s (small group)

- As you proceed with the lesson, think about how you will guide the students by stopping at several points to have them document information and discuss the content. Our suggestion is to start with pairs and then move to small teams once the learners have rehearsed enough to feel comfortable with a larger group.
- At each stopping point, have students discuss the critical concepts and ways the words support their understanding of what is being learned.
  - During discussions of the vocabulary, have students individually crack open their magic book and write on the other side of the magic book one of the following: a sentence using the word, the definition in their own words, or a brief response (incorporating the word) to a question. *Note:* For directions on how to crack open the magic book, see Step 9 of the instructions for creating your magic book on page 117.
  - You may choose to pose some guided questions at this time. As you do this, share with students the page numbers where the information will be found regarding the questions. This gives students a chance to dig into text evidence as you work on the content with them.
  - In the case of a phonics-based activity, you can have students write the meaning of the word or the associated root word.

- After the content of the lesson has been covered, make sure students have had a chance to cover all the words/concepts by writing the reverse side of the magic book.
- Then have students individually revisit the words and images they initially recorded for each vocabulary word. Ask them to cross out words and images that do not apply.
- Next have students turn to the flaps of the magic book to write evidence of what they have learned.
  - You can use this space for students to incorporate answers to curriculum-based questions.
  - In the case of a phonics-based activity, you can have students write different words (or have them draw a visual representing the words) that incorporate a particular sound, blend, prefix, and so forth.
  - If the flaps do not provide sufficient space, have students use blank paper or a journal instead.
- Have students share what they learned with a partner using the academic words to tell about the topic.

Connecting to the "*i*+1"
How does this process move CLD students from the known to the unknown?

- **Sociocultural:** The numerous opportunities to discuss the lesson/text with peers allow students to feel valued in the learning process and engaged in the lesson.
- **Linguistic:** The language on the magic book serves as a scaffold that students can use to express their learning with peers.

- **Academic:** Students' multiple exposures to the new vocabulary words via reading, writing, and discussion promote their retention of the words and overall comprehension of the topic.
- **Cognitive:** The students' metacognitive processes are supported as they are asked to confirm/disconfirm their initial associations with the vocabulary words in light of their new understandings.

AFFIRMATION: A Gallery of Understanding

Directions:

T (Total Group), p (partner),
s (small group), I (Individual)

- When students have finished sharing what they have learned about the topic, have them quiz each other using the magic book.
- As students move toward writing, you can have them pull the magic book apart to "lock in" their learning. Tell them the information is now in their permanent memory.
- Next have students summarize what they have learned or have them produce a different type of writing to demonstrate their language and content gains.
  - Primary students can be given a cloze paragraph in which they simply write the vocabulary words in the blanks. This paragraph can then be glued to a flap on the magic book. Alternatively, they can write the paragraph in their notebooks.

- In the case of a phonics-based activity, you can have students create sentences to show their understanding of the words/ patterns. This task provides students with an authentic context for application of the targeted skills.
- As noted in Step 10 of the instructions for creating your magic book on page 117, you can incorporate multiple small activities on the various sides of the magic book. This strategy can be built upon across multiple lessons to ensure a depth of understanding for students.
- Have students keep their magic book for future use as a study tool.

Author Talk: Affirmation

We know that words are powerful and can provide students with a means of expressing themselves. Yet, at the same time, words become one of the biggest stressors when it comes to comprehension and expression for many CLD students. It is important to support students in understanding how words become part of the conceptual knowledge we need in order to become successful in the classroom and beyond. The Magic Book strategy helps learners determine the meanings of words and phrases in context.

As educators, we need to continually provide students with multiple ways to connect words to the text they are reading. Magic Book is one strategy that can support our efforts to help students make personal connections to, and expand upon, their vocabulary, the academic vocabulary, and curricular concepts. The magic book becomes a "tool in their hand" that students can use both to activate their existing ideas about the vocabulary words and to manipulate the words throughout the progression of the lesson.

Teachers who have used the Magic Book strategy as a way to bridge from students' known words to the new, unknown vocabulary have shared the following tips:

- Place students in pairs (e.g., students with same native language—one with more advanced English proficiency and one at an earlier stage of second language acquisition) and have them work together using one magic book. Allow the pairs to discuss the words from the very beginning and continue working with them as they progress through the lesson.
- After students have finished their magic books, display them on the wall of the classroom so the students can refer to their own understandings of the words as they complete subsequent tasks.
- Keep students' magic books on various topics in separate containers (e.g., shoeboxes) so that they can be used later as study tools for unit/standardized tests.

Affirming Student Ownership: *"I" Get It!*
How does this process celebrate CLD student learning?

- **Sociocultural:** Because students have had numerous opportunities throughout the lesson to develop and articulate their understanding of the target vocabulary, a low-risk environment is maintained during the Affirmation phase as students quiz each other using their magic books.
- **Linguistic:** The continuous nature of the strategy as students return to the vocabulary throughout the lesson, as well as the additional opportunities for peer discussion and collaboration, allow students to gain

proficiency with high-frequency words and the academic vocabulary of the lesson.

- **Academic:** The magic book becomes a personal learning tool that students can use during the lesson and in the future to interact with and demonstrate their understanding of the content.
- **Cognitive:** As students rehearse information with peers, they are able to evaluate their understanding of the vocabulary and content. Using their magic books, students can check for accuracy and revise their understanding as needed.

One Classroom's Perspective
From the 2nd-grade class of Lindsay Blanchard

Activating:

Today was the first day we were working on the strategy of Magic Book. I have several ELL students who range from early production to intermediate fluency. Since the topic of our lesson was nutrition, I knew I needed to do something that would be hands-on and catch my students' attention. Magic Book worked great with my students in writing the six vocabulary words that we chose. I preferred to keep the vocabulary at six words and not eight, since the students were working on this topic for the first time.

The first thing I did with the students was to share with them how the magic book worked. They were quite fascinated by the way they could use their magic books on both sides. I brought all my students onto the carpet and modeled how they were going to write the words on the magic book. Next I divided them into pairs (based on their language proficiencies) and gave them one magic book per pair. To begin the activity, I had the students talk to their partners about the words on the magic book as one partner wrote all the vocabulary words. This phase of the lesson really helped my learners extend their ideas about the words.

Connecting:

Next, I shared the PowerPoint presentation with the students. On the PowerPoint, we had pictures of the words embedded on the slides. That gave my students an idea as to how a word worked within the context of the lesson. As I shared the PowerPoint with my students, I stopped at each slide and had students talk about the words again with each other. This constant sharing of ideas in pairs and small groups really allowed my learners to gain multiple perspectives on the words. As students shared the words this time, I had them turn the magic book over and write the definitions on the other side. As the students talked in pairs and wrote the definitions, I also allowed them to draw pictures relating to the words along with the definitions. Since 2nd-graders tend to respond more

to the pictures, this really helped my students. Also, the visuals really supported the multiple linguistic levels of my students.

As my students worked on the pictures and the meanings of the words on the other side of the magic book, I circulated around the room to listen to some of their conversations. This really gave me an idea as to who was able to follow the words and who needed some more help with them.

(Continued on the next page)

One Classroom's Perspective (*continued*)

Affirming:

To bring the lesson together, I had my students write their own sentences about the words on the side flaps of their magic books. My students were just amazed at how they could use the strategy of Magic Book as they worked throughout the lesson.

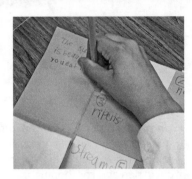

INSTRUCTIONS: Creating Your Magic Book

Materials: A single magic book will require two pieces of construction paper in different colors and a pair of scissors.

Step 1:	Take a piece of the construction paper, make sure it is in landscape orientation, and fold it in half from left to right, making a sharp crease.
Step 2:	Once again, fold it in half from left to right, making another sharp crease.
Step 3:	Fold the paper in half again, but this time fold from the bottom of the paper up. Make another sharp crease. Repeat this step a second time. When the paper is unfolded you should have 16 squares.
Step 4:	Then take a pair of scissors and *on the fold side* cut along the three folds, making sure you cut only to the middle fold of the paper. When you open the paper, you should have three horizontal slits in the middle of your paper.

INSTRUCTIONS: Creating Your Magic Book (*continued*)

Step 5:	Using the second piece of construction paper (a different color than the first piece) repeat Steps 1 and 2. Then open the paper and cut along the fold lines. You will end up with four strips of paper, but each student will need only two of the strips. (You could have two students share the second piece of construction paper. Each student should end up with two strips.)	

Step 6:	Take one of the strips of paper and weave it under the bottom slit in the first piece of construction paper, up through the middle slit, and then back under the top slit.		Your magic book should now look like this:
Step 7:	Take the other strip of paper and weave it up through the bottom slit in the first piece of construction paper, under the middle slit, and up through the top slit.		Your magic book should now look like this:
Step 8:	Fold each outside flap toward the middle.		When you hold the magic book up, you should have a **W**.

Step 9:	To crack open your magic book, fold it loosely (see picture at right) and place each thumb into the center fold. Open the crease by pulling the woven sections apart.	
	Voila! You have cracked open your magic book and created endless possibilities for students' information learning and retention! To return to the starting point, simply pull on the outside flaps that are now tucked under the checkered part pictured here.	
Step 10:	The magical thing is that you can turn your magic book over (so that it looks like an **M**) and then repeat Steps 8 and 9 to crack it open on this side as well!	

STRATEGY

IDEA

I gnite
D iscover
E xtend
A ffirm

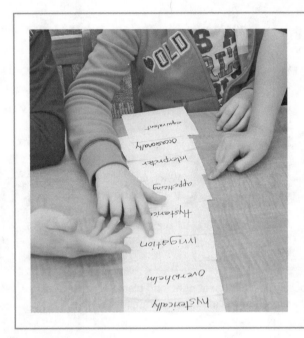

The implementation of this assessment strategy provided me with the insight that many of my CLD students use the context to figure out the meaning of new vocabulary words. Students were able to successfully give definitions and use the vocabulary words correctly in context. The students were excited and engaged throughout the activity. My CLD students, especially the ones identified as special education students, used pictures to show their background knowledge.

—*Amanda Donahey, 2nd-Grade Teacher*

Where Theory Meets Practice

As teachers responsible for enhancing our students' literacy skills, we often ask ourselves: *How can we provide a balanced literacy approach to our students?* In reality, if we think about a balanced literacy approach, we may not be able to find one concrete answer, given the changes we are seeing in society. Our student population has changed drastically and so have the academic, linguistic, sociocultural, and cognitive needs that our students exhibit. Even though we may have diverse perspectives on literacy development, we will all agree that there are certain literacy skills that all of our students need in order to be successful. Oral language skills are one example. One of the most prominent measures of oral language proficiency/linguistic knowledge is vocabulary knowledge (Geva & Yaghoub Zadeh, 2006; Proctor, Carlo, August, & Snow, 2005). Often

for our second language learners, an inability to communicate fluently goes hand in hand with a lack of English vocabulary understanding.

IDEA is one strategy that helps teachers work with students on the enhancement of both oral language skills and vocabulary development. Spycher (2009) found that both English learners and English proficient students in early stages of language development benefited equally from intentional and explicit vocabulary instruction that was a part of rich content instruction; this instruction combined multiple readings of narrative and expository texts with scaffolded opportunities for students to engage in academic talk with the words and concepts they were learning. This is exactly the type of instruction that IDEA promotes.

The "**I**" in IDEA stands for *ignite*. As Swan (2003) reminds us, cooperative learning groups are especially helpful for creating classroom cultures that support students' thinking, strategy use, connections to background knowledge, and engagement with text and vocabulary words. As students work in their small groups to share their first impression of the vocabulary words, they are able to tap into their background knowledge systems (Herrera, 2016).

The "**D**" of the strategy symbolizes *discover*, allowing students to focus on the vocabulary words through a context-based approach to the text. During this portion of the lesson, students are able to use their own words to describe new information gained from texts. Students' sharing of ideas in their small groups provides the teacher with multiple opportunities to help enhance their oral language skills and vocabulary understanding. As students continue working in their small groups and pairs, they are able to initiate dialogue and discover together the meaning and the context of new vocabulary.

The "**E**" of this strategy refers to the *extend* portion of the lesson. During this part, students extend upon their new understanding of the vocabulary words by creating links between the words. Students' language abilities are further strengthened as they connect the vocabulary words in oral or written form. Students work with peers to recall critical information from the text and retell the connections that exist between the words.

The "**A**" of IDEA reminds us as teachers to take time to *affirm* students' learning. Given that teachers cannot frequently meet one-on-one with each student, classroom practices must allow for students to display their thinking so the teacher can become aware of it (Darling-Hammond & Bransford, 2005). At the end of the lesson, the teacher listens to each group share their learning, affirms the efforts of the group, and provides feedback.

MATERIALS & RESOURCES

Materials Needed: Five to seven key vocabulary words • visuals for the vocabulary words • chart paper/paper with key vocabulary words (one for each group of students) • markers/colored pencils • book/text • sticky notes • paper • pencils/pens

---

ACTIVATION: A Canvas of Opportunity

Directions:

i (individual)

- Select five to seven key vocabulary words that are related to the same concept. Explain to students that they will be doing a "word carousel." To do this:
  - Place students in small groups of three or four students.
  - Write the vocabulary words on poster paper (one word per paper) and place one poster at each table.
  - Explain that groups will move from one table to the next, and each group member will record his or her individual thoughts about the word.
  - To help students *ignite* their understandings, encourage them to both write and draw. After recording their own ideas, they should also read what other students have already written about the word on the poster.
  - You can also show students visuals of the words to further ignite their thinking.
- As students work on the posters, circulate around the room to make note of the kinds of things students are recording.

- After the groups have finished with all of the posters, bring the class back together. Place the word posters on a wall where the entire class can see them. Go over the words and revoice some of the associations that students provided for the words.
- Next, explain to students that these initial connections to the words are based on their background knowledge and past experiences. As they read the text, they will see whether or not the way each vocabulary word is used in the text matches the way they initially used/understood it.

Activating the "*i*"
How does this process activate CLD students' existing knowledge?

- **Sociocultural:** Revoicing students' associations with the words for the entire class allows all learners to hear multiple perspectives on the words.
- **Linguistic:** Students have multiple opportunities to write about their initial understandings of the target vocabulary words.

- **Academic:** Students are exposed to academic content vocabulary along with their monolingual English-speaking peers and are provided support through visuals to make meaningful connections to the words.
- **Cognitive:** Students are able to make comparisons between their initial associations to the vocabulary words and those of their peers.

CONNECTION: The Broad & Narrow Strokes of Learning

Directions:

T (Total Group), p (partner), s (small group)

- Keep the word posters displayed in the room so that students can connect to them during the lesson.
- Support students during the lesson as they *discover* the meanings of the words in context by:
  - Talking about the words within the context of the lesson.
  - Reading a text/story in which the words appear.
  - Having students generate and write definitions of the words that reflect their use within the context of the lesson.
- In this phase, be sure to have students make connections back to their initial ideas discussed during the Activation phase. To do this:
  - Have students individually write each vocabulary word on a sticky note.
  - Direct students to record any new discoveries they make about the word during the lesson (i.e., during the course of the read-aloud, individual reading of the text, and/or discussion of the text).

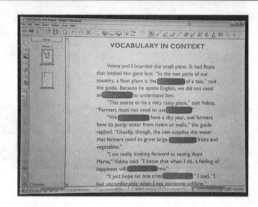

- Have students share their new discoveries with a partner.
- After the content has been covered, have students add their new connections to the group posters they completed during the Activation phase.
- Have students circle the original associations on the posters that came closest to the contextually correct use of the vocabulary words.

Connecting to the "*i*+1"
How does this process move CLD students from the known to the unknown?

- **Sociocultural:** As students work within the context of the lesson to gain new understandings, they continually reflect back on their own background experiences.
- **Linguistic:** CLD students practice writing academic language as they document new discoveries/learnings during the lesson.
- **Academic:** Having students share their new learnings with a partner before bringing them to the larger group

allows them to "test" their learning and clear up any confusion.
- **Cognitive:** As students confirm/disconfirm their original associations with the words, they are able to modify their schemas, as needed, to reflect their more thorough understanding of the words in the context of the lesson.

 ## AFFIRMATION: A Gallery of Understanding

Directions:

**T (Total Group), p (partner),
s (small group), I (Individual)**

- Once the students have finished working with the words and posters, bring the class back together.
- Have students *extend* upon their learning by creating a word chain. To do this:
  - Assign one person from each group to write all of the vocabulary words on index cards. Alternatively, give each group a set of index cards with the words on them. Students at primary levels can use index cards with pictures on them.
  - Explain to the groups that their task is to connect the words/pictures with each other to show the relationships that exist between the words.
  - Have students take turns articulating for one another the connections between the words in their word chain, as based on the story or topic the class just covered.
- After students have had a few minutes to practice, circulate to each group so they can share their word chain

with you and you can *affirm* their understandings. Provide additional support as necessary to ensure that the group has a solid understanding of each word and how the words

relate to one another and the larger topic.
- Next, have each group share their word chain with the rest of the class.
- To get an individual assessment of students' understanding, have each student independently write a paragraph using all of the vocabulary words.
  - *Tip:* If you do this type of assessment, allow CLD students in the preproduction or early production phase of second language acquisition to draw and label their connections in English or write them in their native language.

Author Talk: Affirmation

In talking one day with a teacher about the language development of some students in her 5th-grade class, we kept coming back to the importance of CLD students' oral language development. Students' reading comprehension skills are highly dependent upon their oral proficiency in English. As teachers, we need to provide students with contexts and situations that allow them to continually build their language skills. The IDEA strategy is a great tool for helping students develop their oral language skills, which are most strengthened during the Affirmation phase when students link the vocabulary words and verbally articulate the connections for their classmates. Ideas that teachers have shared to promote language development include:

- Pair students with high and low proficiencies as they work on the strategy. Doing this allows students with limited English proficiency to observe how the language works.
- As you introduce the vocabulary words, show visuals associated with them and have students first share their ideas about the words with a partner before moving to the word posters.
- As students work together to create the word chains, have them also write their word chain associations.

Affirming Student Ownership: *"I"* Get It!
How does this process celebrate CLD student learning?

- **Sociocultural:** Students' negotiation of links between the words with peers allows them to draw from multiple perspectives as they extend upon their learning.
- **Linguistic:** CLD students use all four language domains—listening, speaking, reading, and writing—to demonstrate their understanding of the content.
- **Academic:** As students discuss the relationships among the vocabulary words with peers, they strengthen their overall understanding of the terms and larger concepts.
- **Cognitive:** Students are able to evaluate their understanding of the vocabulary as they hear other groups' alternative arrangements of the words and associated relationships between the terms.

SPOTLIGHT: Early Literacy Connection

Researchers have found that emergent reading, like emergent writing, begins with pictures that help children establish the meaning of the words that make up the stories they will eventually be able to read (Beaty & Pratt, 2007; Neuman & Roskos, 1993). For young children, the majority of the books they are reading (or that are being read to them) are picture books. When children are being read to, the reader significantly influences how the children interpret the texts. When the child becomes the reader of the text, he or she takes on the role of "author" and gets to interpret the meaning of the pictures through his or her own voice and understanding. The IDEA strategy can be adapted for use in early literacy classrooms for just this purpose with the "Picture Me a Story" variant described below.

Picture Me a Story

To implement this version of the IDEA strategy, select six pictures from a picture book with which your students are familiar. Make enough copies of the pictures so that when you pair your students, each pair has a copy of each picture. Explain to the students they are going to be the "authors" of their very own story by working together to put the pictures in order and then tell the class their story using the pictures. Next, give the students time to organize their pictures. After they have finished, circulate around the room to each pair and listen to their story. After all the stories have been told to the class as a whole, talk with your students about what was the same and different about the stories. Emphasize the similarities as well as the differences, reminding students that all authors have different points of view.

Extension. This is also a great activity you can encourage the parents of your children to do at home with pictures from a story or magazine, or even pictures the students draw on their own. The key is to get the students engaged in the act of telling/retelling stories!

One Classroom's Perspective

From the 2nd-grade class of Amanda Donahey

Activating:

I really like the strategy of IDEA, since it helps me work on the vocabulary words with my students and also allows for me to extend their learning about the words to a much deeper level. The many stages of the strategy are really helpful in providing me with an opportunity to construct meaning with my learners. To ignite my students' understanding of the words, I started the activity with a variation of the Vocabulary Quilt (see page 95 of this volume). In order to do this, I put six vocabulary words on each table and then placed my students in groups of two or three. I grouped my students based on their language and academic proficiencies, considering this was the first time my students were seeing the words. We started the activity by having the groups go to each of the words and spend about a minute writing or drawing their initial thoughts about the words. By doing this, my students were able to be exposed to all of the vocabulary words in the chapter.

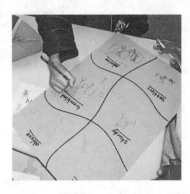

Once the groups were finished working on the words, I gathered the vocabulary words from the tables and had all of the students join me at the carpet. The first thing I did with my students was show them the words one by one, and I read some of the thoughts that they had put on the papers. As I read some of their initial ideas, I also had my students talk to each other regarding how the initial thoughts on the papers connected with the words. I did not give them any correct definitions at this time, since I just wanted to review some of the ideas that my students had put on the paper.

Connecting:

We then gathered in front of the smart board and I pulled up the words on a PowerPoint slide. I had students come up and add pictures from their posters to make connections to what they already knew. Next, I sent my students back to their desks and had them cut apart the words of their vocabulary quilt. I told them I was going to read them a short paragraph from the story, and it was their job to fill in the words that were missing from the paragraph with their vocabulary words. (I covered the words as they appeared in the passage, since I wanted my students to see how the words worked in context.) I read a little bit of the passage, and when I came to the point of the word within the passage, I had my students guess which one of their vocabulary words would fit. I gave stu-

dents some time to think about this, and they wrote the answers on their white boards. This activity served as a great informal assessment for me, since I was able to see if my students were able to understand the idea of context. We went through the entire passage and I asked the students to follow the same procedure. By the end, students were able to see all the vocabulary words written on the screen within a context.

Affirming:

Now that my students had been through many stages of vocabulary development, I wanted them to use the words without a context in front of them. So I asked them to go back to their original groups for this Affirmation phase. To challenge the groups and see what they truly understood about the vocabulary, I gave each group all six words on the original vocabulary quilts. I told them that they now had to connect the words to each other in a meaningful way to show a relationship between the words. As students

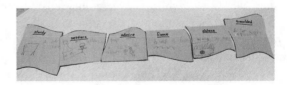

put the words together, I walked around to listen to their connections. As a further extension to the activity and as part of their assessment, I also had my students individually create summaries using all six vocabulary words.

CHAPTER 3

Comprehension: It's Not Real Until It's Rehearsed and Written

DURING A LESSON, students are inundated with a wealth of new information, from academic vocabulary to content concepts. To assimilate this information, they must be able to decode the words they are reading (phonemic awareness and phonics), understand them (vocabulary), and read them accurately and with the proper rate and expression (fluency); finally, they must grasp the overall message of the text (comprehension). Consider how you use all of these skills as you read the following passage:

> Han was very excited about Tết. Because it was January, she was getting ready for the annual Tết celebration with her family and friends, just like her family used to celebrate it in Viêt Nam. Han especially liked eating mung bean rice cakes and bong mai—the plum blossoms. The câu dôi were her favorite of all, though. These poems written about yearning for home and family were really important to her because she and her family now lived in the United States and they missed family members back in Viêt Nam.

Take a moment to reflect on the passage you just read. Were there words with which you were unfamiliar? How did you use your phonemic awareness/phonics skills to help you decipher these words? In what ways did you use context clues to help you determine the meaning of unfamiliar vocabulary (e.g., Tết, bong mai, câu dôi)? Even though some of the vocabulary might have been unfamiliar to you, were you still able to read the passage fluently? Based on what you read, what celebration was Han preparing for? Your answers to these questions illustrate how you use all of your linguistic knowledge and skills to comprehend what you read.

Comprehension: Getting to the Heart of Meaning

Reading comprehension research has been profoundly influenced by schema theory, a hypothesis that explains how information we have stored in our minds helps us gain new knowledge (Reutzel & Cooter, 2012). Schemas (or schemata) can be thought of as a filing cabinet system in our brains, with different drawers and file folders containing different information about concepts (tables, monkeys, cars), events (birthday, school day, haircut), emotions (happiness, anger, sadness), and roles (sibling, parent, teacher) based on our life experiences (R. C. Anderson & Pearson, 1984; Rumelhart, 1980). Each person has distinct schemas based on his or her unique life experiences.

Research has shown that "if the schemata for a particular topic are well developed and personally meaningful, new information is easier to retain and recall, and proficient learners initiate and activate their associations between the new and old learning" (Echevarría et al., 2013, p. 116). For CLD students, the identification of existing schemas is particularly vital, as their culturally influenced schemas may be different from those of a text's intended audience. When we focus first on what our students understand and bring to the lesson, we are able to provide instruction from a *biography-driven perspective* (Herrera, 2016). Biography-driven instruction allows us to get to the heart of who our students are and to use what matters most to them as a vehicle for helping them learn new material.

The strategies described in this chapter not only support teachers in determining what their CLD students already know about an academic topic, key vocabulary, and critical concepts, they also teach students how to monitor their own comprehension and learning throughout the lesson. These strategies help students develop the metacognitive skills they need to successfully overcome difficulties they might encounter when reading text. To understand how strategies can be used to accomplish such a task, let us first define what we mean by metacognition.

Metacognition: More Than Thinking About Your Thinking!

Metacognition was first defined by Flavell (1976) as "one's knowledge concerning one's own cognitive processes and outcomes or anything related to them" (p. 232). Metacognition is often described more simply as the ability to think about your own thinking. This definition, however, tends to downplay the many skills involved in using metacognition for learning. What makes metacognition so powerful when it comes to reading comprehension, for example, is that readers who are metacognitively aware know what to do when they encounter difficulties in text. As N. J. Anderson (2002) notes, "the use of metacognitive strategies ignite[s] one's thinking and can lead to more profound learning and improved performance" (p. 1). Metacognition supports the reader's ability to identify and apply strategies to resolve problems that might occur during the reading process.

According to research by Rea and Mercuri (2006), teachers can encourage schema building and metacognition by

- Helping students build background knowledge and understanding,
- Helping students access the background knowledge they have and use it as a bridge to new learning, and
- Helping students become consciously aware of their thinking processes and the strategies they use to accomplish tasks (p. 47).

This blending of attention to schemas and to metacognition supports CLD students' ability to make conscious decisions when reading text.

To help teach metacognitive skills, Anderson (2002) proposes a model of metacognition that involves:

- Preparing and planning for learning,
- Selecting and using learning strategies,
- Monitoring strategy use,
- Orchestrating various strategies, and
- Evaluating strategy use and learning (pp. 1–2).

In preparing and planning, students are taught how to think about the overall goal and about what they need or want to accomplish from the reading. For selecting and using learning strategies, students need to be taught how to identify and implement specific strategies based on the text and the purpose of the reading. Monitoring of strategy use involves explicitly teaching students how to strategically

monitor their application of learning strategies to make sure they are meeting their overall learning goals. Knowing how to orchestrate and use more than one strategy at a time requires that students have opportunities to practice implementing metacognitive strategies. Finally, students are taught to evaluate the effectiveness of their individual strategy implementation.

Rea and Mercuri (2006) emphasize that for metacognitive strategies to be effective, students must (1) understand the strategy, (2) understand why they need to know it and why it will benefit them, (3) be able to think through the strategy process aloud or voice the strategy in their mind, (4) see examples of the strategy in use, (5) know when and where it is appropriate to use the strategy, and (6) be able to monitor themselves (*Is the strategy working? What should be done if it does not work?*). CLD students need more than cursory exposure to various learning strategies; they need explicit opportunities to learn and apply strategies in ways that support their reading and learning. The goal of metacognition is reached when a student "mobilizes his/her resources to interact with the text to create meaning" (Simonsen & Singer, 1992, p. 202).

Using Peer Support to Enhance Strategy Use

For many CLD students, some of the most valuable resources in the classroom are their peers, particularly their bilingual peers. Peers are the ones who can translate information for English learners when they do not understand what is being said. Peers can often connect with them on a cultural level when many of their other classmates cannot. And peers can provide that sense of "comfort" and "home" when CLD students are feeling lost or overwhelmed in the classroom. Classmates also provide one another with alternative perspectives on the topics, concepts, and academic vocabulary explored in the classroom. Thus, *all* students should be explicitly taught to work collaboratively to help create positive learning situations. If we strategically build upon the assets of our students and actively create a classroom community in which they can learn from one another, we can accelerate not only their comprehension but also their effective application of learning strategies in practice.

In conclusion, the primary questions to remember when selecting strategies are these:

- Which *instructional strategy* would best support the reciprocal teaching and learning process of the teacher and students as they work together to meet the objectives of the lesson?
- What are the biography-driven needs of the students?

- Which *student learning strategies* would best support individual students to succeed on the activities and tasks of the lesson?
- Which grouping configurations would best address the needs of the students and enhance their application of the selected strategy(ies)?

Strategies in Practice

In this chapter you will find descriptions of the following seven BDI strategies, which you can use throughout lesson delivery to increase CLD students' motivation, engagement, language development, comprehension, and academic achievement:

- U-C-ME
- Extension Wheel
- Hearts Activity
- Active Bookmarks
- Mini Novela
- Tri-Fold
- Word Drop

STRATEGY

U-C-ME

U ncover ideas
C oncentrate on the topic
M onitor understanding
E valuate learning

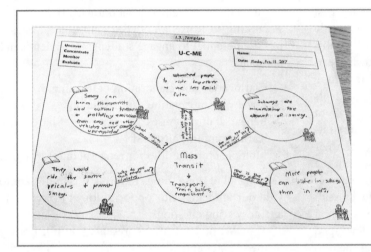

I love the way the strategy aligns with the questions. My kids were attentive and the questions helped them in focusing on the content. Even though I gave students a couple questions initially they were able to come up with questions with no problem. And the questions tied to their ideas perfectly. Great strategy! Lots of discussion was also there. I would definitely like to try it again.

—*Courtney Burkhart, 6th-Grade Teacher*

Where Theory Meets Practice

Focusing on what the teacher or the prescriptive curriculum would ascertain is the most important information to be learned—without guidance or scaffolding—is often next to impossible for CLD students. The language and academic load from both lecture and text require the learner to attend to multiple agendas at once, often making learning mentally, emotionally, and physically exhausting. Thinking maps and other graphic organizers have been touted in research and literature as key to providing comprehensible input that will lead to comprehension of content. However, comprehension difficulties often are related to the fact that readers are not able to get actively involved in the reading process for a variety of reasons, including the learner's reading and language proficiency levels, the teacher's delivery of the lesson, or the student's interest. These challenges are further compounded in the case of our CLD students because the text that is being used often is too far removed from the cultural context of learners.

It is critical for teachers to provide opportunities to students that are more strategic in nature and that help improve learners' textual understanding by having them fully participate in the process of comprehending the text. The objective is not to "provide" students with knowledge, but to support them in organizing, planning for, engaging in, and monitoring their learning and comprehension, so that they can take greater ownership of their own learning process. This is where moving beyond the isolated use of graphic organizers and thinking maps and toward the embedded, strategic use of organizers throughout the lesson does much to benefit the learner. Such hands-on tools can then serve as scaffolds for students' cognitive and metacognitive processes as they actively construct their own understandings.

The U-C-ME strategy begins with the teacher providing a safe opportunity for students to uncover what they know. The teacher then moves toward facilitating the development and selection of guiding questions that will support the community of learners in consciously focusing on what is most important. Questioning is well documented for its benefits to students' language development and learning (e.g., Almeida, 2010; Chin, 2007; Chin & Osborne, 2008;

Davoudi & Sadeghi, 2015; Graesser & Olde, 2003). In order to help advance our CLD students' comprehension skills, we need to utilize strategies that support them in developing, expanding, and challenging their own thinking. The questioning process used in this BDI strategy does just that. It also scaffolds students' development of metacognitive skills.

Metacognition is referred to as one's knowledge concerning one's own cognitive processes or anything related to them. Research has demonstrated that metacognitive skills can be taught (Bransford, Brown, & Cocking, 2000; Chick, n.d.). For English learners who are juggling many demands simultaneously, BDI strategies such as U-C-ME are especially effective in scaffolding this process. Students first make connections to the *known* (knowledge they already bring to the lesson). Teachers are explicit about how this step of making links to their background knowledge is foundational to students' new learning, or understanding of the *unknown*. Through the strategy of U-C-ME, students then determine what more they would like to learn about the content. They document their questions using the strategy's hands-on tool. They use this same tool to track their learning and monitor their comprehension throughout the lesson. As they delve into the process of investigating, collaborating with peers, and answering the personally relevant questions, students' engagement and comprehension are promoted. The student-generated questions, developed with support and guidance from the teacher, lead them to think critically about the content and about the process they undertake in order to answer the questions.

The U-C-ME strategy has been specifically designed to support as well as challenge students' thought processes as a result of questions that are posed on the U-C-ME chart. The "**U**" of U-C-ME emphasizes for students that they first must **uncover** existing knowledge based on what they already know about the topic of the lesson and consider how their knowledge might be related to the lesson content. Research has shown that "the ability to recognize and construct patterns that identify the familiar or not familiar relies on schemas formed by prior knowledge and experiences" (Gregory & Burkman, 2012, p. 38). Students' meaningful connections between their background knowledge (funds of knowledge, prior knowledge, and academic knowledge) and the content promote their willingness to invest in the learning process, despite the previously noted

challenges, and increase the likelihood that their new language and content understandings will transfer to long-term memory (Blachowicz & Fisher, 2000; Jensen, 2006; Sousa, 2011).

Students then are asked to think of specific questions they have about the topic. The "**C**" of U-C-ME moves students toward metacognition as they **concentrate** on answering the questions posed at the beginning of the lesson, thereby focusing on the critical concepts of the lesson. The key in this portion of the lesson is to guide students by "challenging them to link to the past, think beyond, and use questions to discover and uncover new learning" (Herrera, 2016, p. 131). Throughout this portion, learners interact and talk with their peers about what they are learning. According to Kinsella and Feldman (2003), questioning has the potential to engage students in academic talk that allows for

- Clarification and elaboration of learning,
- Review of information as it is taught,
- Rehearsal of responses before they are shared with the learning community, and
- Multiple opportunities for retrieval of information.

Keeping all of these things in mind, it is important to provide our students with opportunities to practice posing and answering questions.

The "**M**" of U-C-ME represents the **monitoring** performed by students when they place answers to their questions on the U-C-ME chart and reflect on the degree to which they understand the related content and vocabulary. Students are also given the opportunity to share and negotiate their answers with their small-group members. As Herrera (2016) notes, this type of structured release to a small group increases the chances that an "$i+1$ response will become part of the group answer" (p. 131).

The "**E**," or final **evaluation** of student understanding, takes place at the end of the lesson as students summarize their key learnings. At this time, students complete the task by referring to their completed tool. This tool, therefore, is used to document the learning that resulted from students' thought processes *throughout* the lesson. As they reflect upon their learning, students are able to evaluate the effectiveness of the learning strategies they used to accomplish the goals of the lesson.

MATERIALS & RESOURCES

Materials Needed: U-C-ME Template (one per student) • poster paper • picture for key vocabulary words • markers/colored pencils • curricular materials • paper • pencils/pens

Template: U-C-ME Template (see page 136); also available for free download and printing from tcpress.com/accelerating

Rubric: Student Assessment Rubric (see page 200); also available for free download and printing from tcpress.com/accelerating

Video: A video clip illustrating implementation of this strategy is available for viewing online at coe.k-state.edu/cima/biographycrt

---

 ACTIVATION: A Canvas of Opportunity

Directions:

i (individual)

During this phase of the lesson, the U-C-ME chart provides a space for you to help your students start thinking of how they will organize their information. Explain how the strategy works by going over the acronym so students understand the progression and also how questioning will help them connect to and understand the content.

- Give each student a blank U-C-ME Template before the lesson.
- As you share the essential question/planned outcome of the lesson, have students write the name of the topic/concept that is the focus of the lesson around the outside of the template's center oval (toward the top of the oval).
- Have each student individually think about the topic and write three or four ideas that they can associate with the topic, using pictures or words, on the back of their chart (toward the top).
- Place students in small groups and have each group orally share what they already know about the topic, including how they know it. This is an important step for English learners, since this oral sharing provides them an anchor for more cognitively demanding tasks to follow.
- Have each group member consider all the ideas shared, choose two or three schematic connections that they think will be most relevant to the lesson, and individually add them within the middle oval in writing and/or with drawings. If there is not enough space, have stu-

dents record them on the back of their chart (toward the middle of the paper). Make sure that students understand the purpose behind making and recording connections between their background knowledge and the topic at the beginning of the lesson.

- Once students have finished recording their ideas on paper, have some of the students share their ideas. Use this opportunity to highlight contributions from students who frequently struggle to make their ideas and voices heard. By this point, all students have had an opportunity to practice articulating their ideas, so they should be more comfortable with sharing their ideas with the larger class.

Instructional Tips:

- As students write, draw, and discuss their ideas, be sure to rotate around the room and document some of their initial ideas. These ideas can be brought into your instructional conversations during the lesson as students work on the creation of their own questions.
- Specific questioning at this time of the lesson directed at particular students or groups can help students focus more on what they already know about the topic and select the more essential ideas for inclusion in the center oval.

Activating the "*i*"
How does this process activate CLD students' existing knowledge?

- **Sociocultural:** Explicit discussion of the importance of making connections to their background knowledge demonstrates to students the power of this step for their continued learning. In this way, students begin to develop their metacognitive skills from the very onset of the lesson. In addition, because the initial connections are based on students' unique knowledge systems, U-C-ME paves the path for students to interact actively with the text at their own level and from their own perspective.
- **Linguistic:** This phase of the strategy provides students with opportunities to orally articulate their initial schematic connections, listen to those of peers, and then

write/draw the most relevant images. Students therefore have multiple opportunities for *i*+1 language input before entering the more cognitively demanding phases of the lesson.
- **Academic:** Through interactions with small group members and the larger learning community, students are guided to narrow their ideas as they make predictions about key information related to the topic.
- **Cognitive:** The U-C-ME chart provides CLD students with a concrete "tool in their hand" to support them in organizing their thoughts and exploring their metacognitive processes.

 CONNECTION: The Broad & Narrow Strokes of Learning

Directions:

T (Total Group), p (partner), s (small group)

 Bridging to the Content— Drawing the *i* into the Lesson

At this time, the U-C-ME chart supports students in connecting to the content in personally relevant ways through the questions that students create. These questions serve as a guide for students to keep track of their own understanding.

- Share pertinent vocabulary words that you think will support students' thought processes as they develop questions.
- Depending upon the text, essential question, and/or the outcome of the lesson, guide students to collaborate in their small groups to create questions that will help them in comprehending the text and making further connections to the content.
  - *Note:* You can begin this process by creating some of the questions yourself. You might develop questions that are tightly tied to the content or that will help students relate to the content on a personal level.
- Have students record one question on each of the spokes radiating from the center oval of the U-C-ME

chart. Explain to students that these questions will guide their learning and their process of monitoring their lesson comprehension and understanding of the text.

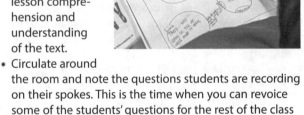

- Circulate around the room and note the questions students are recording on their spokes. This is the time when you can revoice some of the students' questions for the rest of the class in order to provide further direction.
- As students finish forming their questions, ask each group to share a few of their questions with the rest of the class.

Instructional Tip:

- Ensure that student groups are recording questions that require higher-order thinking.

CONNECTION: The Broad & Narrow Strokes of Learning (*continued*)

 Digging into Text

- Explain to students that as the lesson proceeds, they will find answers to their questions and write them in the adjoining ovals. During instruction, make sure to stop periodically to provide students with time to individually monitor their comprehension and use the new information from the text to answer the questions. This step also helps students focus on text evidence.
- Be sure to incorporate opportunities for students to discuss their answers in their small groups as they find them. Encourage them to ask questions of their peers during this time as they come to consensus about the answers.
- After students have finished working with the text, have group members revisit each question and discuss their answers one more time with the group. Encourage them to consider whether new information requires any of the answers to be revised. Have students refer back to the lesson materials/text to evaluate the validity of their answers.
- Next, have each group confirm/disconfirm their predictions regarding the topic-related words/ideas they placed in the center oval of their U-C-ME charts. This step is critical because it allows students to see how their new learnings relate to the ideas they previously had recorded on their U-C-ME charts.

Instructional Tips:

- Make sure to provide students with lots of opportunities for think time during this phase of the lesson. We need to support our students to develop well thought out answers to the questions they have posed. Think time is especially important for English learners.
- Have students record relevant page numbers from the text beside the answer ovals.

Author Talk: Connection

Day after day, we ask ourselves the million dollar question: *How can we ensure that our students are gaining ownership over their learning?* Today as we watched a 4th-grade classroom during their reading time, we found that most of the kids zoomed past the actual reading portion of their reading block. Not many stops were planned during the reading part for the teacher to ask questions and for students to process the text. During our debriefing, one of the main things that surfaced was how questioning is a part of the learning process that allows students to focus on the content but also to formulate their own thought process related to what they are learning.

By providing students with guiding questions at the onset of the lesson, and then revisiting these questions during the lesson, the teacher is able to steer learners toward the main ideas of the lesson and provide a path for them to follow. When teachers allow students to come up with some of the questions themselves, the students take ownership of the learning process. As we have watched this strategy being implemented in different classrooms, we can't help but notice how focused students become when they are allowed to create questions on their own.

The U-C-ME strategy is truly one of the best mediums for supporting students in gaining ownership over their learning process. This strategy provides students with a framework that helps them in guiding themselves throughout the lesson at their own level while also focusing on the major conceptual ideas. U-C-ME structures students' interaction with text, requiring them to read for meaning in order to gather information that is tied to the questions but also to the larger discussion occurring at the classroom level.

Connecting to the "*i*+1"
How does this process move CLD students from the known to the unknown?

- **Sociocultural:** Text–self connections are promoted as students are provided the opportunity to generate questions that reflect what they personally want to know about the topic. Peer interaction supports text–world connections, as each student is able to hear multiple perspectives on the topic. Each viewpoint is reflective of an individual student's culturally bound perspective.
- **Linguistic:** Students engage in academic talk throughout the lesson using their own words and sharing their original thoughts. As students generate and subsequently share answers to their questions, they use academic language naturally throughout the life cycle of the strategy.

- **Academic:** Consistent focus on the questions allows students to have more metacognitive awareness. This in turn helps students gain confidence as they build their academic skills and understanding. Throughout this phase, students are challenged to construct their own meaning as they connect to the text.
- **Cognitive:** Students are stretched cognitively as they are guided to create questions that require higher-order thinking. The consistent documentation of students' ideas on the U-C-ME chart as they seek to answer the questions allows them to track their cognitive connections to the content. The chart serves as a scaffold for the teacher and students as they discuss and engage in the abstract processes of metacognition.

 AFFIRMATION: A Gallery of Understanding

Directions:

**T (Total Group), p (partner),
s (small group), I (Individual)**

At this stage of the lesson, the U-C-ME has become an organized tool that includes students' thought process and their individual connections to the topic. Students have evolved as thinkers, readers, and writers while they worked on finding connections through the U-C-ME chart.

- Return to the essential question/lesson objectives and have students relate how the U-C-ME chart helps them to reflect on their learning. Discuss as a learning community whether the goals of the lesson have been achieved.
- Have students use their completed U-C-ME charts to support their synthesis of learning. To bring the lesson to closure, have students do any of the following:
  - Work individually or in pairs to write a persuasive or narrative paragraph.
  - Use the information in the ovals to answer end-of-chapter questions.
  - Use the information in the ovals to write a paragraph in response to the essential question.
  - Work in small groups to create a class quiz or study guide using the information in the ovals.

Instructional Tips:

- You also can have students do a "connected talk" at the end of the lesson to discuss what they have learned. To do this:
  - Have one student start the connected talk by sharing one thing he or she learned about the topic. Then have each additional student connect his or her idea to what the previous student shared.
  - Encourage students to refer to the answers they have recorded in the ovals of their U-C-ME chart for additional scaffolding of the task.

Affirming Student Ownership: *"I" Get It!*
How does this process celebrate CLD student learning?

- **Sociocultural:** The summation of the whole BDI strategy is very much rooted in students' sociocultural ways. They started the lesson by reflecting upon their own ideas and then focused on the questions that were important to them. The final stage of the lesson allows students to bring their learning to closure by going back to the ways they have individually made sense of the information gathered about the topic.
- **Linguistic:** U-C-ME provides the language support that CLD students need in order to engage fully in the summative assessments planned for the end of the lesson. The U-C-ME chart serves as a repository of words and ideas that students can use as they represent and communicate their learning.
- **Academic:** TThe completed U-C-ME chart provides students with a concrete study tool for reviewing key learnings from the lesson/unit.
- **Cognitive:** Because student thinking is constantly stimulated throughout the lesson, students are supported to reach higher levels of comprehension. Learners have opportunities to strengthen their mental models about the concepts. These new mental models are reflected in students' summarization of ideas and learning.

SPOTLIGHT: Early Literacy Connection

Research has shown that questions "are at the heart of classroom practice" (Marzano et al., 2001, p. 113). In fact, questioning can account for as much as 80% of what occurs in a classroom on any given day (Marzano et al.). Thus, young CLD students should be asked a variety of questions that are appropriate for their age and language proficiency level. The U-C-ME strategy is a great way to model the question-and-answer process while addressing students' needs.

U-C-ME in Pictures!

When initially using the U-C-ME strategy with younger CLD students, use one U-C-ME Template with the whole class. This allows you as the teacher to model use of the strategy through each phase of instruction. When describing each phase on the U-C-ME chart, use a writing utensil of a different color. This allows the students to better understand and remember each distinct stage.

Initially, you can simply ask questions related to the content/story and have the students find the information in the text. Students can then draw a picture to represent the answer for the appropriate bubble. As students get comfortable with generating and asking questions, they can begin to ask their own questions about the vocabulary and content and look for the related information in the text or other resources.

One Classroom's Perspective

From the 6th-grade class of Courtney Burkhart

Activating:

We have been exploring the vocabulary words for the past few weeks that relate to our "Wonders" topic on *Mass Transit.* Today is our first day to read the story, so I decided to use the strategy of U-C-ME with students to focus on the topic of *Transport in the Modern World.* We read about Athens, Greece, last week in our social studies unit so today was a perfect start for the "Wonders" story on mass transit in the modern world. My objective with this story was to help students understand the challenges that would have come with the creation of mass transit in the ancient city.

First I explained the U-C-ME chart to students. Next we moved into writing about three or four ideas that they connected with the topic of *Mass Transit* in the middle circle. I started the lesson by having them just think of mass transit first, so I then could build the lesson toward the actual story. Students were able to individually write quite a few things in the middle circle. Once they were done writing their ideas, I had them share those in their small groups.

I felt like students really contributed quite a bit during this time. They shared and exchanged lots of ideas that they had learned last week as well. I didn't really have to spend so much time asking them questions about what they had learned last week, but rather they themselves brought those into the conversations. As they finished their sharing, I asked some of the students to expand upon their thoughts. One example is when a student shared that they see eco-efficiency with mass transportation. I had the student give his explanation to the rest of the class on why he considers mass transportation as eco-efficient.

Connecting:

After students finished sharing their connections, we moved on to the creation of questions on the spokes. Since this was our first time doing the activity, I started this portion of the lesson by giving my students two questions that I had already prepared. I did this largely because there were a few things I needed them to answer to help connect to the story. As I shared my questions, I also had students think on why I was having them answer these questions by writing them on the spokes. To get the conversation going, I had them share their ideas with partners on why we were answering the questions on the U-C-ME chart.

After we shared our responses, I had them work in groups to create more questions on the spokes of the U-C-ME chart. Students could create their individual questions or they could use their group as a means to come up with the questions. I rotated around the room at this time and helped them as needed. I also restated some of the students' questions. As students finished the questions, we started the reading portion.

I had students chunk the reading and whisper read it first, and then we moved into partner reading. This step really helped since students could discuss their answers

with each other. I told them that this would be the time they would find answers to the questions from the text. We stopped at regular intervals and I had them talk to each other in their small groups to see if they had found the answers. As students came up with the answers, I had them share their answers with the whole class. This step helped my classroom since they became very invested in looking for their answers. As students shared answers with the class, I also had students look for text evidence by pointing to where they found the answer in the text. My students need reminders of this kind since this is what helps them with comprehension. We finished the entire reading and came up with most of the answers from the reading and group discussion. If students couldn't come up with the answers, I had them research for a few minutes using their iPads to find the answers.

One Classroom's Perspective (*continued*)

Affirming:

Now that we had all the answers, I wanted my students to really get into answering my question regarding the challenges that the modern world can face with mass transit. To do this, I had students read through their U-C-ME charts and discuss all of the questions and answers that they had on their charts. I also had them revisit the book at this time, just to make sure they could also point out the text evidence to each other. As they did that I went around and listened to see all of the information they had gathered. Before I had them write their paragraphs, I had them first discuss the challenges they thought were faced in the creation of mass transit in Athens. As we finished that discussion, students moved into writing their paragraphs. I gave them reminders to refer back to their U-C-ME charts to write the paragraph. They did a good job of writing persuasive paragraphs on the challenges of mass transit in an ancient land.

U-C-ME

Name: _____

Date: _____

Uncover
Concentrate
Monitor
Evaluate

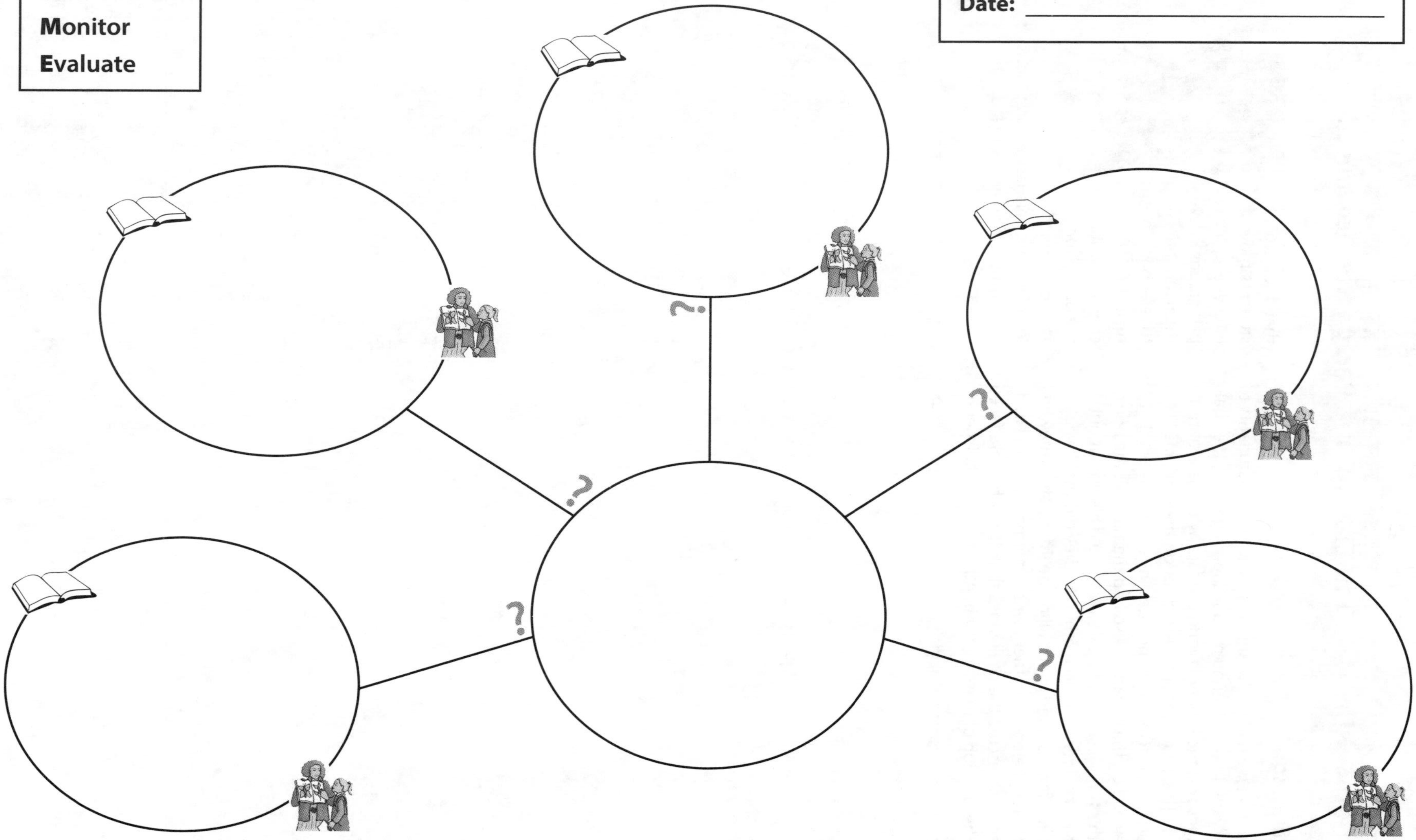

STRATEGY

Extension Wheel

This is a great activity to help students look at the concept of cause and effect, and that is what I did with students today. My students were able to use the visual of the extension wheel to really extend upon their learning. The strategy helped students connect to the content from the very beginning and also helped them in adding to their ideas. Student discussions helped them in extending upon the different parts of the extension wheel. I plan on using this strategy next for sequencing.

—*Megan Valenti, 7th-Grade Teacher*

Where Theory Meets Practice

In schools and classrooms across the nation, we often have discussions that revolve around the question: *How do we help our students expand upon their thought processes and ideas?* We look for ways to help English learners understand how they can convey their thoughts and ideas regarding the text. One way to do this is to connect ideas to what students already know or are familiar with, which in turn will support their overall comprehension and extension of ideas as they focus on a reading task (McIntyre, Kyle, Chen, Kraemer, & Parr, 2008; Turkan, Bicknell, & Croft, 2012).

Also needed are consistent thinking routines tied to strategies that will help students understand how they can expand upon their ideas. According to Salmon (2010), "Thinking routines are a primary strategy for organizing memory; they are crafted to achieve specific goals, such as making connections or deep inquiry" (p. 27). Extension Wheel is a strategy that helps students in making those deeper connections while establishing routines that naturally stretch students' cognition.

We often think about the Extension Wheel strategy as creating a ripple effect to learning as students string together

ideas and document the language and thought processes they are going through as they gather and make sense of information from text. Consider what happens when you throw a stone or pebble into water. The ripple effect in water allows us to see expanded rings, or ripples, in the water. Likewise, in this strategy, once the topic is introduced and students are allowed to dive deep into what they already know—via collaborative conversations, connections to knowledge systems, and embedded teacher and student questioning—they are able to expand upon the topic and see an extended ripple effect of their own ideas.

Teachers implementing this strategy encourage learners to make cultural connections to their own lives and those of their peers, and they focus on the responses they hear as students work with the content. Herrera (2016) states that it is only when we as teachers "actively listen to the hidden messages of student talk" that we can guide learners to interact with the content in ways that stretch them to their zone of proximal development (p. 118). BDI strategies such as Extension Wheel therefore support teachers to prioritize classroom actions that enable them to:

- Access the individual biographies of our students,
- Identify what it is they understand about the lesson, and
- Expand upon their individual learning in meaningful ways.

Extension Wheel offers the teacher a consistent way to help students extend upon their thought processes. The power of this strategy is that it provides students with a framework for the process in the form of a tool. The visual organizer supports CLD students in categorizing information (Zwiers, 2004/2005) and in making meaning as they engage with the text. Drawing on the work of R. T. Vacca and Vacca (2008), Turkan et al. (2012) attest that "active engagement in meaning making with the text is a must for ELLs [English language learners] and all readers" (p. 22).

Extension Wheel also provides students with multiple opportunities to engage in peer sharing as they discuss each of their additions to the wheel. The teacher is able to reinforce these ideas by revoicing what students have shared and validating their personal connections. With each step,

the Extension Wheel strategy provides students with the opportunity to reflect on their own understandings and extend their knowledge of the topic beyond the classroom. As students organize, depict, apply, and evaluate throughout the lesson, they strengthen their cognitive and metacognitive skills.

MATERIALS & RESOURCES

Materials Needed: Extension Wheel Template (one per student) • curricular materials • paper • pencils/pens

Template: Extension Wheel Template (see page 144); also available for free download and printing from tcpress.com/accelerating

Rubric: Student Assessment Rubric (see page 201); also available for free download and printing from tcpress.com/accelerating

Video: A video clip illustrating implementation of this strategy is available for viewing online at coe.k-state.edu/cima/biographycrt

---

ACTIVATION: A Canvas of Opportunity

Directions:

i (individual)

At this stage of the lesson, the extension wheel serves as an advance organizer that supports students in organizing their thoughts from the very onset of the lesson. This strategy provides students with a visual reminder that they will keep expanding upon their thought process as the lesson progresses.

- Place students in small groups of three or four students.
- Give each student a blank Extension Wheel template.
- Share the essential question/content outcomes/objectives of the lesson with students.
- Explain to students how the strategy works and the fact that they will be able to use this tool to expand upon their thought processes and ideas as they proceed through the lesson.
- Have students write the name of the topic/concept that is the focus of the lesson in the center circle of the wheel.
- Ask students to think about the topic/concept and draw an image or write phrases that they associate with it in the center circle.
  - At this stage of the lesson, encourage students to think about their cultural and linguistic connections to the topic/concept. You might say such things as,

"Think of where you may have heard of the topic" or "Have you heard your parents talk about it?" By having students think of situations outside of the school where they may have heard about the

topic, we provide additional pathways for students to connect to the topic.
  - Depending upon your topic and how in-depth you want your students to go, you may have them start this portion of the lesson by writing their initial associations on a separate piece of paper and then, based on the conversations they have with their peers about their original ideas, they can transfer the most pertinent information to the center circle.

Instructional Tip:

- Rotate around the room so you can observe the connections that students are making. Document some of these connections for later use when students get into the text/content of the lesson.

Activating the "*i*"
How does this process activate CLD students' existing knowledge?

- **Sociocultural:** The initial phase of this strategy provides students with a way to actively express themselves through the lens of their own knowledge systems, which can then lead to subsequent engagement and understanding of the text.
- **Linguistic:** Allowing students to first document as many connections and ideas as possible before narrowing their focus is particularly beneficial for English learners. These initial words, images, and ideas provide a

basis for students to voice their opinions and connections throughout the lesson.
- **Academic:** The Extension Wheel strategy leads students to start owning their own learning process from the onset of the lesson.
- **Cognitive:** Ways of knowing in the classroom are clearly tied to our students' culture-bound ways of understanding the world. This phase of the strategy prepares students to explore the content using a less linear path.

 CONNECTION: The Broad & Narrow Strokes of Learning

Directions:

T (Total Group), p (partner), s (small group)

 Bridging to the Content— Drawing the *i* into the Lesson

During this phase of the lesson, the extension wheel becomes a tool for students to expand upon their initial connections. Through the readings and ongoing discussions, the extension wheel supports learners in continually expanding upon their thinking.

- Once the students have finished writing/drawing their ideas, have them discuss their initial thoughts and connections in their small groups.
- Then have students share some of their ideas with the whole class. *Note:* Since students will have already shared in smaller groups, it will be easier for them to share now with the whole class.
- Next, share the academic vocabulary with students.
  - You may want to use a combination of content- and skill-specific vocabulary, since this might help students to create their extensions.
  - Allow students to discuss their understanding of the vocabulary words with a partner.

Instructional Tips:

- Encourage students to provide rationales for their initial ideas so that other group members will understand their perspectives and you will be able to tap into students' knowledge systems.

- You can have students write the vocabulary words on the side of the extension wheel so they have those words to refer to as they discuss ideas with peers and expand upon their extensions.

 Digging into Text

- At this time, explain to students that they will be using the reading or the content of the lesson to expand on the first ring of the wheel.
- You can do this step in multiple ways. The whole purpose is to have students look for ways they can extend upon the topic in the middle of the wheel using text evidence and their own interpretations of the text as they read.
  - You can have students read in their small groups by jigsawing the text. Then group members collaborate to find extensions they can make to the topic in the middle.
  - You also can have students partner-read and work on finding extensions as partners.
  - To support students with this step, make sure to circulate to each group, look at their extensions, and redirect if needed.

(Continued on the next page)

CONNECTION: The Broad & Narrow Strokes of Learning (continued)

- Make sure to stop at several points during the reading to ensure that the students are able to find plenty of extensions to add to the first ring while also understanding the reading/text.
  - With each extension, have students discuss their ideas with each other.
  - Encourage students to use the academic vocabulary during their discussions.
  - Provide opportunities for groups to share ideas with the whole class.
- Have students work together to find further extensions of the ideas now recorded on the first ring of the wheel. This time, the groups will add ideas to the second ring of the wheel, with two new ideas/extensions per one extension from the first ring.
  - You can have students write phrases or words to show their expansions on the rings.
  - Students can also draw visuals to share their extensions on the rings of the wheel.
  - Remind students to consider ways the concepts connect with the world outside the classroom.
- After students finish putting the expanded ideas on the second ring, bring the class together and have groups share their ideas with the whole class or with another small group.
- Because the whole purpose of the activity is for students to expand upon their thought process, you may want the students to add a third ring as well. To do this, have students expand upon only certain ideas from the second ring.
  - To support this additional extension process, visit each group and circle on the students' extension wheels the ideas you now want them to expand upon.
  - Make sure to have students expand upon the things that will help them move toward your overall goal/outcome for the lesson.

Instructional Tips:

- Revoicing plays a crucial role at this time. Periodically, bring the class together to revoice some of the things that students have written/drawn on their wheels. For example, a teacher might say, "I noticed that Yugang's group put _____, _____, and _____ on the first ring. I really like that because it shows how they were personally connecting to the topic . . . or . . . how they found the evidence in the text."
- As one group is sharing, have the other students individually use their extension wheels to add details they are hearing.
- Have groups include on the wheel extensions the page number of the text that supports their connection.

Connecting to the "*i*+1"
How does this process move CLD students from the known to the unknown?

- **Sociocultural:** Through the negotiation of extensions and discussions on how the topic should be expanded, students are able to learn from each other while bringing in their own knowledge systems. This in turn helps in the creation of a true community of learners.
- **Linguistic:** This phase provides students with opportunities to use listening, speaking, reading, and writing to convey their points of view, consider others' perspectives, find text evidence, and document learning.

- **Academic:** The continual expansion of ideas and emphasis on connections beyond the classroom allow the lesson to become a discovery process for each student, as he or she connects to the academic concept at individual, local, and global levels.
- **Cognitive:** Students must reflect upon all the ideas shared by their peers as they make decisions about which ideas to record on the wheel. This process requires students to use higher-order thinking as they filter through the information and determine the most important and relevant details.

AFFIRMATION: A Gallery of Understanding

Directions:

**T (Total Group), p (partner),
s (small group), I (Individual)**

At this point in the lesson, students use the extension wheel to extend further upon their own thoughts. They are ready to assume individual ownership over their learning and take it to writing.

- After groups finish recording ideas on the wheel, ask the students to write a narrative or expository summary of the points identified on the wheel.
  - Students can complete this task individually or in pairs.
  - Depending upon the target skill for the lesson, have students incorporate words that connect to that skill (e.g., cause and effect, sequencing) to create their summaries.
  - Remind students to incorporate the vocabulary words in their writing.
- Allow students to share their writing with peers from another group.
- The completed extension wheels can serve as a scaffold

for students as they complete any curriculum-specific tasks at the end of the lesson. These might include writing a response to the essential question or to an end-of-chapter essay/short-answer prompt.

Instructional Tips:

- You can accommodate student preferences and varying levels of language proficiency by:
  - Allowing students to alternatively create a pictorial summary of the key ideas that also incorporates some of the vocabulary words.
  - Having students work on a cloze passage where they use the ideas from the extension wheel and the vocabulary words to complete the passage.
  - Having students write two or three sentences summarizing the key points learned from the lesson while using vocabulary/concepts from the extension wheel.

Author Talk: Affirmation

The authors of this book have a unique opportunity to regularly observe teachers perform the art of teaching in their classrooms. It has become increasingly clear that what keeps learning going for many students are their personal connections to the content and the teacher's artistry in helping them see how these connections matter for their learning and that of the classroom community. The BDI strategies in this book aim at helping teachers bring the art into the science of their day-to-day instruction. In this respect, the Extension Wheel strategy is no different from the others. It provides a cognitive tool for students that allows the teacher to get an inside look at what matters most to learners as they explore the content. The strategy also provides students the freedom to follow learning paths that are meaningful for them.

In the end, what is exciting about the Extension Wheel

strategy is that it allows students to use academic vocabulary, phrases, and ideas throughout the lesson as they work together to expand upon their thoughts, which are rooted in the academic concepts and students' personal connections to the world. Using the Extension Wheel Template, students are able to document their background knowledge and then add their new understandings as the lesson progresses. CLD students' language and comprehension expand as we build upon the foundational knowledge that they bring to the lesson, as well as their evolving thoughts about the language and content. We have seen teachers use the Extension Wheel strategy for concepts/skills such as cause and effect, main ideas and details, sequencing, characterization, multiplication, and science formulas. The list is endless. Simply keep the biographies of your classroom community in mind and give it a try!

Affirming Student Ownership: "I" Get It!
How does this process celebrate CLD student learning?

- **Sociocultural:** The completed extension wheels provide students with a tangible product to share with peers and reinforce the idea that all students participated in the construction of knowledge.
- **Linguistic:** Because students' expansions are tied to a single topic, their associations help them use language to elaborate on their learning at a much deeper level than might otherwise be possible. Interactions with peers also provide English learners with language support.

- **Academic:** The Extension Wheel strategy supports all students in providing written evidence of their learning. Students can draw upon the many levels of their extension wheels to summarize their ideas about the topic, including applications beyond the classroom.
- **Cognitive:** This phase of the strategy provides students with an additional opportunity to stretch their thinking about the topic as they listen to alternative points of view represented in peers' writing.

One Classroom's Perspective

From the 7th-grade class of Megan Valenti

Activating:

To connect to students' prior knowledge, I used the strategy of Extension Wheel with the bell ringer work that we did today. I started the lesson by having students think of an action they took over the last week as well as the reason for that action. As I did this, I shared some examples provided by students in other classes so they knew what the expectations were. Since today was our cause-and-effect day and we were using the strategy of Extension Wheel for the first time, I wanted them to have some examples in front of them. Their task was to individually come and write on the board what their own cause-and-effect examples were from the week. After they had finished, I brought everyone together and, using their examples, I took what they produced toward cause-and-effect relationships. We discussed how their actions, for instance, were the effect of something they had thought about—their intent (cause).

I gave them some time to talk to each other about some of the ideas they shared and how sometimes a

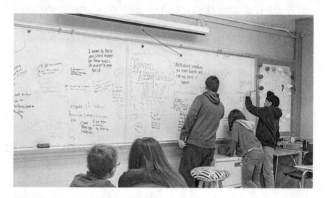

cause can have lots of effects. To help them move into these associations with extension wheel, I used the example of a ripple effect in water by having them think of what happens to water when we throw a stone in it. We used this example to discuss how our cause-and-effect ideas on the extension wheel would be like that. One cause can have multiple effects. Today we would be using an article to add our causes and effects on the extension wheel.

One Classroom's Perspective (continued)

Connecting:

We used the article "Memory Test for Dogs" to have students work on their extension wheels. I took them back to the example of the ripple effect on water and shared how they were to extend upon the wheel using the cause (memory test for dogs) and identify the effects of it through the article. I scaffolded this part quite a bit for students so they could see how the extension wheel would work for them and how they were to add the events within the wheel.

now and then I also shared with the group some of the things I saw students writing on their wheels. We continued expanding our ideas on the

As we got into the article, I had them stop at several points, discuss with their partners, and add their ideas to the wheel. As students added more ideas to the wheel, we stopped and discussed with the whole class. Every

wheel regarding the effects of our topic. Throughout this time, students read and discussed with partners to expand upon their topic.

Affirming:

Now that the students had their completed extension wheels, I had them create sentences using signal words to show cause-and-effect statements. As they did this, I had them use their extension wheels to connect the cause-and-effect statements from their wheels. However, their challenge was to use the signal words that I had provided them as they connected the parts of their sentences. As students completed this task, I had some share their sentences with the rest of the class.

TEMPLATE: Extension Wheel

Name: _____

Date: _____

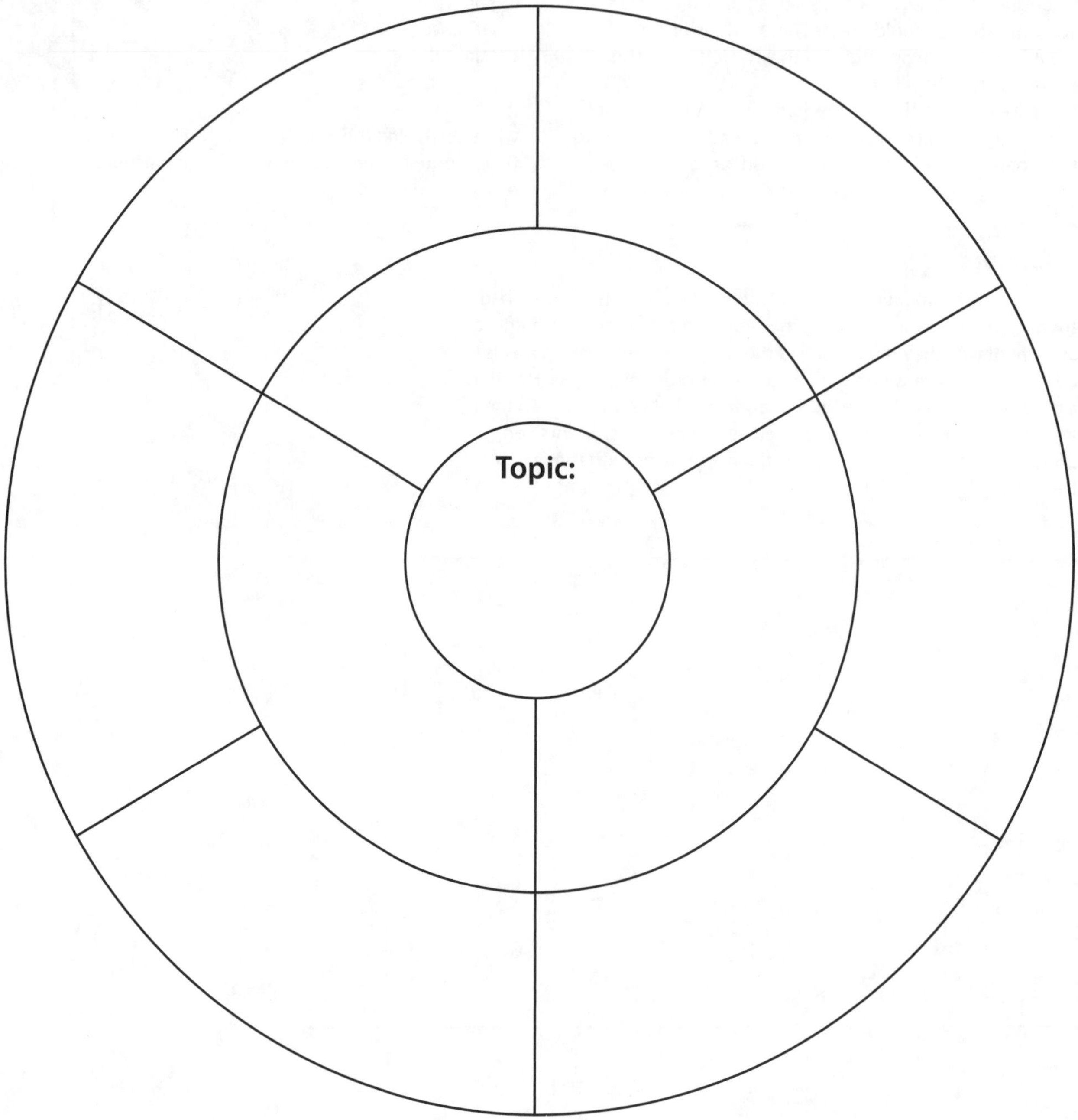

Topic:

STRATEGY

Hearts

The Hearts activity [strategy] allows the teacher to reach the students academically. It helps us understand what they know, what they have gone through, and the academic connections they are making to the text so we can meet their needs. It also provides us with insight into their writing skills.

—*Jennifer Bowden, 6th-Grade Teacher*

Where Theory Meets Practice

The ability to articulate one's views about a topic or issue often requires the learner to make a connection to the topic, understand new information, and come to some conclusion related to what he or she believes about the topic. Students also need to have the language and vocabulary to make this happen. The Hearts strategy provides learners with a concrete tool for thinking about the topic and sharing what they already know. Strategic planning and use of Hearts as a BDI strategy guides the student from the abstract to the specific as the learner moves from generating ideas, to relating them to a subset of ideas, and then to relating them to something specific. As the teacher bridges into the text and teacher-directed lesson, the same sequence takes place using the content of the lesson to move from big ideas, to evidence, and eventually to the main idea or theme. Beyond this, the Hearts strategy immediately creates the conditions for listening, speaking, reading, and writing to occur in a setting that supports instructional conversations (CREDE, 2014; Tharp, Estrada, Dalton, & Yamauchi, 2000).

This strategy supports teachers' ability to listen to and observe what students bring as background knowledge; such efforts can greatly enhance teaching and learning in practice (Marzano, 2004). Herrera (2016) elaborates on this concept of getting to know our students, stating, "To understand what our students know and how they communicate that knowledge, we must first understand the cultural constructs that shaped them *before* they arrived in our classrooms" (p. 78). Yet getting at these cultural constructs can sometimes be difficult, particularly when students are hesitant to share information from their background knowledge. Strategies such as Hearts encourage the learner to share throughout the lesson. These connections to students' lives outside of school increase the relevance of the lesson and promote the teacher's use of questions that require higher-order thinking and are rooted in what the learner produced.

Note: Given the specific nature of this strategy, two sets of directions are included. The first set is recommended for Grades K–2. The second set is recommended for Grades 3–8. Each set has its own template, and the directions have been written to reflect the specific academic, linguistic, and cognitive needs of the targeted grade levels. However, the overall goal of helping students make meaningful connections to the text by linking the "known" to the "unknown" is the same for all grade levels, K–8.

MATERIALS & RESOURCES

Materials Needed: Hearts Template appropriate to grade level of students (nested hearts for Grades K–2 or split heart for Grades 3–6; one per student) • electronic/enlarged copy of template to post at the front of the room (optional) • markers/colored pencils • pencils/pens

    Note: Blank paper can easily be used instead of a template, especially with older students. Students can draw the heart(s) and label them according to strategy directions.

Template: Hearts Template, two versions, one suitable for Grades K–2 and another suitable for Grades 3–8 (see pages 152, 153); also available for free download and printing from tcpress.com/accelerating

---

 ACTIVATION: A Canvas of Opportunity

Directions (Grades K–2):

i (individual)

- Give each student a Grades K–2 Hearts Template.
- Explain to students that they are going to be doing an activity in which they will expand upon a topic through questioning.
- To get students started, tell them they are going to *activate* their thinking. Pose one or two questions such as the following to help them connect the topic to something happening in their community or the world: "Think about _____ [the topic]. What movie or picture do you see in your head?"
- Have students discuss the question with a partner and individually write their responses in the largest heart (labeled **Activate**) to document the ideas they activated.
  - Depending on the age and language proficiency level of your students, this can be done in the form of pictures, words, or abbreviated sentences.
  - Remind students that they can share in whatever language they choose.
  - Allow students to add any ideas learned from peers during this time as well.

- As partners are sharing, circulate from group to group and listen to what is being shared. As students are sharing, write their responses on sticky notes. Put these sticky notes on the Hearts Template at the front of the room.

- Return to the whole group and have students share with the class their individual responses. To support their sharing, revoice specific responses from the partner conversations (see sticky notes).
- Bridge into the text you are going to read and set the stage for what students will be writing or drawing in the second heart.

ACTIVATION: A Canvas of Opportunity (continued)

Directions (Grades 3–8):

i (individual)

- Explain to students that they are going to be doing an activity that will help them explore cultural and vocabulary connections to the text they will be reading.
- Give each student a Grades 3–8 Hearts Template.
- Introduce the topic of the lesson and ask students to think about ways they connect to it by using personal experiences, information from books they have read, or things they have heard on the news or from other people (e.g., their family or friends).
- Place students in groups of three or four and have them discuss the different connections they make to the topic.
- To extend the group discussion, pose the following types of questions to the whole group and have students take turns sharing one idea connected to the topic in their small groups:
  - *Broad question:* When you think of _____ [the topic], what comes to mind as it relates to the past, the world, or _____ [something else]?
  - What impact will this have, or how might/do people feel about it?
  - What personal connections do you have with _____ [the topic]?
- Next, have students individually write ideas from their group discussion in the **Activate** part of their individual hearts. Encourage students to draw pictures or write words that they associate with the topic, making sure to allow students to write in their native language (L1) if they choose to do so.

Activating the "*i*"
How does this process activate CLD students' existing knowledge?

- **Sociocultural:** The collaborative learning component helps CLD students understand how ideas can be elaborated in multiple ways, depending on a person's point of view (culture). By recognizing the validity of each perspective, as well as their own prior knowledge about the topic, students will realize they have words or images that set the stage for making associations and connecting to new learning.
- **Linguistic:** As the teacher actively listens to what students share with their peers, the teacher has an opportunity to gain insight into *how* students know what they know. This gives the teacher links that he or she can use to connect to students' native language and known vocabulary during the working phase of the lesson. Listen to their words and ask yourself: *Where are they coming from in their responses?*
- **Academic:** The initial phase of the Hearts strategy sets the stage for peers at different levels to share the vocabulary and content knowledge they already bring to the lesson.
- **Cognitive:** This strategy helps students organize their thoughts related to the central topic and document them on paper as the lesson unfolds.

CONNECTION: The Broad & Narrow Strokes of Learning

Directions (Grades K–2):

T (Total Group), p (partner), s (small group)

- Next, explain to students that they will use the middle heart (the medium-sized heart) during the lesson to record their learnings and specific connections to the text.
- Explain that you are going to give students a new set of questions that will help them set a purpose for their reading. These questions can be displayed for students on the board or with a projector.
- We recommend that you give your students a combination of literal and inferential questions. Questions for this stage could include:
  - What is happening in the story/chapter related to the topic?
  - What are the characters feeling?
  - What do you think is the main idea of the story/text?
  - How can we apply what we learned from the story in the real world?
- Have students work together in small groups to preview the text and predict answers to one or more of the questions posed.
- Read a portion of the text and have students stop and discuss in their small groups the specifics of the topic as related to the questions posed.
- After students have finished their discussion, have each group agree on one answer for each question that they will individually record in the **Connect** section of their template and share with the whole class. Depending on the biographies of your students, they can use key words, phrases, sentences, or pictures to document their connections.

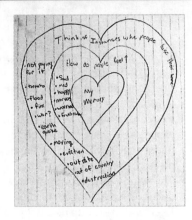

- Call on each group to share their answer for each question with the whole class. As students share answers, record them on sticky notes and add them to the whole-class Hearts Template at the front of the room. (If projecting the template, use a marker or type to add the connections to the medium-sized heart.)
- Have students continue this process of reading, discussing, and documenting their learnings until the text has been completed.
- Make sure to incorporate time for students to reflect on similarities and differences between their original associations to the topic (documented on the **Activate** heart) and their new learning.

CONNECTION: The Broad & Narrow Strokes of Learning (*continued*)

Directions (Grades 3–8):

T (Total Group), p (partner), s (small group)

- Before you have students read the text, give them a new set of questions that will help them set a purpose for their reading. We recommend that you give your students a combination of direct and inferential questions. Keep the questions closely aligned with the first set of questions you asked during the opening of the lesson. Sample questions for this Connection phase, when students work with and practice vocabulary and learn new information, include
  - *Broad question:* When you think of _____ [the topic], what comes to mind as it relates to the past, the world, or _____ [something else]?
  - What impact will this have, or how might/do people feel about it?
  - What personal connections do you have with _____ [the topic]?
  - As you read/listen to the teacher or talk with your peers about what is happening in the story/text, what can you cite that would provide evidence of _____ [something]?
  - What makes you think that? Be specific, and choose words from the text to help support your answer.
  - What are the characters feeling?
  - What are some of the key issues the author is focusing on?

  - What are some of the main ideas or "lessons" we can take away from the story?
  - How can we apply in the real world some of the learnings we gained from the text?

- After students have read a portion of the text or after you have led part of the discussion, have students stop and discuss in their small groups the specifics about the topic related to the questions posed.
- As groups come to consensus on their answers, have them write their ideas in the **Connect** portion of their individual hearts.
- Have small groups share ideas with the whole class. Revoice student connections as part of your instructional conversation on the topic.
- As chunking of the complex text occurs, ask students to individually refer to their opening statements in the **Activate** portion of their template to find similarities and differences between their predictions/thoughts and those of the author/text.
- Have students continue this process of reading, discussing, and documenting their learnings until the text has been completed.

Connecting to the "*i*+1"

How does this process move CLD students from the known to the unknown?

- **Sociocultural:** Through instructional conversations, students and the teacher are provided the opportunity to listen to different perspectives. This is an essential component to creating an environment of mutual respect and understanding.
- **Linguistic:** Language is taken to *i*+1 when the conditions are set and opportunities given for use of both social and academic language. During the Connection phase, the learner listens to and has opportunities to articulate what is important. Students rehearse academic vocabulary in authentic ways, which helps to establish it for use in the future.

- **Academic:** As the teacher provides new information and facilitates talk among the students, he or she is also formatively assessing learning. Elaboration or clarification, on the part of both students and the teacher, is essential to students making strong connections to new learning. This phase also provides an opportunity for the teacher to connect the known (knowledge documented at the opening of the lesson) to the unknown (new learning).
- **Cognitive:** The Hearts Template serves as a "tool in the hand." For the student, it provides a roadmap of what is important. For the teacher, it documents what and how students have processed the content and vocabulary.

AFFIRMATION: A Gallery of Understanding

Directions (Grades K–2):

T (Total Group), p (partner), s (small group), I (Individual)

- Once students have completed the outer (**Activate**) and middle (**Connect**) rings of their heart, have them turn the page over.
- On the reverse side of their Hearts Template, have students individually summarize their key learnings by focusing on at least one of the following types of connections:
  - Text to self
  - Text to text
  - Text to world

  Note: Students at the preproduction or speech emergent stages of second language acquisition should be given the option of writing this passage in their native language or with the support of a more proficient peer or paraprofessional.
- Encourage students to provide an illustration to accompany their writing.
- After students have completed their writing, have them read their work to a partner.

- Circulate around the classroom and listen to students' sharing of their summaries so you can revoice critical connections with the entire class.
- Depending on the text/topic, you can also have students:
  - Draw a visual representation of the text and write a short description.
  - Use the information on their Hearts Template to do a compare-and-contrast diagram/chart.
  - Write questions about the story based on the information from their Hearts Template and use it to quiz their peers.

Directions (Grades 3–8):

T (Total Group), p (partner), s (small group), I (Individual)

- Once students have individually recorded their ideas in the **Activate** and **Connect** parts of their Hearts Template, have them turn it over.
- Have students use the page to individually summarize their learnings. Depending on the topic and essential question/lesson objectives, students might:
  - Work in small groups to role-play an exchange between characters in the story. Their writing should

explain the causes for, as well as the effects of, the exchange.
  - Individually write a persuasive paragraph explaining why a certain idea related to the topic is good or bad for the world.
  - Use the ideas on their Hearts Template to answer end-of-chapter questions individually.
  - Work with a partner to create a visual and written explanation that compares and contrasts their initial ideas with what was learned from the author.
- Encourage learners to use the completed Hearts Template as a tool for articulating and defending their ideas/positions and using key vocabulary as they write.

Affirming Student Ownership: "I" Get It!
How does this process celebrate CLD student learning?

- **Sociocultural:** Students are able to use their ideas from the Hearts Template to help them summarize their learning in their own words and from their own perspectives.
- **Linguistic:** The completed Hearts Template provides evidence of the vocabulary that has been gained throughout the lesson. It serves as a tool for scaffolding students' writing or oral presentation of learning.

- **Academic:** The Hearts Template provides both the teacher and the learner with notes on what has been discussed and read throughout the lesson. In this way, learners have visual links to important information from the text/lesson as they write, discuss, and complete end-of-lesson activities.
- **Cognitive:** Students' metacognition is promoted as they use their completed Hearts Template to reflect on the progression of their learning throughout the lesson.

One Classroom's Perspective
From the elementary school class of Deborah Hesse

Activating:

When planning this lesson I wanted to make sure my students understood different types of storms. The Hearts activity [strategy] was a great activity for getting to the heart of the prism model [learners' biographies]. Students had the opportunity to think about times they were frightened because of storms, to share experiences with each other, and to make connections with the main character in the story. Students interacted with and learned from each other. No matter what stage of language acquisition they were in, they were able to share and express their feelings and experiences and document them on their individual hearts.

Connecting:

The second part of Hearts took students from the known to the unknown using all three memory functions (sensory, working, permanent) and helped my students make associations to new vocabulary. The use of individual, partner, team, and whole-group instruction further enhanced my students' learning. As we proceeded with the reading of the book, students used their background knowledge as a resource to learn new vocabulary. By having them document their learning on their hearts, I was really able to take the lesson to an *i*+1 level using the information my students had already put on their hearts. One of the best things we discovered as a class was that there were many cognates (*tornado, hurricane, torrential, typhoon, precipitation, catastrophe, temperature, map*) that could be incorporated into the lesson.

Affirming:

At the end of the story, I had students compare/contrast their memories with the main character's experience. I encouraged my students to use information from their heart to support them with their writing. In particular, I emphasized using cognates to enhance their understanding. Not only did we model/share personal experiences, we also used the first page of our story booklet to write/draw what students thought the title of the book, *Riding Out the Storm,* meant. They also used a map to share storm experiences by locating geographical areas for certain types of storms based on where students were from. After the students' stories were complete, we shared them as a whole class.

TEMPLATE: Hearts (Grades K–2)

Name: _____

Date: _____

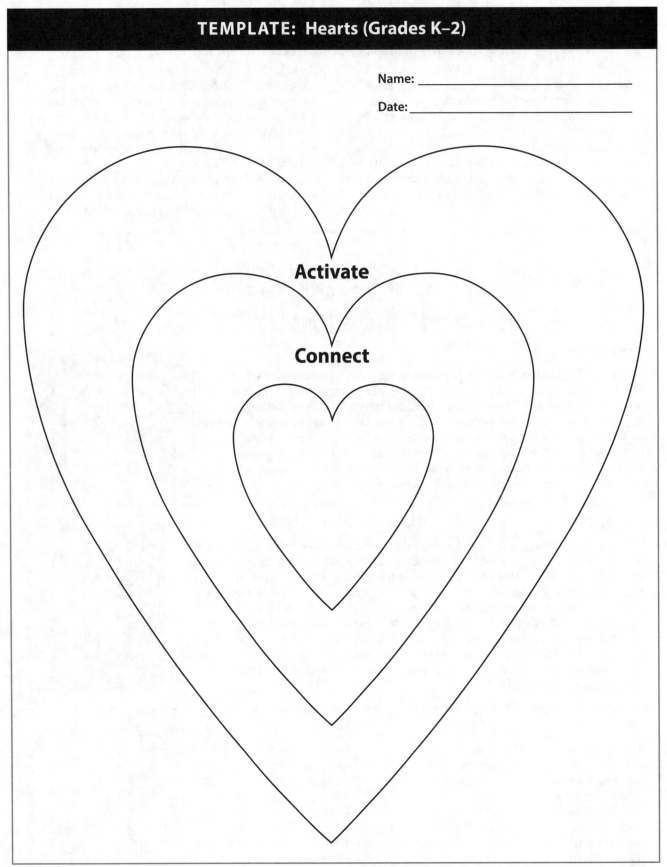

Activate

Connect

TEMPLATE: Hearts (Grades 3–8)

Name: _____

Topic: _____

Date: _____

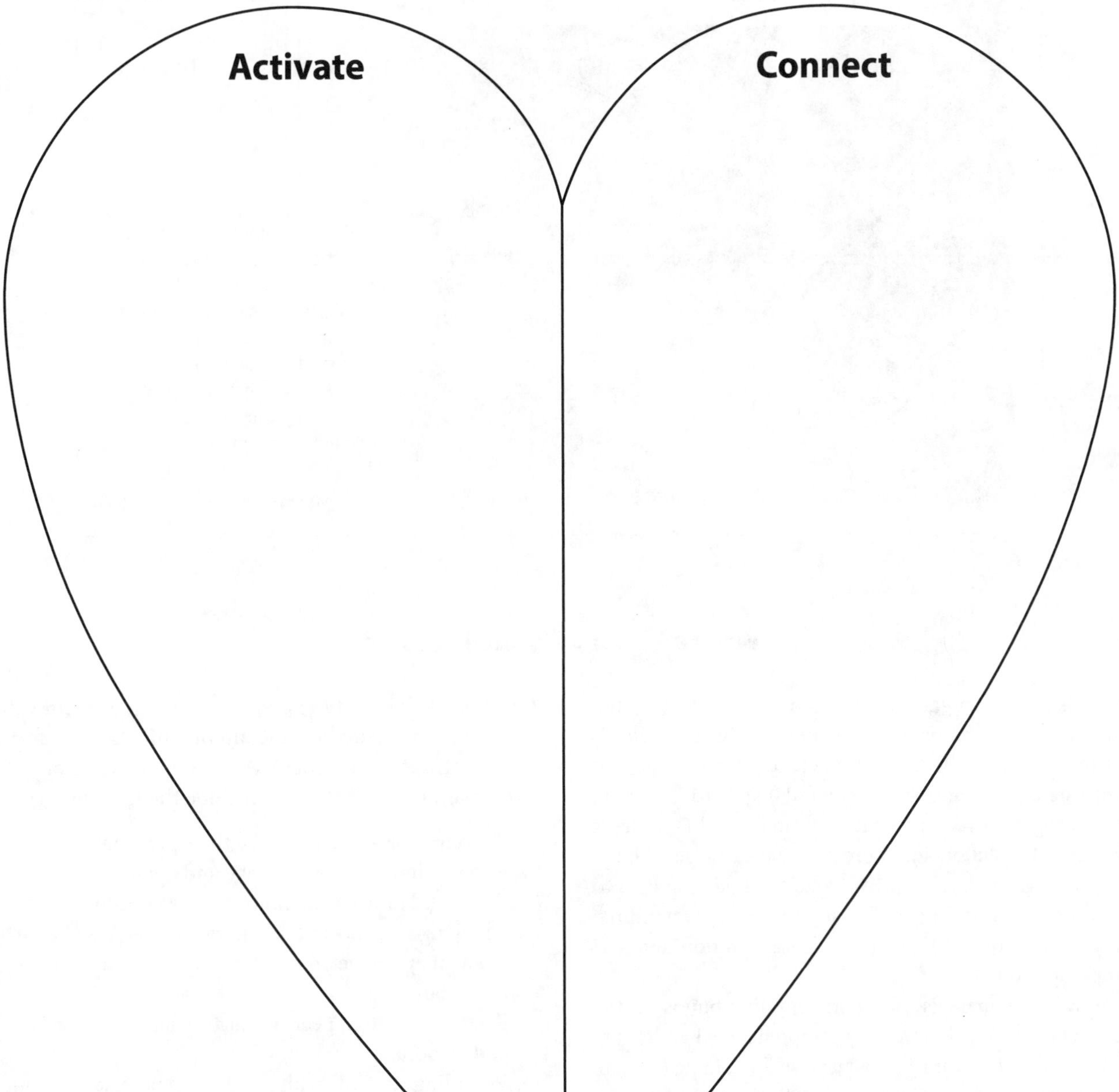

Activate

Connect

STRATEGY

Active Bookmark

This strategy allows students to check their progress and make sure they comprehend the material. It also allows them to take ownership of their learning. As the students write questions, note taking becomes part of this process, which leads toward prediction and summarization skills.

—*Sabina Hacker, ESL Coordinator*

Where Theory Meets Practice

Students often struggle to focus on key concepts when reading. One of the primary reasons for this difficulty is that they often get "lost" in all the text. When the goal of comprehension is not being achieved, explicit instruction on metacognitive reading strategies can help CLD students take corrective action and more effectively engage with the text (Herrera et al., 2014). By explicitly modeling how to monitor their thinking and assess their understanding, teachers promote CLD students' metacognition and text comprehension.

Active Bookmark is a BDI strategy that builds on the idea that readers will more fully comprehend what they are reading if they first construct a purpose for reading (Tovani, 2000). After having students work with the target vocabulary and make predictions about the overall topic/text, active bookmarks serve as a scaffold and guide students in posing questions about the information as they read. The strategy also serves to get students talking about what they understand as they read. Using the text as the foundation for their questions and talk helps students extract new con-

tent knowledge, and the bookmark provides them with a concrete tool for processing and organizing the information (J. Hill & Flynn, 2006). Additional benefits of Active Bookmark for CLD students include the following:

- Encouraging students to use their personal experiences to link to new language and content.
- Focusing students' attention on key concepts/ideas.
- Allowing students to take charge of their own learning as they decide on questions to write on their bookmark.
- Partnering with a peer to clarify, share information, and elaborate.
- Providing students with a tool they can use to monitor their comprehension and scaffold their peer discussions.

The Active Bookmark strategy keeps CLD students engaged in all phases of the reading process: before, during, and after. Research has found that this type of active engagement is one of the essential characteristics of a good reader (Gregory & Burkman, 2012; Smartt & Glaser, 2010). According to Harris, Graham, Mason, and Friedlander (2008), before, during, and after reading strategies can be translated as **TWA**, or:

- **THINK** before reading
- Think **WHILE** reading
- Think **AFTER** reading

Active Bookmark ensures that all students are provided the support they need to engage in these reading processes.

MATERIALS & RESOURCES

Materials Needed: Active Bookmark Template (one per student) • curricular materials/texts • pencils/pens

Template: Active Bookmark Template (see pages 161–162); also available for free download and printing from tcpress.com/accelerating

Checklist: Student Academic Behavior Checklist (see page 202); also available for free download and printing from tcpress.com/accelerating

---

ACTIVATION: A Canvas of Opportunity

Directions:

i (individual)

- Introduce the Active Bookmark strategy by telling students that they are going to be monitoring their own learning as they read the text. They will do this by posing and answering questions as they interact with the text and their peers.
- Place students in small groups of four students based on their biographies. In the Activation phase, students benefit from starting with a student who can support their language (i+1). Have students complete the name, title, and date portion of the bookmark.
- Ask students to turn their active bookmark to the side that has **Vocabulary** written at the top. Have students write the five vocabulary terms that you have selected because of their importance for students' comprehension of the text. *Note:* Longer readings can have more than one bookmark.
- Have students look at the words and draw or write words they associate with the target vocabulary in the space provided. Observe students as they work to note connections and periodically revoice ideas to support students' brainstorming.

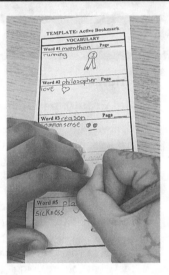

- Share the title and the cover page of the story (or the chapter/section title of the text) with students. Ask them to look at the vocabulary words and share with a partner or predict what the story might be about. Students can also discuss what they already know about the topic and the vocabulary words.
- Have students in their small groups talk about their predictions related to the story/topic. As students predict what the story is about, ask them to reflect on their personal/background experiences to see if they can find a connection to the text.
- Circulate around the room to listen to students' predictions and connections.

Activating the "*i*"
How does this process activate CLD students' existing knowledge?

- **Sociocultural:** As students develop and share their predictions, they focus on their own background experiences that connect with the vocabulary and the text.
- **Linguistic:** The Active Bookmark strategy provides learners with a language scaffold at the onset of the lesson. The bookmark tool supports students during communicative interactions with peers in this phase and throughout the remainder of the lesson.
- **Academic:** Allowing students to first make predictions about the text supports them to activate their back-ground knowledge on the topic so they are primed to make connections between the new information and what they already know.
- **Cognitive:** As students discuss their predictions with group members, they are challenged to support their ways of thinking. The ideas they documented on the active bookmark about the vocabulary words provide them with possible links they can use to justify their predictions.

 CONNECTION: The Broad & Narrow Strokes of Learning

Directions:

T (Total Group), p (partner), s (small group)

- Next, have students turn their bookmark to the side with questions. Explain that they will be using questions to guide their reading throughout the lesson.
- To help students understand how to use the active bookmark, read a short piece of the text and model how we can pose questions during reading to make predictions and to further our understanding of the text.
  - Talk about your thinking process so students can "see" what you are doing.
  - You might say something like the following: "I like how the text _____. But it makes me wonder _____. My question is: _____?
- To show students how to document their questions, write your sample question on an active bookmark that is displayed electronically or drawn on the board as an enlarged model.
  - Be sure to explain that students should note the number of the page from the text that corresponds to the question that they write.
  - You can also have predetermined questions for the students to focus on as they partner or individually read the text.
- Also, explain to students that there are different ways we can find answers to the questions we pose. *Sometimes the answer is right there in the text, sometimes we*

have to read a little bit more to find the answer to our question, or sometimes we have to use what we know and our imagination to come up with an answer.

- Have students individually or with a partner work on their active bookmarks as they read a short section of the text/story.
- Encourage students to stop frequently (e.g., after every paragraph) to see if they have a question they could pose and write down. If questions are predetermined, have students write down the page where the answer was found and compare their answer with that of a friend.
- Instruct students to write the answers to their questions if they come across them in the text. They can write the answers on their bookmark if there is room, or they can write them on a blank piece of paper or in a journal.

CONNECTION: The Broad & Narrow Strokes of Learning (*continued*)

- Facilitate the process by having students stop periodically (at predetermined points or based on what students are writing) to discuss with a partner what they have understood from the text.
  - Encourage students to use the prompt located below the questions on their bookmark to support their sharing (*What I understand from the reading so far is . . .*).
  - After students have summarized what they have understood thus far, have them share the question(s) they have written. Students also can share whether they have found or figured out the answers.
  - Circulate around the room to listen to students' conversations.
- Bring the class back together to discuss as a whole group what is being learned.
  - Revoice key ideas that were shared by partners.

- Highlight various types of questions, including those that likely will be answered by the text and those that might require personal thinking.
  - Reinforce the skill(s) that are part of the lesson.
- Have students work with a partner to revisit the vocabulary words.
  - Ask them to write the page number on which each word was used/defined.
  - Have them discuss their new understandings of the words.
  - Encourage them to compare their new ideas about the words with their initial recorded thoughts.
- The active bookmark can be used in the Connection phase in multiple ways. Ultimately, it serves to focus learners, provide them with opportunities to talk about what they understand from the text, compare ideas with peers, and achieve higher levels of comprehension.

Author Talk: Connection

Teachers in the field have used the Active Bookmark strategy to extend students' learning and language development while they engage in independent reading. However, we have also seen teachers pair students based on their biography-driven needs so that they can collaboratively pose and answer the questions on their bookmarks. For students in the initial stages of English language development, this approach is particularly effective because they can work with a more proficient peer to support their reading of the text.

To answer the self-generated questions, students often need to use higher-order thinking skills. Many times the answer is not explicitly stated in the text. As observers, we have had the pleasure of watching students actively engage in this process, seeing firsthand how this strategy builds their cognitive skills. Perhaps the power of this strategy is best illustrated by the experience of an ESL teacher, who

shared this story after implementing the strategy with her 6th-grade students:

> As I was walking around, I noticed students going slower instead of zooming through the text. I also noticed the students feeling at ease to share with their group and listening to their peers. I thought we had a variety of higher-level questions, and many of the questions asked were not in the text. The students realized they would need to look for outside resources to find the answer.

In this example, Active Bookmark readily engaged students in the learning process, and they took ownership of their learning. For such reasons, we feel this is one of the best strategies for helping CLD students become more independent readers. While the strategy still provides them with the scaffolding they need, it also requires them to be active thinkers.

Connecting to the "*i*+1"
How does this process move CLD students from the known to the unknown?

- **Sociocultural:** Students are encouraged to draw upon their background knowledge to infer answers to their text-related questions.
- **Linguistic:** Documenting their questions (and related answers) in writing provides students with an authentic reason to practice writing in English.

- **Academic:** The Connection phase supports students' comprehension of the vocabulary, the text, and the larger topic.
- **Cognitive:** The Active Bookmark strategy helps students monitor their own learning. In addition, it supports greater investment in the learning process, as they select what they want to focus on when reading.

AFFIRMATION: A Gallery of Understanding

Directions:

**T (Total Group), p (partner),
s (small group), I (Individual)**

- Have each student within the small group switch partners. Have students take turns asking their questions and sharing what they have learned with their new partner. When partners answer the questions, the students who asked the questions get to confirm/disconfirm the answer and share their response.
  - Encourage partners to think especially hard about questions that require the reader to make an inference. If their answers to such questions differed, they can discuss the thought process they used to arrive at their answer. If differences still remain, encourage students to share their perspectives with you. Capitalizing on these moments can yield insights that can be used to further the learning of the entire class.
- Bring the class back together as a whole group and have volunteers share their questions and the process they went through to find the answers (i.e., did they

find the answer in text, did they have to infer the answer, or would they have to seek out additional resources to find the answer?).
- Have students use their completed bookmarks as a scaffold to write a summary of the text/story. They can also use the bookmark to respond to the essential question or complete end-of-lesson curricular tasks. Remind students to use the vocabulary words as they articulate their thoughts in writing.

Affirming Student Ownership: *"I"* Get It!
How does this process celebrate CLD student learning?

- **Sociocultural:** Students are able to hear peers' content-based connections/questions as well as to have their own voices heard. Students' culture-bound ways of understanding and interpreting will influence their individual perspectives.
- **Linguistic:** The Active Bookmark strategy prompts students to use academic language to articulate the answers to their questions orally and then express their learning through writing.

- **Academic:** Students have an opportunity to hear, discuss, and evaluate alternative perspectives on the answers to their questions, which helps to solidify their overall understanding of the text.
- **Cognitive:** Students' completed active bookmarks provide them with a tool they can refer back to as they assess their understanding of the text and synthesize their own learning.

SPOTLIGHT: Early Literacy Connection

The Active Bookmark strategy is a great way to model the thought process a reader engages in when reading. For younger students, this modeling is particularly important, as they may not know how to ask questions when reading. Boyd-Batstone (2006) notes that shared experiences like this help students understand the way readers perceive and interpret the meaning of a story.

To engage younger CLD learners in these questioning processes, teachers can implement the following activity.

Our Questions

Post a large piece of chart paper at the front of the class to document students' questions. Begin by reading a story aloud to students. Stop at key points and ask a question about what you are reading. Record these questions on the chart paper, along with the related page numbers from the text. This allows the class to easily refer back to the text.

After modeling this process several times for your students, ask them to pose questions they have. As students share their questions, document them on the chart paper. Continue reading the story. As you encounter answers to the questions you and your students have posed, go back to the chart paper and document the answers.

It's the *"i"* Thing

With the strategy of Active Bookmark, we can focus on multiple skills needed for comprehension, a paramount goal of core instruction. Students start with exploring their background knowledge related to the vocabulary and make predictions about the text. Then they proceed with the many steps of active monitoring as they use the active bookmark to track their thinking. Learners chunk information as they move through the text and interact with peers to confirm and advance their understanding. The strategy provides innumerable avenues for teachers to differentiate instruction for students. Learners can generate questions at their own cognitive, academic, and linguistic levels. Alternatively, the strategy provides the teacher with the flexibility to provide predetermined questions for students to use to guide their reading. This strategy supports all students in being active readers and is ideal for text of all kinds.

One Classroom's Perspective

From the 7th-grade class of Kendra Metz

Activating:

We have been studying Ancient Greece. The next main topic was the *Golden Age of Athens.* I chose five vocabulary terms to focus on: *marathon, reason, philosopher, Delian League,* and *plague.* First I had the students add these words to their bookmarks. Then they added words and pictures for each one. I explained to the students that they should add any words they could think of or pictures they associated the word with. After students completed this individually, I gave them 2 minutes to compare notes and talk to each other before I shared the topic of the day with them. With this step, we recapped what *Golden Age* meant.

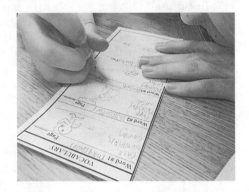

Connecting:

Now that we had some expectation of where we might be headed, I asked students to share a text-book with their neighbor. I explained to them that they would read a page and then add a big question (something we could discuss) to their book-marks. I explained to them that a big question isn't one with a simple answer like a quiz question. I provided some sample question starters based on the book, such as "What led to . . . ?" "What happened when . . . ?" so students understood the expectations. Then, to model what we would do, I read aloud the first page and came up with a question similar to what I was looking for. I instructed students to read one page, turn and summarize/recap, and then write a question (read, recap, write). Students took off after that and wrote down several questions as they moved ahead.

I could tell that some students were going faster than others, so I asked those who were working more quickly to turn and quiz each other over the questions they had written and to make sure the partner could answer thor-oughly. I explained that it would be ideal if they could use one or more of our vocabulary words.

Once all the partners had completed the reading, we put up a large piece of chart paper and collected the big ideas of our reading selection. Once the kids (or I) felt the big things were listed, I asked where each of the vocabulary terms fit. Could we make sure each of them fit in our big ideas?

Affirming:

As we completed our bookmarks, students turned to their partners to restate the big ideas, using the vocabulary terms, with the listener provid-ing the feedback on usage or adding information. Lastly, these big ideas statements were left up for students to refer to as they wrote five sen-tences, using one of the vocabulary words in each.

TEMPLATE: Active Bookmark (front)

Name:

Title:

Date:

Guiding Question #1   Page ____

Guiding Question #2   Page ____

Guiding Question #3   Page ____

Think. Discuss.

What I understand from the reading so far is . . .

Name:

Title:

Date:

Guiding Question #1   Page ____

Guiding Question #2   Page ____

Guiding Question #3   Page ____

Think. Discuss.

What I understand from the reading so far is . . .

Name:

Title:

Date:

Guiding Question #1   Page ____

Guiding Question #2   Page ____

Guiding Question #3   Page ____

Think. Discuss.

What I understand from the reading so far is . . .

TEMPLATE: Active Bookmark (*back*)

VOCABULARY

Word #1   Page ____

Word #2   Page ____

Word #3   Page ____

Word #4   Page ____

Word #5   Page ____

VOCABULARY

Word #1   Page ____

Word #2   Page ____

Word #3   Page ____

Word #4   Page ____

Word #4   Page ____

VOCABULARY

Word #1   Page ____

Word #2   Page ____

Word #3   Page ____

Word #4   Page ____

Word #5   Page ____

STRATEGY

Mini Novela

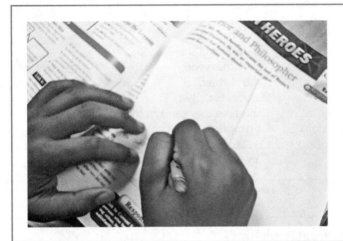

Mini Novela really gave my students an alternate way of considering the ways to summarize learning. We started the activity by getting involved in a task that took shape with students' high interests. Students were able to use their understanding of the vocabulary words to create their personal summaries in the form of a mini novela. This strategy truly spoke to my students, and the best part was they were able to work in small groups and capitalize on each other's language skills.

—*Jessica Larsen, 6th-Grade Teacher*

Where Theory Meets Practice

Effective teachers seek to understand and build upon students' strengths and interests. Students from CLD families possess a wealth of cultural knowledge and experiences that can be used to enhance their literacy development (Moll, 2001). The Mini Novela strategy taps into the cultural phenomenon of telenovelas (short-lived soap operas) that are shown in countries all over the world. These telenovelas are well known for their dramatic short stories of the characters' lives. Most run for only one season. Tapping into the storytelling aspect of telenovelas, Mini Novela combines cultural knowledge, drawing, and writing to help students understand key vocabulary and concepts within the texts they read.

When CLD students are able to use their cultural experiences, it gives them a sense of belonging and can increase their ability to learn the English language (Wong Fillmore, 2000). Thus, Mini Novela has been purposefully designed to allow students to share their cultural connections to key vocabulary terms at the beginning of the lesson. According to Herrera (2016), when educators begin the lesson by capitalizing on students' cultural connections, they greatly increase the likelihood of the students' active engagement throughout the lesson.

During the lesson, the Mini Novela strategy engages students in drawing to support their writing development. Routman (2005) found that allowing students to draw first stimulated their story writing. Cognitively, drawing becomes a rehearsal for their understandings, ideas, thoughts and words (Wessels & Herrera, 2014). In this strategy, drawing serves as a scaffold that encourages CLD students to become more independent writers. After students have drawn a visual representation of a portion of the text in their mini novela, they then write a sentence to explain their illustration. Students use their drawings to generate ideas about what to write and to further elaborate on their thinking. For those with limited English-speaking ability, the pictures they have drawn help them to recall and use a wider range of academic vocabulary words than they might otherwise incorporate. Because this strategy provides students with multiple opportunities to revisit the text and summarize it in their own words, it is ideal for supporting their cognitive and metacognitive skills as well as their linguistic understandings (Chamot & O'Malley, 1994).

MATERIALS & RESOURCES

Materials Needed: Blank mini novela booklet (one per student) • blank sheets of paper • curricular materials • scissors • stapler • pencils/pens

Instructions: Creating Your Mini Novela (see page 168)

ACTIVATION: A Canvas of Opportunity

Directions:

i (individual)

- Following the instructions at the end of this strategy description (page 168), either make mini novela booklets for the class ahead of time or provide students with the materials and guide them through the process of constructing their own mini books.
- Post six to eight vocabulary words specific to the topic on the board and give each student a blank piece of paper.
- Have students individually create their first impressions of the words by either illustrating what the word means or writing the meaning of the word.

- After the students have finished documenting their initial connections to the words, have them turn to a partner and share their ideas with the partner. Tell students that at this time they can add their partner's words to their own words on the paper.
- As students discuss the words with each other, circulate around the room to listen to their ideas.

Activating the "*i*"
How does this process activate CLD students' existing knowledge?

- **Sociocultural:** The collaborative nature of the activity allows students to hear alternative perspectives and helps them create relationships with peers that can support their learning outcomes.
- **Linguistic:** The low-risk learning environment fostered by this strategy allows students to document their first impressions of the vocabulary words in a way that is meaningful to them. This, in turn, supports students' sharing of their perspectives with peers.

- **Academic:** This phase allows students to make and record their existing academic knowledge of the vocabulary words before being influenced by the perspectives of a peer.
- **Cognitive:** Students strengthen their visualization skills as they form and record mental pictures related to the vocabulary words.

CONNECTION: The Broad & Narrow Strokes of Learning

Directions:

T (Total Group), p (partner), s (small group)

- Share with the class that during the lesson they will be working to summarize their learning in the form of a mini novela. Explain to students that the Mini Novela strategy will involve their drawing visuals and using the language that is most meaningful to them.
- If you have access to the necessary technology, you can share a few short clips of a telenovela with students.
- Once you have explained the gist of the task, share with students the topic of the lesson or the book that will be

read. If using a book, start by showing the cover of the book, and ask students to predict what the book will be about.

CONNECTION: The Broad & Narrow Strokes of Learning (*continued*)

- Allow students 1 minute to individually predict what the book or lesson might be about.
- Have students share their thoughts with a partner.
- Place students in small groups of three or four students and give each student a blank mini book (unless they created their own at the beginning of the strategy).
- Read the selected text (or cover the content of the lesson), stopping periodically to have students discuss the content with their small group.
- After students have finished discussing their ideas about a given text selection/concept, have them use one page of their blank mini book to draw a description of their individual summary, using mini novela format. In order to do this:
  - Have them reflect back on the telenovela clips they watched and think of the ways the language was being used.
  - Explain that the purpose of the mini novela is to make their summaries interesting and appear like a story.
- Next encourage students to write a narrative to accompany their illustrations. Encourage them to incorporate the target vocabulary words.
- Continue this process until you have finished the entire book or lesson.

Connecting to the "*i*+1"
How does this process move CLD students from the known to the unknown?

- **Sociocultural:** This phase encourages students to connect to their background knowledge as they make predictions about the text/topic.
- **Linguistic:** Discussing their personal learning and understandings with peers supports CLD students' ability to extend upon their vocabulary and written language skills in their summaries.

- **Academic:** As students work on the summaries, they have the opportunity to monitor their comprehension of the lesson's concepts and vocabulary.
- **Cognitive:** When students create their own summaries at the end of every passage/concept discussion, they are supported in comprehending manageable chunks of the text/segments of the lesson.

AFFIRMATION: A Gallery of Understanding

Directions:

**T (Total Group), p (partner),
s (small group), I (Individual)**

- Have students put the finishing touches on their mini novelas.
- Then have students take turns sharing their mini novelas with each other in their small groups.
- As students are sharing their ideas, have them add to their mini novelas if they come across anything interesting that can expand upon their summaries.
- Once the students have finished sharing their summaries, have them return to the initial impressions of the vocabulary words that they recorded during the Activation phase. Ask students to confirm/disconfirm their original thoughts by underlining ideas related to the lesson. Have them add new learning as needed to clarify the meaning of the words.

- *Extension activity:* If the strategy was used with a picture book, show students the book's illustrations and have them compare those illustrations with their own.

Author Talk: Affirmation

Mini Novela is a great strategy to share with CLD families as a home–school connection. Many countries around the world have types of television programs much like the tele-novelas that are so popular in Spanish-speaking countries. The Mini Novela strategy encourages students and their families to use their imagination, create visual images, and actively participate in the act of storytelling. Storytelling is a tool for socialization through which ideas, perspectives, and cultural customs are passed down to future generations. Stories shared within a family setting are a treasure trove of cultural information and insight into students' lives.

Teachers can encourage families to make their own mini novelas and then have the students bring these stories back to the classroom to share with their classmates. Parents should be encouraged to create the stories in their native language. They can also be invited to read the stories aloud to the class. The drawings start to tell the story regardless of the language of the text. Students can then translate and explain the story to the class in English.

Affirming Student Ownership: "I" Get It!
How does this process celebrate CLD student learning?

- **Sociocultural:** A continual sharing of ideas helps students appreciate the knowledge and ideas of their peers and become more confident in themselves as learners.
- **Linguistic:** As students share their mini novelas, they gain experience in orally articulating their written work.

- **Academic:** The completed mini novela serves as a showcase of each student's understanding of the language and concepts of the lesson.
- **Cognitive:** As students review their initial impressions related to the vocabulary words, they are able to evaluate the accuracy/relevance of their prior knowledge.

SPOTLIGHT: Early Literacy Connection

Some CLD students may be able to draw detailed pictures; however, they may not have the ability to communicate the details verbally or in writing because they lack sufficient skills in the English language. The Mini Novela strategy allows students to rely on visuals to help them relay their understanding of the concept. Young learners may not be developmentally ready to produce writing to accompany their visuals. Some of the ways teachers have made connections between this strategy and early literacy include the following activities.

About Me

At the beginning of the school year, teachers always ask their students to share a little something about themselves. Mini Novela can help students share about themselves in a very nonthreatening yet meaningful way. Give each student in the class a blank mini book or four or five pieces of paper stapled together. As you hand out the mini books, ask students to create a story about themselves. They can simply draw pictures or they can draw and write on the paper. After the students have finished creating and sharing their mini novelas at school, they can be allowed to take them home to share with their parents.

Show Me the Pictures

As you read a book to students, have them use blank mini books to create their own mini novela summaries using only pictures. After students have finished, have them share their mini novela with a partner.

One Classroom's Perspective

From the 6th-grade class of Jessica Larsen

Activating:

Today was the first day we were working with the topic of the life of Marcus Aurelius in our social studies unit. In my small group of students that I was working with as a Tier 2 group, I have students who are from many different countries. My students are at multiple language levels. I knew that I wanted an activity that would provide students with an opportunity to express themselves in a meaningful way and that would include students' own words. So I started the lesson by pulling six words from the chapter and sharing them with students on sticky notes. I put the sticky notes with one word each on a big poster paper. As I posted the words, I had my students create their impressions by talking to each other about the word. This activity really helped my students activate their understanding, since I have students at multiple levels of language proficiency in my class.

Connecting:

Once we were done sharing the words, I explained to my students that they were going to be creating mini novelas using their booklets. First I shared with them a short clip of how a novela looks. Since I have a lot of students from Latin American countries, my students were able to connect to them right away. Next I shared with them that they were going to create their own summaries in a mini novela format. This was a great opportunity for my students since a lot of them like to draw their ideas.

We started the activity by first reading a little from the book. At specific points we stopped and discussed what we read. After the discussions and the sharing, students proceeded with creating their own mini novelas. Individ-

ually they took their mini books and created the pictures that came to their mind as they thought of the life of Marcus Aurelius. At the same time, they gave phrases to their visuals to make them sound like dialogues from a novela. Some of them did a description of Marcus's life as if he was living in present times and sharing his own story in a novela format.

Affirming:

Once the students were done creating their novelas, I had them go to their social studies book one last time and add any other ideas specific to Marcus Aurelius's life, to help them connect with the text and look for more details. Once students were done with that, I had everyone come to the front of the room and share their novelas with the class. This was a great activity since it really helped my students see how they can represent the life of a historic figure using their own summaries. My students took great pride in creating these mini books. As students finished sharing their novelas, we looked at our social studies

book and compared our illustrations with those in the book. At this time I also allowed students to add more descriptions to their novelas if they found something interesting in their peers' summaries. I plan on using this strategy to teach students the skill of summarizing.

INSTRUCTIONS: Creating Your Mini Novela

Materials: A single Mini Novela will require one sheet of paper and a pair of scissors.

Step 1:	Take a piece of paper, making sure it is in landscape orientation (long edges at top and bottom), and fold it in half from left to right, making a sharp crease.
Step 2:	Turn the page so it is once again in landscape orientation. Then fold it in half from left to right and make a sharp crease.
Step 3:	One last time, turn the page so it is in landscape orientation. Once again, fold it in half from left to right and make a sharp crease.
Step 4:	Unfold the paper until you have four rectangles (the paper will be folded in half at this point). Take a pair of scissors and, *on the fold side,* cut along the center fold, making sure you **cut only to the middle fold** of the paper. When you open the paper, you should have one horizontal slit in the middle of the paper.
Step 5:	To make your mini novela, slip one hand through the slit in the middle of the paper. Using your other hand, grab one side of the paper and pull it out slightly to make the shape of half of a diamond.
	Slowly take your first hand out of the paper. With this hand, grab the other side of the paper and pull it out to complete the diamond.
Step 6:	Holding the top and bottom points of the diamond, pull them away from each other as far as possible to make the pages of your mini novela.
Step 7:	You should have eight pages in total. Simply flatten them together, making sure that each page has a solid crease.

STRATEGY

Tri-Fold

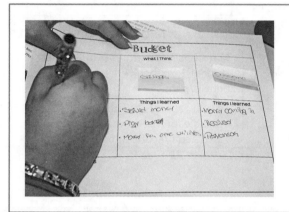

The Tri-Fold strategy provided me with evidence of student learning from the beginning of the lesson through to the end. I had a clear understanding of what the students brought to the lesson in the way of prior knowledge because of their initial sticky notes. Students were really able to make deep connections between what they read and what they already knew by reevaluating their ideas.

—*Reesa Darby, 5th-Grade Teacher*

Where Theory Meets Practice

According to research by Gregory and Kuzmich (2014), sequencing is an important literacy skill for students to develop because it helps them with the writing process and in being able to relate a series of events. To be successful at sequencing information from text, students should first understand the structure of the text. Tompkins (2007) recommends that teachers "consider the structure of the text as they decide how to introduce an informational book, what type of graphic organizer or diagram to make to help emphasize the big ideas, and what points to emphasize in discussions" (p. 318). By first evaluating the text in this way, teachers are able to provide their students with a structured approach to reading and analyzing the material. With such guidance, students have an opportunity to focus on the big ideas in the text rather than becoming overwhelmed by less important information, which also helps them with academic language development.

Tri-Fold is a BDI strategy that allows students to chunk information and analyze it at their own level, thereby promoting their comprehension. The tri-fold tool becomes an interactive graphic organizer for students. It serves all three basic functions of graphic organizers described by Díaz-Rico (2008):

- The tool is *generative*, in that students work to complete the organizer.

- It is *representative*, because it scaffolds students' thinking as they manipulate ideas and construct their content understanding.
- The tri-fold is *evaluative*, as it provides evidence of content and language growth that supports teachers in assessing students' learning.

Beyond these basic functions, the tri-fold tool as used throughout this strategy supports students in igniting associations to their background knowledge (funds of knowledge, prior knowledge, academic knowledge), bridging to new learning, and interacting with peers throughout the progression of the lesson.

As we support students in understanding the content of lessons, we must provide them with learning strategies for working with the text that will increase their comprehension and internalization of key concepts. Summarization is one such skill that can be especially helpful for CLD students. For learners who are new to the expectations traditionally associated with summarization in U.S. schools, and for other learners as well, Herrera (2016, p. 54) recommends the following:

- First identifying key concepts from a passage or lesson and then asking students to locate textual explanations/support for each concept or to record points of the lesson related to each concept.

- Providing explicit instruction on how to differentiate key information from supporting details.
- Incorporating opportunities for students to work together to practice differentiating essential information from nonessential details.
- Supporting students in individual summarization tasks by providing a hand-held scaffolding tool, such as a foldable or a graphic organizer, to help guide their thinking.
- Providing students with examples of written summaries and modeling for students how information contained on a scaffolding tool can be used to develop a written summary of content knowledge.

As we bring writing to the forefront, we pay special attention to students' development of academic language, as it is necessary for creating topic sentences, using transitions effectively, and editing (Gersten, Baker, et al., 2007).

The Tri-Fold strategy provides CLD students with a scaffolding tool and explicitly models processes for both sequencing and summarization. Students collaborate to share their individual perspectives on the text. Because students are able to apply the strategy throughout the lesson to explore sequences of ideas/events, they are able to gain greater prowess with using the academic language of the lesson to discuss relationships among concepts or events.

MATERIALS & RESOURCES

Materials Needed: Tri-Fold Template (one per student) • textbook • paper (one piece per group) • pencils/pens

Template: Tri-Fold Template (see page 176); also available for free download and printing from tcpress.com/accelerating

---

ACTIVATION: A Canvas of Opportunity

Directions:

i (individual)

- Place students into groups of four or five students, and give each student a Tri-Fold Template.
- Depending upon the skill/topic of the day, ask students first to individually think of any concepts or images they associate with the topic. Have them record their ideas on the back of their template.
- After students have individually brainstormed and documented ideas, have them discuss what they have written within their small groups. As students discuss their ideas, have them share what prompted their thinking.
- Circulate around the room while students discuss in order to gather some of the ideas they are sharing.

- Next, have students consider everything that has been discussed up to this point and individually select ideas to draw or write (using L1 or L2) in the "Our Connections" (middle) column of the tri-fold.
- As students work, be sure to observe and document some of their ideas so that you can use these with the rest of the class later.

Author Talk: Activation

As educators, it is easy to approach instruction with specific expectations in mind. Yet when working with CLD students, it is important to remember that their cultural background serves as their "template for the organization of knowledge" (Byers & Byers, 1985, p. 28). In other words, the cultural background of CLD students greatly influences the way they individually think about the academic content presented to them in the classroom setting. Being aware of this, and using students' culturally driven understanding as a springboard from which to build greater depth of understanding, greatly enhances their comprehension.

Tri-Fold is a strategy that is heavily embedded in the content and the language of the lesson. Because it stems from students' own thinking and gradually moves them toward more meaningful understanding of the text, it is ideal for supporting students in continually adding to and revising their schemas. Teachers are most effective at implementing the Tri-Fold strategy when they listen closely to what their students are saying. Specifically, they need to note the verbal as well as the nonverbal cues of their students and build upon these. Effective teachers look for patterns in their students' responses, because these patterns are indicative of students' understanding as well as their areas of confusion. Gathering what the community of learners has produced helps the teacher determine how to lead whole-group instruction.

Activating the "*i*"
How does this process activate CLD students' existing knowledge?

- **Sociocultural:** The Tri-Fold strategy provides CLD students with an academic avenue to express their culturally bound perspectives. Providing consistent opportunities for students to see their thinking and language valued by the teacher builds their self-confidence about what is possible within the classroom.
- **Linguistic:** Students' oral sharing of their initial connections allows them to express their ideas using the words/language they have available. It also provides them an opportunity to begin to gather the words necessary to support their full engagement in the lesson.

- **Academic:** Students who are culturally and linguistically diverse often are not given the opportunity to make public the academic knowledge they have available to them from previous schooling. The Tri-Fold strategy provides a low-risk opportunity for all students to share what they already know.
- **Cognitive:** CLD students are provided with a process for documenting their understanding in a systematic way. This process, which begins with their own thinking, will evolve throughout the lesson to incorporate new ideas, concepts, and vocabulary.

CONNECTION: The Broad & Narrow Strokes of Learning

Directions:

T (Total Group), p (partner), s (small group)

- Continue with the lesson and explain to students that they are going to focus on sequencing ideas/events related to the topic using the "Things I Learned" (left) column of the tri-fold.
- Ask students to do a jigsaw of the text, paying special attention to the events covered. Alternatively, students may read the text in pairs or individually.
  - If you plan on using the jigsaw, have each student in the small group take a different part of the story/chapter and silently read it. As they finish with this portion, have them share their summary of the portion they read with the rest of the group. Once each member has finished sharing, have students individually add their learnings in the "Things I Learned" column.
  - If the text is read individually, we recommend that class be brought back together every 5–7 minutes and guided to write on their tri-fold and discuss ideas in pairs or small groups.
  - At each stopping point, allow time for students to evaluate what they have written to determine how the information reflects the critical content/concepts from the text.

- Have students write the relevant page number of the text to provide evidence for each idea.
- As students progress through the process, alternating between reading and documenting their learning, take time to facilitate the connections that will help them answer the essential question or attain the objectives of the lesson.
  - Remember to make links to some of the ideas students shared in the Activation phase.
  - Be sure to provide students plenty of opportunities to share their ideas with each other.
  - Listen to students' conversations for insights to revoice for the benefit of the individual, small group, and entire class.
- After students have finished reading the text, have them come back together and discuss with their small group what they have understood from the text.

Connecting to the "*i*+1"

How does this process move CLD students from the known to the unknown?

- **Sociocultural:** Students' ongoing discussion with peers to check understanding and determine key events helps make learning more meaningful for CLD students. Peers have opportunities to share past experiences and consider new perspectives.
- **Linguistic:** Careful consideration of your CLD students' language proficiency when dividing the text for the jigsaw activity can allow you to differentiate the amount of reading each student receives to reflect his or her individual linguistic abilities.
- **Academic:** All students are held accountable for taking part in the learning process, reporting and discussing key information and ideas from the reading with the rest of the group.
- **Cognitive:** The partner/small-group interaction during application of the Tri-Fold strategy prompts students to engage in ongoing monitoring of their own understanding of the text as they respond to ideas and articulate key concepts with their peers.

AFFIRMATION: A Gallery of Understanding

Directions:

T (Total Group), p (partner), s (small group), I (Individual)

- After students have reviewed their learning with their small group, have them individually evaluate the extent to which their original connections recorded on the tri-fold relate to their new learning.
- Next have students summarize their ideas in the "Summary" (right) column.
  - If students need additional support, allow them to work with a partner.
  - Students may choose to highlight aspects of their group discussion or their overall learning from the lesson.
- Then have group members work together to create a timeline of their combined events on a separate sheet of paper.
- You can also have students use their tri-folds as a means to talk about different text structures (e.g., cause and

effect, compare and contrast). Have students categorize the ideas on their tri-folds to illustrate their understanding of the text structure.
- Have students keep their completed tri-folds to use as study tools. You can have students paste them in their notebooks or journals. Doing so allows students to refer to them easily as they move to other concepts.

Affirming Student Ownership: *"I"* Get It!
How does this process celebrate CLD student learning?

- **Sociocultural:** Students work collaboratively to express their combined learning in the form of a timeline. This process promotes respect and appreciation for one another as individuals and as fellow learners.
- **Linguistic:** CLD students are engaged in practicing and using grade-level content vocabulary throughout the lesson, which supports their ongoing development of academic English language skills.

- **Academic:** All students are held to the same high expectation of gaining a deeper understanding of the content concepts. Students are supported in engaging as full participants in each activity of the Tri-Fold strategy.
- **Cognitive:** The tri-fold serves as a scaffolding tool to promote CLD students' ability to actively construct meaning, negotiate understanding, and document their comprehension of curricular concepts.

SPOTLIGHT: Early Literacy Connection

Recognizing sequencing and the correct order of events in a story is a critical skill for young students to develop. Identifying the beginning, middle, and end of a process helps children to remember the procedure and understand that most steps have a logical sequence. However, for young learners, the concept of sequencing can be very abstract. You can best teach the concept through a hands-on activity.

The Tri-Fold strategy is great for making sequencing more concrete and understandable. Young CLD students learn while discussing, investigating, creating, and discovering with other students. As students become familiar with the beginning–middle–end structure of a story, they begin to make decisions about content and process, requiring less teacher support and allowing more interactive learning to occur (Cooperstein & Kocevar-Weidinger, 2004).

To modify the Tri-Fold strategy for young CLD students, teachers can implement the following adaptation.

Activation:

When initially using the Tri-Fold strategy to support students' understanding of the sequential elements of beginning, middle, and end, start by having them complete the sequence of an event from their own lives.

* Fold a piece of chart paper into three sections.
* Explain to the students that they are going to learn about the concept of beginning, middle, and end.
* On the folded chart paper, start in the middle section and draw something that you did before school this morning (e.g., brushed your teeth). Then write a sentence at the bottom of the page describing that picture.
* Next, move to the first (left) section—beginning—and draw an event that happened directly before the event that was drawn in the middle section. Again, write a sentence at the bottom of the page describing the picture.
* Finally, move to the last (right) section—end—and draw something that happened directly after the middle

event. Again, write a sentence at the bottom of the page describing the picture.
* Explain to the students that they are going to create their own tri-fold of their own personal events.
* Have students brainstorm possible personal events that they could write about on their tri-fold and then share their ideas with a partner.
* Have each pair share one of their ideas with the whole class.

Connection:

* Have the students fold a piece of paper into three parts. *Note:* Depending on the age and abilities of the students, you might pre-fold the paper for them.
* Next explain that they are going to draw a picture of a personal event in the middle section and leave space at the bottom of the page for writing.
* Then in the first (left) section—beginning—have the students draw something that happened directly before the event they drew in the middle section. Again, they need to leave space at the bottom for writing.
* In the last (right) section—end—have the students draw an event that happened right after the one depicted in the middle section, leaving space at the bottom for writing.
* After the three pictures are drawn, have the students verbally share their sequence of events with their partner.

Affirmation:

* Next, have students write a sentence for each picture.
  ◎ If students struggle with writing, they can dictate their sentence to you or another adult.
  ◎ Alternatively, students can simply write the name of the action/event for each picture.
  ◎ Encourage partners to support one another in this process.
* Have each pair of students share their tri-folds with at least one other pair of students.

One Classroom's Perspective

From the 5th-grade class of Reesa Darby

Activating:

I know that my students enjoy learning more about new subjects and are very curious by nature. These students bring various types of background knowledge to our class discussions, and because of this I knew that their group discussions would be rich. The Tri-Fold activity [strategy] allowed students to tap into their schemas about the topic of working with satellites before they were expected to learn more and share their knowledge. This gave some of my hesitant learners a chance to get comfortable with the topic at hand before instruction began. The students were given the opportunity to think individually about the prior knowledge they had about the topic and use sticky notes to record that knowledge. I made sure to

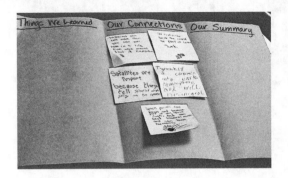

explain to the students when introducing the activity that they would be adding to their knowledge of the subject and that their thinking might change as we continued.

Connecting:

During the lesson, students were placed in four groups, each containing four students. I selected group members by using data on the students' reading comprehension and fluency levels. Because the students were grouped for mixed abilities, the arrangement allowed for some peer teaching to occur. After students had created an individual list of their prior knowledge, they shared with their teammates.

The reading for the day was divided among students in each team using the jigsaw method. Students were given pages to read in their book, and then after all were done reading, they were asked to come up with no fewer than three key ideas they had learned from their reading. They also were asked to reevaluate their prior knowledge on the sticky notes.

I had a clear understanding of what the students brought to the lesson in the way of prior knowledge

because of their initial sticky notes. I was also able to determine how their thinking changed because they were asked to reevaluate their learning and remove their "prior knowledge" sticky notes if they felt they did not relate to the topic after they had done their reading. By tracking the students' self-evaluation, I was able to see how well they had read the information in the book, and could see where I needed to fill in the gaps in their knowledge.

Affirming:

Finally, each group created a team summary of their learnings. The student summaries helped by providing a conclusion to what the students knew and had learned through their reading for the day.

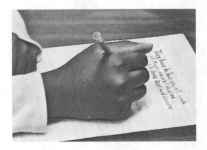

Tri-Fold

Things I Learned	Our Connections	Summary

STRATEGY

Word Drop

I appreciated that the strategy employed both individual and group work. The individual work allowed me to quickly walk around the room and assess each student's understanding. The small groups allowed more students to share their prior knowledge than if we had worked as a whole class. I felt that the whole class had a better understanding of the selected vocabulary after completing the Word Drop.

—*Jessica Golden, 5th-Grade Teacherr*

Where Theory Meets Practice

The application of metacognitive strategies helps students to pay conscious attention to their thinking. According to research by Quiocho and Ulanoff (2009), practicing metacognitive strategies repeatedly serves to "increase the self-confidence of ELLs as it helps them build academic language by making connections to what they already know and deliberately focusing on strategy application" (p. 127). Focused metacognitive strategy instruction has the potential to enhance CLD students' comprehension at the opening, during the work time, and at the closing of the lesson.

Word Drop is a BDI strategy that uses advance organization to provide students with a tool they can use to become more efficient learners and active participants. Focused attention on key vocabulary at the onset of the lesson guides students to be more aware of what they are going to learn. Through the activities incorporated in this strategy, students are supported in making connections between existing word knowledge and the content they are learning. This attention to key vocabulary helps students develop a deeper level of word knowledge so that they can use the vocabulary across content areas; by comparison, students who memo-

rize vocabulary terms are said to have only a surface level of word knowledge (Beck et al., 2013).

During the lesson, students learn how to monitor their comprehension and become strategic in their learning as they read, respond, write, and discuss what they are learning with peers. When teachers ask students to focus on the connections they are making between the key vocabulary and the text/lesson, they are better able to actively listen and make meaningful links to content. When text-centered activities are supported by one-on-one interaction with peers, small-group discussions, and whole-group synthesis, these links to content and language are further reinforced.

Finally, using the Word Drop strategy supports students in becoming reflective learners throughout the lesson. By producing two different levels of definitions, individual and group—students are able to monitor their own production and language development over the course of the lesson. Individual summaries using the key vocabulary that are produced at the end of the lesson provide evidence of each student's level of understanding. In addition to the academic benefits of using metacognitive strategies like Word

Drop, Herrera (2016) notes that these strategies also "help to demystify the learning process and to lower CLD students' anxiety, which is often provoked by being in a linguistically demanding learning environment" (p. 108). With the support of this strategy's built-in tool, students are able to focus more fully on comprehending and using language as they work with others to explore new concepts.

MATERIALS & RESOURCES

Materials Needed: Word Drop Template (one per student) • curricular materials • pencils/pens

Template: Word Drop Template (see page 183); also available for free download and printing from tcpress.com/accelerating

ACTIVATION: A Canvas of Opportunity

Directions:

i (individual)

- Select four key vocabulary words that are crucial to students' comprehension of the lesson concepts.
- Provide each student with a Word Drop Template. Have students individually write the preselected vocabulary words in the center of each of the four clouds (one word per cloud).
- Have students look at each vocabulary word and think of any words or images that come to mind based on their background knowledge.
- Have students individually document their connections to each word by writing ("dropping") three connections in the raindrops below each cloud.

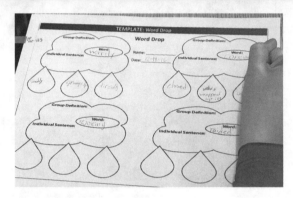

- Encourage students to use L1 and/or picture prompts as needed.
- Allow only 3–4 minutes for students to drop their words/pictures on the page.

Activating the "*i*"
How does this process activate CLD students' existing knowledge?

- **Sociocultural:** Providing students with the opportunity to select three connections to their background knowledge to individually document validates what students already know. This recorded knowledge gives teachers concrete information that is relevant to learners that they can use to build upon and make meaningful links to during instruction.
- **Linguistic:** Giving each student time to individually document his or her knowledge lowers the affective filter and allows students at different stages of second

language acquisition to show what they know without the pressure of producing oral language.
- **Academic:** The Activation phase of Word Drop provides teachers with a nonthreatening way to assess the level of word knowledge that each student brings to the lesson.
- **Cognitive:** Students are challenged to think metacognitively about the vocabulary from the onset of the lesson. They are also provided an element of choice as they determine which connections to document for further use as the lesson progresses.

CONNECTION: The Broad & Narrow Strokes of Learning

Directions:

T (Total Group), p (partner), s (small group)

- Place students in small groups of four or five students. (*Note:* Strategically use your knowledge of students' L1 and English language proficiency levels to create supportive groups.)
- Have students share their connections with a partner.
  - As students complete this activity, circulate around the room and note the academic vocabulary that students have already recorded on their templates. Listen for connections that you can later revoice for the entire class.
- Proceed with the lesson. As the key vocabulary words are encountered in text, have students discuss the meaning of each word with a partner (another member of their small group).
- After the text selection has been read, assign each group a portion of the text in which one or more of the vocabulary terms is located.
- Have students work in their small groups to create a group definition for each word in their assigned portion of text. Have students write their definitions in the top half of each cloud.
  - Remind students to use information from the text as well as the information that they and/or other students have already dropped on their raindrops to help them come up with the definition.
  - Reminding students to revisit their initial connections will help them create a more meaningful and compre-

hensive definition. They will be able not only to confirm/ disconfirm their initial understanding but also to embed personal associations with the vocabulary word.

- Circulate around the room and support groups as needed as they create their definitions.
- Have each small team share their group-generated definition with the whole class.
- As each group shares, have students fill in the definitions for the vocabulary terms that were not part of the group's reading (in this way, all students will have definitions for each term).
- Once all groups have shared and each student has filled in the definitions for all the vocabulary terms on their individual word drops, have them talk to their peers once more to make sure they understand the meaning of each vocabulary term. *Tip:* Verify that each student has filled in a group definition for all the vocabulary terms on their individual word drops. Provide individual support to any students who might need it at this time.

Connecting to the "*i*+1"

How does this process move CLD students from the known to the unknown?

- **Sociocultural:** Each student is considered a valuable member of the learning community who has information on his or her word drop that can be used to support peers as they construct group definitions.
- **Linguistic:** Students are engaged in reading, speaking, listening, and writing tasks that promote academic language development in a safe and supportive language environment. Allowing students to stop at regular intervals during the reading to discuss ideas with a partner promotes comprehension and supports students' con-

tinued engagement in the cognitively demanding process of reading.
- **Academic:** Students are able to make sense of the academic content presented in the text in various ways and with multiple levels of support from their peers and the teacher. Scaffolding through peer interaction is an essential element of this strategy.
- **Cognitive:** Students develop their metacognitive skills as they use selective attention and contextual cues to locate text evidence and negotiate the definition of the vocabulary with group members.

AFFIRMATION: A Gallery of Understanding

Directions:

**T (Total Group), p (partner),
s (small group), I (Individual)**

- To assess students' individual understanding of the target vocabulary, have them write a sentence in the bottom half of each cloud in which they use the corresponding vocabulary word.
  - Allow students who need additional language support to work with a partner to write the sentence.
- Next, have students individually write a summary of what they learned over the course of the lesson on the back of their Word Drop Template.
  - Ask students to use at least three vocabulary words that were most meaningful to them.
  - For students who need extra linguistic support, consider accommodations such as the following:
    - Allow students to work with a partner.
    - Provide students with a cloze paragraph.

- Allow students to use both their native language and English, incorporating pictures where necessary to communicate their understanding.
- Have students share their summaries with a partner to show all that they have learned.

Author Talk: Affirmation

Have you ever heard the saying "the classroom was alive and buzzing with activity"? This is exactly the type of learning environment that the Word Drop strategy fosters. It actively engages CLD students in the learning process and promotes student interaction throughout the lesson. When observing this strategy in practice, it is always fascinating to see the transformation that takes place: students are up and out of their seats, actively engaging in discussion, and sharing ideas that promote their learning and comprehension. As Kerry Wasylk, a 4th-grade teacher, noted:

This strategy gave my students a chance to organize their own thoughts before being taught new content. They were each allowed to enter the lesson on their

own level. They had the choice of writing or drawing their thoughts on the page. Next, my students were able to meet their social needs by having role models in the classroom during partner and small-group discussion. Students of all abilities would be able to participate in this lesson on their level while learning important grade-level content.

The more we can do as educators to promote our students' cross-cultural interactions and connections to key vocabulary through strategies such as this, the more likely we are to promote meaningful and long-term content learning for our CLD students.

Affirming Student Ownership: *"I" Get It!*
How does this process celebrate CLD student learning?

- **Sociocultural:** Individual writing allows all students to express their learning from their own unique perspectives. These perspectives have roots in the background knowledge that students documented and discussed earlier in the lesson.
- **Linguistic:** Students are able to use their individual and group-generated resources to support their writing of sentences and paragraphs in English.

- **Academic:** This strategy enables students to engage with the authentic assessment tasks in ways that are appropriately challenging. All students are supported in writing sentences that reflect key academic connections to the text/lesson.
- **Cognitive:** Students are able to monitor their own understanding and self-assess via the individual sentences and the summaries they produce to demonstrate their understanding of the content and key vocabulary.

SPOTLIGHT: Early Literacy Connection

The Word Drop strategy is an excellent strategy for promoting young learners' exposure to, and active discussion of, key content vocabulary. Research has shown that students best understand the meaning of words when their senses, background knowledge, and emotional responses are engaged (Boyd-Batstone, 2006; Marzano, 2003). Multisensory instruction, for example, helps learners use their senses (visual, auditory, tactile, and kinesthetic) to store and retrieve information (Wolf, 2001). Such instruction sends information to the brain along multiple pathways simultaneously (Currie & Wadlington, 2000).

Creative Connections

To modify the Word Drop strategy, you will need a poster-sized version of the Word Drop Template so that all the students can see it. Introduce each word by saying it aloud; have the students repeat the word. Next, write the vocabulary word in the center of one of the clouds. As you spell the word, have the students practice spelling the word through skywriting (writing the word in the air). After all the words have been recorded on the word drop poster, orally discuss the words and any connections that the students can make with the vocabulary. You can incorporate pictures from the text or other visuals related to the vocabulary. Such pictures, photos, or illustrations provide concrete, visual support for students' understanding. This strategy also provides a great opportunity to bring in multimedia resources such as video clips, auditory samples, and so forth to help enhance students' multisensory connections to the newly introduced vocabulary.

As you encounter the words in the context of meaningful literature, pause to discuss how the words are used in that context. This further extends students' learning and understanding of the words. Then work together as a class to develop a student-friendly definition of the word. Write the definition in the "group definition" section. After the entire story has been read aloud, revisit the word drop poster and discuss how each of the words could be used in a sentence. Have several students share possible sentences and then write one of those sentences on the poster.

One Classroom's Perspective

From the 1st-grade class of Della Peréz

Activating:

Before the lesson I wanted to encourage the students to write in their native language or draw what they thought of when they heard the target vocabulary words from our story, *The Knight and the Dragon,* by Tomie DePaola. The Word Drop strategy is perfect for 1st-graders to use because the more advanced students can write the words in English and my students who are still acquiring English can either draw a representation of the word or write words in their native language. As a teacher, this is also an eye-opening experience for me, because I get to see the background knowledge that the students already bring

to the lesson. This insight helps me to know where to begin my instruction before I even open the book!

Connecting:

I told the students before I started reading the story that their job was going to be to listen for the key vocabulary words on their Word Drop Templates. When I got to one, they had to raise their hands so I knew that we would have to stop at the end of that page and discuss the word. As I began reading, I was really surprised at how attentive the students were. They really listened for the key vocabulary and were quick to signal me when they heard one of the words. After the students had signaled me, I would stop at the end of the page and we would identify which word(s) they had heard and discuss them as a whole group. Then I told them their job was to come up with a definition for the word in their small groups based on our discussion. As each group discussed and wrote down their defintions, I checked to make sure they were on the right track by talking to each group sepa-

rately. After all the groups were done, I had them share their definitions with the class before we continued reading the story. By the time we finished the story, all the students had their group definitions of the vocabulary words filled out on their Word Drop Templates.

Affirming:

To be sure the students really understood the meaning of the words, I had them individually use each word in a sentence. I told the students to be sure to use the words and pictures as well as the group definitions they created from our story to help them come up with meaningful sentences. Finally, to assess students' overall comprehension of the story, I asked each one to write a summary of what the story was about on the back of their Word Drop Template. The only rule was that they had to use at least three of the vocabulary words from the front of the word drop in their summary. After reading the individual student sentences and summaries, I could see the students had a much deeper understanding of the terms and the story.

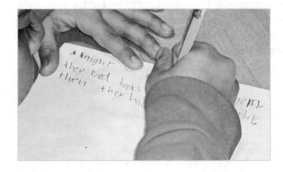

This was especially evident with the more limited English speakers, who were able to create much richer and more detailed sentences than they had in previous lessons!

Name: _____

Date: _____

Word Drop

Group Definition:

Word:

Individual Sentence:

Group Definition:

Word:

Individual Sentence:

Group Definition:

Word:

Individual Sentence:

Group Definition:

Word:

Individual Sentence:

This template can be printed double-sided to accommodate additional vocabulary words.

Available for free download and printing from tcpress.com/accelerating

PART III

Empowering Ourselves to Dismantle Both Visible and Invisible Walls

Why Are We Stuck?

Since the publication of *A Nation at Risk* (National Commission on Excellence in Education, 1983), education reform and legislated learning agendas have recurrently dominated the landscape of professional practice for teachers. Such efforts have tended to accentuate a *technocratic consciousness* about how to change or fix schools, teaching, and instruction (Herrera & Murry, 2016; Leopard, 2013; McLaren, 1994). This *technocratic–instrumental perspective* on teaching and teacher learning has advocated deference to so-called educational experts, a teacher-proofing of the curriculum, and a devaluing of teachers' own innovations and decisionmaking in their classrooms (Herrera & Murry, 2016; Jackson, 2015; Leopard, 2013).

The pattern of this perspective tends to be a long-standing and familiar one. Following a top-down protocol, state and/or district bureaucrats or administrators decide what reforms and agendas are needed to *fix* education. District administrators then contract perceived experts, who specify what critical behaviors in the classroom will attain the objectives of the reform. Teachers learn to replicate these behaviors and follow prescribed protocols throughout the average school day. Instructional coaches and others often monitor classrooms to ensure that teachers do not deviate from these expectations for teaching and learning.

In turn, the technocratic targeting of these behaviors and protocols of teaching is designed to enable the accelerated and efficient coverage of prescribed (so-called *essential*) content by specific time or quota benchmarks throughout the school year. Ultimately, highly standardized student assessments are designed or selected to ensure that target student outcomes of the reform are achieved. Proponents assert that this very structured and functionalist perspective on teaching and learning efficiently and instrumentally tightens teacher behavior, concentrates on the basics, ensures accountability, and produces effective schools (Leopard, 2013; Pink & Borman, 1991).

Not surprisingly, a range of debatable assumptions, dogmatic premises, negative effects on teaching, damaging outcomes, and unimpressive results have been associated with the technocratic–instrumental perspective (D. Hill & Kumar, 2012; Jackson, 2015; Pearl, 1991). For example, the perspective has been variously criticized as very top-down, authoritarian, conservative, assimilationist, quick-fix driven, mechanistic, linear, disengaging, and inconsistent. In particular, the perspective tends to promote one-size-fits-all approaches to, and strategies for, teaching that fail to account for increasing levels of diversity in classrooms (D. Hill & Kumar, 2012; Jackson, 2015; Leopard, 2013). Increasing numbers of CLD students bring different kinds of background experiences, cultural heritage, academic knowledge, preferred ways of knowing, mental models for problem solving, language assets and needs, and more to our classrooms. The technocratic viewpoint mistakenly assumes, among other things, that a trickle-down model of professional development, from expert to coaches to teachers, will maintain the fidelity of implementation necessary to ensure predictable outcomes for our increasingly diverse student population (Bett, 2016).

Teachers as Agents of Change

In this book, we offer an alternative perspective on teacher *professional* development. We focus on providing teachers with the strategies, tools, supports, and encouragement they need to be true professionals in the classroom. Teachers are best positioned to build relationships with their students that provide the foundation for all successful teaching and learning endeavors. Teachers are able to listen to what students say, watch how they interact with peers, and see what they produce as they engage with the curriculum.

Teachers are called to be decisionmakers and advocates for instructional practices that are best for their students—combining insights from research and theory, their own expertise, and knowledge of their specific community of learners.

We view the biography-driven instructional strategies and ideas presented throughout the chapters of this book as professional development that not only is grounded in Krashen's *i*+1, Vygotsky's zone of proximal development, and culturally responsive teaching but also stems from an understanding of everyday realities that teachers across the nation face. The strategies presented in this resource do not provide a formulaic approach to curriculum and instruction. Rather, they aim at helping teachers create opportunities within the classroom that can provide a platform for creating a sustainable inside-out/bottom-up change process.

Through consistent implementation of BDI strategies as tools for addressing each student's biography (i.e., academic, linguistic, cognitive, and sociocultural dimensions), teachers create a classroom culture that has the power to positively change students' self-concepts, levels of engagement, and educational trajectories. In such spaces, communities of learners build momentum together, using their own funds of knowledge, prior knowledge, and academic knowledge as catalysts for individual and collective learning. Through this type of pedagogical change, teachers can make a lasting impact on the school culture. Long-term benefits of sustainable, high-quality teaching and learning that enhances a sense of community and inclusion for all students and subgroups include the kinds of student growth, tangible outcomes, and academic gains that policymakers, employers, administrators, teachers, parents, and students themselves crave.

A Glimpse of What's Possible

Educators who consistently implement the BDI strategies often have shared the sentiment that their use of the strategies leads to a kind of *democratic citizenship* as they increase student voice and participation in the classroom, regardless of the subgroup being represented. The processes involved in their implementation of the strategies help teachers to prioritize their actions, focusing on students' social/emotional development while simultaneously scaffolding learners' use of academic language and comprehension of the content. One teacher we interviewed shared with us how the DOTS strategy supported her in meeting the needs of all students in her 3rd-grade classroom:

I found that through the implementation of the DOTS chart, one student, who will have her IEP for next school year, [benefited particularly]. . . . She always needed a lot of extra support, a lot of repetition. Since she had all the words in front of her, like in the text that we read and then on the paper that we recorded on, when we got to the writing part, it was a lot easier for her because she wasn't just sitting there trying to think . . . 'cause she wouldn't be able to come up with all those words on her own. She needs lots of support. So since it was all right in front of her, she felt more confident and proud of herself because, for her, it was taking her words from her work to write at the end of the week. And I think that was something she felt successful in, whereas in a lot of other things she didn't always feel so successful, since it was so difficult. . . . Thinking about the other students . . . for the high-level kids, they were really excited about the DOTS chart. It made the research part of it more exciting as they found other words and synonyms and thoughts that they could record . . . and there are the typical kids who would write a lot anyway at the end of the week, but because we gave them . . . higher-level academic language, their writing, I think, was [at] a higher level.

—*Beth Livingston*

As teachers consistently check their own habits of mind and modify the way they implement any given strategy in real time, based on what students produce, they are able to support students in developing the targeted skills, processes, and understandings. If they see that students are struggling, responsive teachers take action to reroute them through instructional conversations, provide opportunities for them to negotiate the curriculum through interactions with peers, and continually create bridges between what they already know and the challenging curriculum. This type of *reflective–transformative* perspective on teaching and learning emphasizes the capabilities of those closest to the students to

- Preassess and accommodate student needs and assets,
- Differentiate instruction accordingly,
- Tailor authentic postinstructional assessments to reflect what was taught and the way it was taught,
- Examine instructional outcomes, and
- Critically reflect upon self and praxis, as a means to ongoing and systematic improvement and efficacy (Herrera, 2016; Herrera & Murry, 2016; D. Hill & Kumar, 2012; Mezirow, 1997).

The teachers with whom we are privileged to collaborate often share that it is through the implementation of BDI strategies that they are able to create conditions where language and knowledge production begin with the learner, and all sources of capital—including social, linguistic, cognitive, and academic—are used to accommodate and differentiate instruction. Drawing on the wealth of assets that students bring, these teachers use BDI strategies to create conditions where culture-bound ways of knowing are valued and where all students, regardless of their background, are held to high expectations and provided access to grade-level content. Such teachers monitor and attend to their students' states of mind and social/emotional needs without losing the rigor required for academic achievement. Teachers find the BDI strategies to be flexible enough to allow for creativity and implementation with students across grade levels and content areas. The benefits of these strategies for both teachers and students are reflected in the words of this 3rd-grade teacher we interviewed:

> We like to use the same strategy over and over again for vocabulary and our ELA units because we've found that [with] the Vocabulary Quilt and some of the changes that we have made, the more they [students] are able to use that strategy, and become really strong at using that strategy, the more beneficial it is. So, we use the Vocab Quilt at the beginning of every "Wonders" week. And then we . . . use a modification of Linking Language with that as well. So, they kind of go hand in hand, and we use that every week. It's gotten to be very fast, very efficient, and very effective. Because they [the learners] know what to expect, they know what their roles are, they know what their jobs are. It's collaborative but it also has the independent piece, so we know that everybody is accountable. But they also have that security of . . . working as a part of a group. So the Vocab Quilt is something that we use religiously. The kids love it. They know what to expect.
>
> With Science and Social Studies, we like to . . . use a variety of strategies for the vocabulary and for note taking. And that's where it helps them because when we get out a new note taking guide or a new foldable, or a flipbook, or a tri-fold, or a mini book—something like that—for the new Social Studies unit, they know we've switched over to a new topic and they know that that's going to be the thing they use throughout the entire unit. So, for ELA we stay pretty consistent with that strategy and then in Science and Social Studies, like I said, we use just a wide array of strategies . . . and tools that the kids have learned to expect.
>
> . . . We do have a lot of second language learners here, and so we always like to do the big building background piece. And we like everything for them to have ownership over it. . . . Last year we really tried to switch up the vocab for ELA every week, but we found that it was taking us a long time to teach it, we didn't get the most out of it, we were spending a lot of time going through the routine and the procedures, and we didn't get to spend as much time on the bulk of what the vocab *was*. So, this year we said, okay, we're going to try a couple [of BDI strategies] out at the beginning of the year and see what fits these kids—which one gets the most ideas on paper, and the most conversation to happen. And that was the Vocabulary Quilt. So, that's the one that we started with. And then as we went on, we saw . . . where they need a little extra support, and that's how we made modifications. It was like kind of a running document.
>
> . . . I think one of the things that works really well for me is that I am trying to constantly make adjustments according to what's happening in the classroom. . . . So, for example, if I see that the context clues are translating for them [the students] as a definition, I am not just going to let it continue that way. I am going to stop and create additional supports to let them see we're dealing with two different things here. We can use those to get us where we need to be [definitions], but we're not at that point yet.
>
> —*Lauren Langhofer*

In this account, we hear the teacher describe how the BDI strategies provide students with distinct paths for learning. With repeated use, the instructional strategies become student-owned learning strategies. As this teacher notes, the students know what to expect, and the strategies provide tools that the teacher can use to support the learning of the classroom community. The most powerful teaching happens when educators such as this teacher respond situationally to the needs that arise during the course of instruction. Such responsiveness to students supports every learner in achieving.

Change Begins with Each of Us

Central to faculty renewal, program/curricular innovation, and schoolwide continuous improvement is faculty and staff willingness to engage in *critical reflection* on critical incidents in the classroom/school and outcomes of choices and actions in practice (Herrera & Murry, 2016; Mezirow, 1997). Teachers' choice and volition in their own context and professional learning are more important than any reform, initiative, or agenda. We each must recognize that we have the power to take the next step and to make a difference for students. Sometimes this requires us to unlearn and rethink the way we teach. Consider the experiences of the following teacher, who in an interview candidly shared with us his own professional journey:

> I think I have a unique perspective over most of my colleagues here . . . as far as working with the BDI program. I came into here [this elementary school] as a middle school teacher. I taught 7th grade for 10 years, and this year is my first year in an elementary classroom. One of my biggest concerns was developing that safe environment. . . . In a middle school classroom my demeanor and my questioning technique and my discussion technique [were] effective for me. However, I noticed at the beginning of the year some of the things I would do in a middle school classroom did not work with 4th-graders at all. For example, cold calling. I would cold call and, probably an old school teacher technique, that when I see a student who's off task, cold call them, pull them back. Or just make sure everyone's just kind of focused. What I saw, especially in the ELL population in my room, was I scared them—not scared, but I definitely noticed within the first couple of days of actual instruction that I was not able to foster the kind of safety I needed to foster for those kids to feel comfortable. So, and I don't say this to make you or any of your team feel good, but you were a savior for me, to be honest. When I started to implement the BDI strategies, what I saw immediately was 100% engagement by all kids. . . . For example, we started with some simple turn and talk and some of the vocabulary strategies but I immediately gained— as a professional, as a teacher—a certain comfort level that I was doing the right thing for my kids to develop that safety piece where they started taking risks. They were engaged with each other and sharing their ideas.
> —Dave Thomas

The benefits of BDI were only possible for the CLD students in this teacher's classroom because he was willing to set aside pride, check his desire for control, and re-examine his techniques for creating low-risk opportunities for student talk. Ultimately, he opened up his classroom to the kinds of reciprocal processes and conversations that make school a safe space for all students to learn.

Student Knowledge Is ALWAYS Evolving

Student knowledge expands and transforms with each passing minute. Teachers' introspection/understanding of evolving student knowledge often is based on their ability to observe the ever-changing academic and linguistic behaviors in their classrooms. The views one 3rd-grade teacher expressed to us when interviewed make evident the critical need for each of us to be attentive to our students, in ways that go beyond simply knowing how they are faring on curriculum-based and standardized assessments.

> So looking at my students as individuals is really important in really tailoring biography-driven instruction. Every student comes in with a different background, different set of skills, different history, and I start the year with starting to get to know those students with, you know, the CLD Student Biographies—kind of a modified version of that—getting to know them at the beginning of the year. But the important thing to remember is their biography is always evolving, so the student you get at the beginning of the year is not necessarily the same student that you have in December or March. And so if you're a highly involved teacher, you're always monitoring those changes. And if they're growing, [thinking about] what you can do to extend that. And if they're not, if they're falling behind or just kind of staying stagnant, [trying to understand] why that is happening . . . [to] get to the root of those things. Meet with parents. Go to their homes. Knock on their door; find out what's going on. Or have an old-fashioned conversation and just sit down and try to get to the bottom of those things. Because good instruction goes a lot further when you know what your students are dealing with and who they are as individuals.
> —Lauren Langhofer

The BDI strategies in this book support teachers in building into every lesson opportunities for students to develop relationships and make their knowledge and thinking public. Through these efforts and through interactive opportunities for dialogue, teachers lower students' affective filters and gain insights into their ever-evolving background knowledge as well as their cognitive processes and social/emotional states as they make sense of the lesson's content and language. In this way, teachers can approach instruction in ways that are meaningful and relevant to students' lives, inside and outside of the classroom.

Lesson Planning and Lesson Delivery Are Not Mutually Exclusive

In the last few years the authors of this book have had the pleasure of visiting classrooms across different districts and states. Often the chatter in the classrooms presents diverging scenarios where either the students are doing something because they want to do it and want to be there or the students are merely doing it because the teacher said so. In the classrooms where the students do things because they want to, one theme that recurrently emerges is respect of students' autonomy and voice and a consistent showcasing of individual accountability as a by-product of an often messy, yet seamless, implementation of learning procedures, habits, and processes (not to be confused with simplistic routines and disciplinary actions). Through numerous brown-bag lunches and roundtable discussions, we have tried to figure out why a certain teacher's classroom looks a certain way. Frequently we find ourselves gravitating toward a teacher's perspective on lesson planning.

We often think that the results of our teaching lie in the way that we plan lessons, because it is through lesson planning that we envision (1) what our students bring to the table and (2) what it is that they are capable of within the confines of the outcomes we plan. However, if this were true, then what about the variances we often face in classrooms in the form of outbursts of aggressive student behavior or lack of motivation among certain learners? No amount of effective lesson planning can account for these variables. Yes, lesson planning might provide us with a sense of confidence in being able to execute a "perfect" lesson intentionally designed to lead to the planned outcomes, but it will not be able to help us respond to the ever-changing academic, social/emotional, cultural, linguistic, and cognitive realities of students within the classroom. This is where the emphasis on lesson *delivery* comes into play.

When we focus on our preplanned classroom actions and processes *and implement them in accordance with the biographies of our students,* we as teachers succeed and, in turn, our students succeed. Effective teachers enter the lesson with their lesson plan, knowing that it is *tentative* and *contingent* on what students produce. At times, following through with the lesson as initially planned would be an inefficient use of time, as students might demonstrate in the Activation phase that they already know many of the concepts. At other times, simply moving forward without listening to what students have to say means that we leave them behind in our wake and the only people arriving at the destination of the lesson are we teachers!

Biography-driven instruction (Herrera, 2016) provides the underlying, methodological foundation for the BDI strategies in this book. Through BDI, teachers are supported in developing an *interpretive paradigm,* in which they interpret the community context in which they teach and reflect on implications for themselves and for their students. Teachers who implement BDI gain a holistic perspective on their learners, considering their biopsychosocial histories as well as the school-situated aspects of who they are. This understanding of our students enables us not only to plan our lessons but also to execute them effectively as we orchestrate instruction, keeping in mind the individual and the collective biographies represented in our classrooms. BDI creates the conditions and situations necessary for teachers and learners to collaborate, combining knowledge from the "unofficial space" of students' lives and the "official space" of the curriculum to jointly create knowledge together in the "third space" (Gutiérrez, Baquedano-López, & Tejeda, 2003).

A Final Word

The strategies in this book are not intended to provide you with a magic solution to the daily complexities that you encounter in teaching. Such a solution does not, and never will, exist. Instead, we aim to provide you with pieces that you as a teacher, and as a professional, can put together to develop frameworks, lessons, and personalized tools that work for *your* classroom and that can respond to the needs of *your* students, regardless of the initiative being implemented in your district.

Accelerating Literacy for Diverse Learners

Classroom Strategies That Integrate
Social/Emotional Engagement
and Academic Achievement, K–8

SECOND EDITION

by **Socorro G. Herrera, Shabina K. Kavimandan,**
Della R. Perez, & Stephanie Wessels

DON'T MISS THE COMPANION WEBSITE FOR THIS BOOK:

coe.k-state.edu/cima/biographycrt

featuring

CLASSROOM VIDEOS

See real-world implementation of the strategies,
showing how they

- Accelerate learning
- Promote social/emotional growth
- Foster student-to-student relationships

SUPPORTING MATERIALS FROM THE BOOK

- Templates
- Rubrics
- Checklists

TEACHER-CREATED MATERIALS

Teachers using the strategies in their own classrooms provide
supporting materials they have designed

APPENDIX

Strategy Rubrics and Checklists

CHAPTER 1 *Images as Catalysts for Culturally Driven Connections*

Pictures and Words: Student Academic Behavior Checklist   192

Mind Map: Student Assessment Rubric   193

Listen Sketch Label: Student Academic Behavior Checklist   194

Story Bag: Student Assessment Rubric   195

CHAPTER 2 *Rigor: Leveraging Words Toward Academic Achievement*

DOTS: Student Academic Behavior Checklist   196

Pic-Tac-Tell: Student Assessment Rubric   197

Vocabulary Quilt: Student Academic Behavior Checklist   198

Thumb Challenge: Student Academic Behavior Checklist   199

CHAPTER 3 *Comprehension: It's Not Real Until It's Rehearsed and Written*

U-C-ME: Student Assessment Rubric   200

Extension Wheel: Student Assessment Rubric   201

Active Bookmark: Student Academic Behavior Checklist   202

All of these rubrics and checklists are available for free download and printing from tcpress.com/accelerating

Pictures and Words

Student Academic Behavior Checklist

Name: _____   Topic: _____

Academic Behaviors	Score*			Comments
	1	2	3	
Assesses personal understanding of the word at the beginning of the lesson.				
Shares background knowledge and academic connections to the words with a peer.				
Makes connections between his or her background knowledge and the topic/ vocabulary, and documents the connections in writing and/or with nonlinguistic cues (pictures).				
Participates in collaborative conversations with peers and listens in ways that demonstrate care and respect.				
Works with peers to define the meaning of key vocabulary from the text and helps group reach a consensus.				
Builds on and makes meaningful links between comments shared by others about the summary of key learnings at the end of the lesson.				

*Scoring (Optional):   1 = Beginning   2 = Developing   3 = Accomplished

Mind Map

Student Assessment Rubric

Name: _____ **Topic:** _____

Category	Beginning 1	Emerging 2	Developing 3	Accomplished 4
Linguistic and Nonlinguistic Representations	Only one type of representation, linguistic or nonlinguistic, is included on completed mind map. Few words or pictures reflect the topic.	Both types of representation are included on completed mind map. Some words and pictures reflect the topic.	Both types of representation are included on completed mind map. Most words and pictures reflect the topic.	Both types of representation are included on completed mind map. Words and pictures reflect high levels of topic comprehension.
Vocabulary Development	Completed mind map does not include any key vocabulary words.	Completed mind map includes few key vocabulary words and no connections to the content.	Completed mind map includes key vocabulary words with connections to the content that demonstrate some level of comprehension.	Completed mind map includes key vocabulary words with connections to the content that demonstrate a high level of comprehension.
Connections between Mind Map and Summary Paragraph	No connections are made between concepts on the mind map and the final summary paragraph.	Minimal connections are made between concepts on the mind map and the final summary paragraph.	Some concepts and details on the mind map are integrated into the final summary paragraph.	Numerous concepts and details on the mind map are integrated into the final summary paragraph.

Comments

Listen Sketch Label

Student Academic Behavior Checklist

Name: _____   Topic: _____

Academic Behaviors	Score*			Comments
	1	2	3	
Individually produces an example of figurative language in the native language or in English.				
Willingly shares with peers an example of figurative language from background knowledge.				
Works collaboratively with peers to interpret student-generated examples of figurative language.				
Works collaboratively with peers to distinguish connotations (associations) from denotations (definitions) of figurative language in context.				
Individually sketches pictures that illustrate the meaning of figurative language in context.				
Individually labels each sketch in a way that demonstrates understanding of the figurative language, word relationships, and nuances of word meanings.				

*Scoring (Optional):   1 = Beginning   2 = Developing   3 = Accomplished

Story Bag

Student Assessment Rubric

Name: _____   Topic: _____

Category	Beginning 1	Emerging 2	Developing 3	Accomplished 4
Working with a Partner	Partners do not work together.	Partners do some work together.	Partners are starting to listen and share with each other.	Partners work collaboratively throughout the activity.
Story Bag Retell	Few, if any, story bag items are in the correct sequence.	Some story bag items are in the correct sequence.	Most story bag items are in the correct sequence.	All story bag items are in the correct sequence.
Connections Between Story Bag and Summary Paragraph	Minimal, if any, connections are made between the story bag and the final summary paragraph.	Few connections are made between the story bag and the final summary paragraph.	Some connections are made between the story bag and the final summary paragraph.	Numerous connections are made between the story bag and the final summary paragraph.

Comments

DOTS
(<u>D</u>etermine, <u>O</u>bserve, <u>T</u>alk, <u>S</u>ummarize)
Student Academic Behavior Checklist

Name: _____   Topic: _____

Academic Behaviors	Score*			Comments
	1	2	3	
Writes words (in L1 or L2) or draws pictures in the boxes that represent his or her background knowledge (family, community, school).				
Orally shares initial connections to the topic with a peer and responds to the peer by asking questions to clarify ideas or seek additional information.				
Participates in discussion with peer(s) and builds upon ideas, as demonstrated through oral conversation and/or "borrowing" words and writing them on the DOTS chart.				
Independently connects words inside the DOTS chart to the target vocabulary as his or her understanding of the words in context expands throughout the lesson.				
During the lesson, places additional words related to the topic inside the DOTS chart to show increased knowledge of the academic concepts and language.				
Writes summary sentences/paragraphs that explicitly show connections between his or her own words and the target vocabulary.				
Presents a clear and coherent summary that demonstrates his or her understanding of the topic, is well organized, and is written at his or her linguistic level.				

*Scoring (Optional):   1 = Beginning   2 = Developing   3 = Accomplished

Pic-Tac-Tell

Student Assessment Rubric

Name: _____ Topic: _____ Score: _____

Criterion	Emerging 1	Developing 2	Distinguished 3	Score
Key Vocabulary	The student may/may not have used three key vocabulary words within the sentences. There is limited evidence that the student understood the meanings of the vocabulary terms.	The student used three key vocabulary words within the sentences, but it is clear that the student did not understand the meaning of one or more vocabulary terms.	The student used three vocabulary words within the sentences, and it is evident that the student understood the meanings of the vocabulary terms.	
Content Connections	The student's sentences included vague, unclear content connections based on what was learned from the lesson.	The student's sentences included general content connections based on what was learned from the lesson.	The student's sentences included strong, detailed content connections based on what was learned in the lesson.	
Strategy in Practice	The student's sentences rarely, if ever, connected the three vocabulary words selected using the Tic-Tac-Toe pattern.	The student's sentences somewhat connected the three vocabulary words selected using the Tic-Tac-Toe pattern.	The student's sentences connected all three of the vocabulary words selected using the Tic-Tac-Toe pattern.	

Additional Notes

Vocabulary Quilt

Student Academic Behavior Checklist

Name: _____   Topic: _____

Academic Behaviors	Score*			Comments
	1	2	3	
Individually documents connections to background knowledge (home, community, school) using pictures and/or words in L1 or L2.				
Shares written or pictorial associations with peers and articulates his or her rationales for the word(s) or picture(s) used.				
Predicts what the lesson or text will be about based on the key vocabulary words on the vocabulary quilt.				
Writes the definitions of key vocabulary words in his or her own words as they are encountered in text and documents these definitions (i.e., using sticky notes) for verification.				
Works collaboratively with peers to come to consensus on the definitions of key vocabulary words by using context cues from the reading and discussions about the academic content.				
Writes a summary, individually or with a partner, that demonstrates his or her understanding of the key vocabulary in context.				

*Scoring (Optional):   1 = Beginning   2 = Developing   3 = Accomplished

Thumb Challenge

Student Academic Behavior Checklist

Name: _____   Topic: _____

Academic Behaviors	Score*			Comments
	1	2	3	
Records individual connections on sticky notes using words (L1 or L2) and/or pictures.				
Willingly shares background knowledge connections to the key vocabulary with a peer.				
Interacts with a peer by taking turns to define the key vocabulary.				
Clearly explains to a peer the meaning of each vocabulary word with relevant details from the text or lesson.				
Writes sentences/paragraphs that demonstrate his or her understanding of the key vocabulary words.				

*Scoring (Optional):   1 = Beginning   2 = Developing   3 = Accomplished

U-C-ME
(Uncover, Concentrate, Monitor, Evaluate)
Student Assessment Rubric

Name: _____   Topic: _____

Category	Beginning 1	Emerging 2	Developing 3	Accomplished 4
Individual Connections	Includes only one individual connection in the center of the U-C-ME chart.	Includes two or three individual connections in the center, but they are vague and show no evidence of the peer discussion.	Includes four or more individual connections in the center that are clear and reflect the peer discussion.	Individual connections (four or more) in the center are clear and show extensive connections to the peer discussion.
Posed Questions	Questions posed are limited to yes/no questions.	Questions posed require some thoughtful consideration regarding the topic.	Questions posed elicit elaboration and discussion related to the topic.	Questions posed require in-depth analysis, elaboration, and higher-order thinking.
Summary	Summary does not include key information from the U-C-ME chart.	Summary includes some of the key information from the U-C-ME chart and is somewhat well organized.	Summary includes most of the key information from the U-C-ME chart and is well organized.	Summary includes all of the key information from the U-C-ME chart, and its organization reflects relationships among the questions and key details.

Comments

Extension Wheel

Student Assessment Rubric

Name: _____   Topic: _____

Category	Beginning 1	Emerging 2	Developing 3	Accomplished 4
Expansion of Ideas	Information presented on the different rings is disjointed and not connected to the topic.	Information presented on the different rings is somewhat connected to the topic, and there are minimal connections between the concepts in different rings.	Information presented on the different rings is connected to the topic, and there are some connections between the concepts in different rings.	Information presented on the different rings is explicitly connected to the topic, and the concepts in each ring build upon those in the ring at the level below.
Ties to Key Vocabulary and Critical Concepts	Information on the rings does not include key vocabulary or reflect critical concepts.	Information on the rings minimally includes key vocabulary or reflects critical concepts.	Information on the rings includes some key vocabulary and somewhat reflects critical concepts.	Information on the rings includes most key vocabulary and reflects critical concepts.
Sentence Formation	Student-created sentences do not include information from the wheel.	Student-created sentences include some information from the wheel and allude to the topic, but do not clearly demonstrate the relationships between the two.	Student-created sentences include key words and phrases from the wheel and somewhat demonstrate the relationships between the critical concepts and the topic.	Student-created sentences include a high level of information from the wheel and demonstrate the relationships between the critical concepts and the topic.

Comments

Active Bookmark

Student Academic Behavior Checklist

Name: _____   Topic: _____

Academic Behaviors	Score*			Comments
	1	2	3	
Makes predictions that are logical, sequenced, and reflect personal connections to the text.				
Willingly shares predictions with peers.				
Determines relevant questions and provides a rationale for questions posed when asked.				
Reads and finds answers to questions posed.				
Participates in peer discussions regarding predictions, questions, and connections to the text.				
Produces a written summary that incorporates information from his or her individual active bookmark and clearly demonstrates his or her point of view or understanding of the text.				

*Scoring (Optional):   1 = Beginning   2 = Developing   3 = Accomplished

References

Aisami, R. S. (2015). Learning styles and visual literacy for learning and performance. *Procedia—Social and Behavioral Sciences, 176,* 538–545. Available at www.sciencedirect.com

Almeida, P. A. (2010). Questioning patterns and teaching strategies in secondary education. *Procedia—Social and Behavioral Sciences, 2,* 751–756. Available at www.sciencedirect.com

Ambrose, S. A., Bridges, M. W., DiPietro, M., Lovett, M. C., & Norman, M. K. (2010). *How learning works: 7 research-based principles for smart teaching.* San Francisco, CA: Jossey-Bass.

Anderson, N. J. (1999). *Exploring second language reading: Issues and strategies.* Boston, MA: Heinle and Heinle.

Anderson, N. J. (2002). The role of metacognition in second language teaching and learning. *ERIC Digest.* Available at https://www.ericdigests.org/2003-1/role.htm (ED463659)

Anderson, R. C., & Pearson, P. D. (1984). A schema-theoretic view of basic processes in reading. In P. D. Pearson, R. Barr, M. L. Kamil, & P. Mosenthal (Eds.), *Handbook of reading research* (pp. 255–291). White Plains, NY: Longman.

Anderson, V., & Roit, M. (1993). Planning and implementing collaborative strategy instruction for delayed readers in Grades 6–10. *Elementary School Journal (Special Issue: Strategies Instruction), 94*(2), 121–137.

Au, K. H. (2002). Balanced literacy instruction: Addressing issues of equity. In C. M. Roller (Ed.), *Comprehensive reading instruction across the grade levels: A collection of papers from the Reading Research 2001 Conference* (pp. 70–87). Newark, DE: International Reading Association.

August, D. (2004, May 1). *The work of the national literacy panel.* Presentation at the Reading Research Institute of the International Reading Association, Reno, NV.

August, D., Carlo, M., Dressler, C., & Snow, C. (2005). The critical role of vocabulary development for English language learners. *Learning Disabilities Research and Practice, 20*(1), 50–57.

August, D., & Hakuta, K. (Eds.). (1997). *Improving schooling for language minority students: A research agenda.* Washington, DC: National Academy Press.

Ausabel, D. P. (1968). *Educational psychology: A cognitive view.* New York, NY: Holt, Rinehart, & Winston.

Bartholomé, T., & Bromme, R. (2009). Coherence formation when learning from text and pictures: What kind of support for whom? *Journal of Educational Psychology, 101*(2), 282–293. doi: 10.1037/a0014312

Beaty, J. J., & Pratt, L. (2007). *Early literacy in preschool and kindergarten: A multicultural perspective* (2nd ed.). Columbus, OH: Prentice Hall.

Beck, I. L., McKeown, M. G., & Kucan, L. (2013). *Bringing words to life: Robust vocabulary instruction* (2nd ed.). New York, NY: Guilford Press.

Benson, C., & Lunt, J. (2011). We're creative on a Friday afternoon: Investigating children's perceptions of their experience of design & technology in relation to creativity. *Journal of Science, Education & Technology, 20,* 679–687.

Bett, H. K. (2016). The cascade model of teachers' continuing professional development in Kenya: A time for a change? *Cogent Education, 3*(1). Available at http://www.tandfonline.com/doi/full/10.1080/2331186X.2016.1139439

Bhattacharya, J., & Quiroga, J. (2009). *Learning English & beyond: A holistic approach for supporting English learners in after school.* Emeryville, CA: California Tomorrow.

Blachowicz, C. L. Z., & Fisher, P. J. (2000). Vocabulary instruction. In M. L. Kamil, P. B. Mosenthal, P. D. Pearson, & R. Barr (Eds.), *Handbook of reading research* (Vol. 3, pp. 503–523). Mahwah, NJ: Lawrence Erlbaum.

Blachowicz, C. L. Z., & Fisher, P. J. (2014). *Teaching vocabulary in all classrooms* (5th ed.). Upper Saddle River, NJ: Pearson Education.

Bobe, G., Perera, T., Frei, S., & Frei, B. (2014). Brain breaks: Physical activity in the classroom for elementary school children. *Journal of Nutrition Education and Behavior, 46*(4), S141. doi: 10.1016/j.jneb.2014.04.116

Boerma, I. E., Mol, S. E., & Jolles, J. (2016). Reading pictures for story comprehension requires mental imagery skills. *Frontiers in Psychology, 7.* doi: 10.3389/fpsyg.2016.01630

Bortnem, G. (2008). Teacher use of interactive read alouds using nonfiction in early childhood classrooms. *Journal of College Teaching & Learning, 5*(12), 29–44.

Boston, G. H., & Baxley, T. P. (2014). *Connecting readers to multiple perspectives: Using culturally relevant pedagogy in a multicultural classroom.* Tallahassee, FL: EdConnections.

Boyd-Batstone, P. (2006). *Differentiated early literacy for English language learners: Practical strategies.* Boston, MA: Allyn & Bacon.

Braden, R. A. (1996). Visual literacy. In D. H. Jonassen (Ed.), *Handbook of research for educational communications and technology* (pp. 491–520). New York, NY: Simon & Schuster.

Bransford, J. D., Brown, A. L., & Cocking, R. R. (2000). *How people learn: Brain, mind, experience, and school.* Washington, DC: National Academy Press.

Brumberger, E. (2011). Visual literacy and the digital native: An examination of the millennial learner. *Journal of Visual Literacy, 30*(1), 19–46.

Buzan, T. (1989). *Use both sides of your brain* (3rd ed.). New York, NY: Plenum.

Buzan, T. (2003). *The mind map book: How to use radiant thinking to maximize your brain's potential.* London, UK: BBC Books.

Byers, P., & Byers, H. (1985). Nonverbal communication and the education of children. In C. B. Cazden, V. P. John, & D. Hymes (Eds.), *Functions of language in the classroom* (pp. 3–31). Prospect Heights, IL: Waveland.

Calderón, M. (2007). *Teaching reading to English language learners, Grades 6–12: A framework for improving achievement in the content areas.* Thousand Oaks, CA: Corwin.

Calderón, M., August, D., Slavin, R., Durán, D., Madden, N., & Cheung, A. (2005). Bringing words to life in classrooms with English language learners. In E. H. Hiebert & M. L. Kamil (Eds.), *Teaching and learning vocabulary: Bringing research to practice* (pp. 115–136). Mahwah, NJ: Lawrence Erlbaum.

Center for Research on Education, Diversity & Excellence (CREDE). (2002). *The standards for effective pedagogy and learning.* Berkeley, CA: Author, University of California, Berkeley.

Center for Research on Education, Diversity & Excellence (CREDE). (2014). *The CREDE five standards for effective pedagogy and learning.* Available at http://manoa.hawaii.edu/coe/credenational/the-crede-five-standards-for-effective-pedagogy-and-learning/

Chamot, A. U., & O'Malley, J. (1994). The cognitive academic learning approach: A model for linguistically diverse classrooms. *Elementary School Journal, 96,* 259–273.

Chick, N. (n.d.). *Metacognition.* CFT Teaching Guide. Nashville, TN: Center for Teaching, Vanderbilt University. Available at https://cft.vanderbilt.edu/guides-sub-pages/metacognition/

Chin, C. (2007). Teacher questioning in science classrooms: Approaches that stimulate productive thinking. *Journal of Research in Science Teaching, 44*(6), 815–843.

Chin, C., & Osborne, J. (2008). Students' questions: A potential resource for teaching and learning science. *Studies in Science Education, 44,* 1–39.

Coady, M., Hamann, E. T., Harrington, M., Pacheco, M., Pho, S., & Yedlin, J. (2003). *Claiming opportunities: A handbook for improving education for English language learners through comprehensive school reform.* Providence, RI: Brown University and the Northeast and Islands Regional Laboratory.

Collier, V. P., & Thomas, W. P. (2009). *Educating English learners for a transformed world.* Albuquerque, NM: Fuente Press.

Cooper, J. D. (1986). *Improving reading comprehension.* Boston, MA: Houghton Mifflin.

Cooperstein, S. E., & Kocevar-Weidinger, E. (2004). Beyond active learning: A constructivist approach to learning . *Reference Services Review, 32*(2), 141–148.

Coyne, M. D., McCoach, D. B., Loftus, S., Zipoli, R., & Kapp, S. (2009). Direct vocabulary instruction in kindergarten: Teaching for breadth vs. depth. *Elementary School Journal, 110,* 1–18.

Cummins, J. (1981). The role of primary language development in promoting educational success for language minority students. In C. F. Leyba (Ed.), *Schooling and language minority students: A theoretical framework* (pp. 3–49). Los Angeles, CA: California State University at Los Angeles, Evaluation, Dissemination and Assessment Center.

Cummins, J. (1989). Language and affect: Bilingual students at home and at school. *Language Arts, 66,* 29–43.

Cummins, J. (2001). *Language, power, and pedagogy: Bilingual children in the crossfire.* Philadelphia, PA: Multicultural Matters.

Cunningham, P. M., Moore, S. A., Cunningham, J. W., & Moore, D. W. (1999). *Reading and writing in elementary classrooms: Strategies and observations* (4th ed.). White Plains, NY: Longman.

Currie, P., & Wadlington, E. (2000). *The source for learning disabilities.* East Moline, IL: Linguisystems.

Curtis, A., & Bailey, K. M. (2001). Picture your students talking: Using pictures in the language classroom. *ESL Magazine, 4*(4), 10–11.

Darling-Hammond, L., & Bransford, J. (Eds.). (2005). *Preparing teachers for a changing world: What teachers should learn and be able to do.* San Francisco, CA: Jossey-Bass.

Davoudi, M., & Sadeghi, N. A. (2015). A systematic review of research on questioning as a high-level cognitive strategy. *English Language Teaching, 8*(10), 76–90. doi: 10.5539/elt.v8n10p76

de Jong, E. J. (2011). *Foundations for multilingualism in education: From principles to practice.* Philadelphia, PA: Caslon.

de Jong, E. J., & Harper, C. A. (2005). Preparing mainstream teachers for English language learners: Is being a good teacher good enough? *Teacher Education Quarterly, 32*(2), 101–124.

Dewey, J. (1938). *Experience and education.* New York, NY: Collier Books.

Díaz-Rico, L. T. (2008). *Strategies for teaching English language learners* (2nd ed.). New York, NY: Pearson.

Díaz-Rico, L. T. (2013). *Strategies for teaching English learners* (3rd ed.). Upper Saddle River, NJ: Pearson.

Donovan, M. S., & Bransford, J. D. (Eds.). (2005). *How students learn: History, mathematics, and science in the classroom.* Washington, DC: The National Academy Press.

Duke, N. K., & Carlisle, J. (2011). The development of comprehension. In M. L. Kamil, P. D. Pearson, E. B. Moje, & P. P. Afflerbach (Eds.), *Handbook of reading research* (Vol. IV, pp. 199–228). New York, NY: Routledge.

Duke, N. K., & Pearson, P. D. (2001). How can I help children improve their comprehension? Ann Arbor, MI: Center for the Improvement of Early Reading Achievement (CIERA).

Echevarría, J., Vogt, M. E., & Short, D. J. (2013). *Making content comprehensible for English learners: The SIOP model* (4th ed.). Boston, MA: Pearson.

ERIC Clearinghouse on Languages and Linguistics. (1994). *Funds of knowledge: Learning from language minority households.* Washington, DC: Author. (ED367146)

Fisher, D., & Frey, N. (2008). *Word wise & content rich.* Portsmouth, NH: Heinemann.

Fisher, D., & Frey, N. (2015). Meaningful vocabulary learning. *Educational Leadership, 72*(6), 77–78.

Flavell, J. (1976). Metacognitive aspects of problem-solving. In L. Resnick (Ed.), *The nature of intelligence* (pp. 231–236). Mahwah, NJ: Lawrence Erlbaum.

Forman, E. A., Larreamendy-Joerns, J., Stein, M. K., & Brown, C. A. (1998). "You're going to want to find out which and prove it": Collective argumentation in a mathematics classroom. *Learning and Instruction, 8*(6), 527–548.

Gay, G. (2010). *Culturally responsive teaching: Theory, research, and practice* (2nd ed.). New York, NY: Teachers College Press.

Gentry, J. R. (1987). *Spel . . . is a four-letter word.* Portsmouth, NH: Heinemann.

Gersten, R., Baker, S. K., Shanahan, T., Linan-Thompson, S., Collins, P., & Scarcella, R. (2007). *Effective literacy and English language instruction for English learners in the elementary grades: A practice guide.* Washington, DC: National Center for Education Evaluation and Regional Assistance, Institute of Education Sciences, U.S. Department of Education. (NCEE 2007-4011)

Gersten, R., Dimino, J., Jayanthi, M., Kim, J., & Santoro, L. (2007). *Teacher study groups as a means to improve reading comprehension and vocabulary instruction for English learners: Results of randomized controlled trials.* Signal Hill, CA: Instructional Research Group.

Geva, E., & Yaghoub Zadeh, Z. (2006). Reading efficiency in native English-speaking and English-as-a-second-language children: The role of oral proficiency and underlying cognitive-linguistic processes. *Scientific Studies of Reading, 10*(1), 31–57.

Gipe, J. P. (2014). *Multiple paths to literacy: Assessment and differentiated instruction for diverse learners, K–12* (8th ed.). Upper Saddle River, NJ: Pearson Education.

Goldenberg, C., & Wagner, K. (2015, Fall). Bilingual education: Reviving an American tradition. *American Educator, 39*(3), 28–32, 44.

Graesser, A. C., & Olde, B. A. (2003). How does one know whether a person understands a device? The quality of the questions the person asks when the device breaks down. *Journal of Educational Psychology, 95,* 524–536.

Greenberg, J. B. (1989, April). *Funds of knowledge: Historical constitution, social distribution, and transmission.* Paper presented at the annual meeting of the Society for Applied Anthropology, Santa Fe, NM.

Gregory, G. H., & Burkman, A. (2012). *Differentiated literacy strategies for English language learners: Grades K–6.* Thousand Oaks, CA: Corwin.

Gregory, G. H., & Kuzmich, L. (2014). *Data driven differentiation in the standards-based classroom* (2nd ed.). Thousand Oaks, CA: Corwin.

Gunning, T. G. (2006). *Closing the literacy gap.* Upper Saddle River, NJ: Pearson Education.

Guthrie, J. T., Rueda, R. S., Gambrell, L. B., & Morrison, D. A. (2009). Roles of engagement, valuing and identification in reading development of students from diverse backgrounds. In L. Morrow & R. S. Rueda (Eds.). *Handbook of reading and literacy among students from diverse backgrounds* (pp. 195–215). New York, NY: The Guilford Press.

Gutiérrez, K. D., Baquedano-López, P., & Tejeda, C. (2003). Rethinking diversity: Hybridity and hybrid language practices in the third space. In S. Goodman, T. Lillis, J. Maybin, & N. Mercer (Eds.), *Language, literacy, and education: A reader* (pp. 171–187). Trent, UK: The Open University.

Harris, K. R., Graham, S., Mason, L. H., & Friedlander, B. (2008). *Powerful writing strategies for all students.* Baltimore, MD: Brookes.

Harvey, S., & Goudvis, A. (2007). *Strategies that work: Teaching comprehension to enhance understanding* (2nd ed.). York, ME: Stenhouse.

Hattie, J., & Yates, G. (2014). *Visible learning and the science of how we learn.* New York, NY: Routledge.

Herrera, S. (2010). *Biography-driven culturally responsive teaching.* New York, NY: Teachers College Press.

Herrera, S. (2016). *Biography-driven culturally responsive teaching* (2nd ed.). New York, NY: Teachers College Press.

Herrera, S. G., Cabral, R. M., & Murry, K. G. (2013). *Assessment accommodations for classroom teachers of culturally and linguistically diverse students* (2nd ed.). Boston, MA: Allyn & Bacon.

Herrera, S. G., Kavimandan, S. K., & Holmes, M. A. (2011). *Crossing the vocabulary bridge: Differentiated strategies for diverse secondary classrooms.* New York, NY: Teachers College Press.

Herrera, S. G., & Murry, K. G. (2016). *Mastering ESL/EFL methods: Differentiated instruction for culturally and linguistically diverse (CLD) students* (3rd ed.). Boston, MA: Pearson.

Herrera, S. G., Perez, D. R., & Escamilla, K. (2014). *Teaching reading to English language learners: Differentiated literacies* (2nd ed.). Boston, MA: Allyn & Bacon.

Herrera, S., Perez, D., Kavimandan, S., Holmes, M. A., & Miller, S. (2011, April). *Beyond reductionism and quick fixes: Quantitatively measuring effective pedagogy in the instruction of culturally and linguistically diverse students.* Paper presented at the annual conference of the American Educational Research Association, New Orleans, LA.

Hill, D., & Kumar, R. (Eds.). (2012). *Global neoliberalism and education and its consequences.* New York, NY: Routledge.

Hill, J., & Flynn, K. (2013). *Classroom instruction that works with English language learners* (2nd ed.). Alexandria, VA: Association for Supervision and Curriculum Development.

Irvine, J. J. (1990). *Black students and school failure: Policies, practices, and prescriptions.* New York, NY: Praeger.

Jackson, T. O. (2015). Perspectives and insights from preservice teachers of color on developing culturally responsive pedagogy at predominantly white institutions. *Action in Teacher Education, 37*(3), 223–237.

Jensen, E. (2000a). *Brain-based learning* (rev. ed.). San Diego, CA: The Brain Store.

Jensen, E. (2000b). Brain-based learning: A reality check. *Educational Leadership, 57*(7), 76–80.

Jensen, E. (2006). *Enriching the brain.* San Francisco, CA: Jossey-Bass.

Jensen, E. (2008). *Brain-based learning: The new paradigm of teaching* (2nd ed.). Thousand Oaks, CA: Corwin.

Kinsella, K. (2005). *Preparing for effective vocabulary instruction.* A publication of Aiming High: A Countrywide Commitment to Close the Achievement Gap for English Learners. Available at http://www.scoe.org/docs/ah/AH_kinsella1.pdf

Kinsella, K., & Feldman, K. (2003). *Active learning: Structures to engage all students. High school teaching guidebook for universal access.* Upper Saddle River, NJ: Pearson Education.

Krashen, S. (1985). *The input hypothesis: Issues and implications.* London, UK: Longman.

Krashen, S. D. (2009). *Principles and practice in second language acquisition* (Internet edition). (Original work published 1982.) Available at http://www.sdkrashen.com/content/books/principles_and_practice.pdf

Krussel, L., Springer, G. T., & Edwards, B. (2004). The teacher's discourse moves: A framework for analyzing discourse in mathematics classrooms. *School Science and Mathematics, 104*(7), 307–312.

Kwon, O. N., Ju, M. K., Rasmussen, C., Park, J. H., & Cho, K. H. (2008, July). *Roles of teacher's revoicing in an inquiry-oriented mathematics class: The case of undergraduate differential equations.* Paper prepared for a Topic Study Group of the 11th International Conference on Mathematical Education, Monterrey, Mexico. Available at http://tsg.icme11.org/document/get/541

Lado, A. (2004). *Reading stories with the earliest-stage children.* Handouts for the Preconvention Institute on March 30, 2004, at the 38th annual convention and exhibit, TESOL 2004, Long Beach, CA.

Ladson-Billings, G. (2009). *The dreamkeepers: Successful teachers for African-American children* (2nd ed.). San Francisco, CA: Jossey-Bass.

Langer, J. A. (2001). Beating the odds: Teaching middle and high school students to read and write well. *American Educational Research Journal, 38,* 837–880.

Lent, R. C. (2012). *Overcoming textbook fatigue: 21st century tools to revitalize teaching and learning.* Alexandria, VA: ASCD.

Leopard, D. (2013). *Teaching with the screen: Pedagogy, agency, and media culture.* New York, NY: Routledge.

Maria, K. (1990). *Reading comprehension instruction: Issues and strategies.* Parkton, MD: York Press.

Marzano, R. J. (2003). *What works in schools: Translating research into action.* Alexandria, VA: Association for Supervision and Curriculum Development.

Marzano, R. J. (2004). *Building background knowledge for academic achievement: Research on what works in schools.* Alexandria, VA: Association for Supervision and Curriculum Development.

Marzano, R. J., Pickering, D. J., & Pollock, J. E. (2001). *Classroom instruction that works: Research-based strategies for increasing student achievement.* Alexandria, VA: Association for Supervision and Curriculum Development.

Marzano, R. J., & Toth, M. D. (2014, March). *Teaching for rigor: A call for a critical instructional shift. Why essential shifts in instruction are necessary for teachers and students to succeed with college and career readiness standards.* A Learning Sciences Marzano Center Monograph. West Palm Beach, FL: Learning Sciences Marzano Center.

McGee, L. M., & Richgels, D. J. (2014). *Designing early literacy programs* (2nd ed.). New York, NY: Guilford Press.

McIntyre, E., Kyle, D. W., Chen, C., Kraemer, J., & Parr, J. (2008). *Six principles for teaching English language learners in all classrooms.* Thousand Oaks, CA: Corwin.

McLaren, P. (1994). *Life in schools: An introduction to critical pedagogy in the foundations of education* (2nd ed.) New York, NY: Longman.

Mezirow, J. (1997). Transformative learning: Theory to practice. *New Directions for Adult and Continuing Education, 74,* 5–12. doi: 10.1002/ace.7401

Moll, L. C. (2001). The diversity of schooling: A cultural-historical approach. In M. de la Luz Reyes & J. J. Halcón (Eds.), *The best for our children: Critical perspectives on literacy for Latino children* (pp. 13–28). New York, NY: Teachers College Press.

Moll, L. C., Amanti, C., Neff, D., & Gonzalez, N. (1992). Funds of knowledge for teaching: Using a qualitative approach to connect homes and classrooms. *Theory into Practice, 31*(2), 132–141.

Nagy, W. E. (2003). *Teaching vocabulary to improve reading comprehension.* Urbana, IL: National Council of Teachers of English.

National Center for Education Statistics. (2012). *The nation's report card: Vocabulary results from the 2009 and 2011 NAEP Reading Assessments* (NCES 2013-452). Washington, DC: Institute of Education Sciences, U.S. Department of Education.

National Commission on Excellence in Education. (1983). *A nation at risk: The imperative for educational reform.* Available at https://eric.ed.gov/?id=ED226006

National Governors Association Center for Best Practices & Council of Chief State School Officers (NGA & CCSSO). (2010). *Common Core State Standards for English language arts & literacy in history/social studies, science, and technical subjects.* Washington, DC: Author.

National Research Council. (1998). *Preventing reading difficulties in young children.* Washington, DC: National Academy Press.

Neuman, S., & Roskos, K. (1993). *Language and literacy learning in the early years: An integrated approach.* Fort Worth, TX: Harcourt Brace Jovanovich.

Noddings, N. (2005). *The challenge to care in schools: An alternative approach to education* (2nd ed.). New York, NY: Teachers College Press.

O'Connor, M. C., & Michaels, S. (1996). Shifting participant frameworks: Orchestrating thinking practices in group discussion. In D. Hicks (Ed.), *Discourse, learning and schooling* (pp. 63–103). Cambridge, UK: Cambridge University Press.

Oxford, R. L. (1990). Styles, strategies, and aptitude: Important connections for language learners. In T. S. Parry & C. W. Stansfield (Eds.), *Language aptitude reconsidered* (pp. 67–125). Englewood Cliffs, NJ: Prentice Hall.

Paivio, A. (2006, September–October). *Dual coding theory and education.* Draft chapter for the conference on Pathways to Literacy Achievement for High Poverty Children. Ann Arbor, MI: The University of Michigan School of Education.

Pearl, A. (1991). Systemic and institutional factors in Chicago school failure. In R. R. Valencia (Ed.), *Chicano school failure and success: Research and policy agendas for the 1990's* (pp. 273–320). New York, NY: Falmer.

Peregoy, S. F., & Boyle, O. F. (2017). *Reading, writing, and learning in ESL: A resource book for K–12 teachers* (7th ed.). New York, NY: Longman.

Pink, W. T., & Borman, K. M. (1991). *Community involvement and staff development in school improvement.* Chicago, IL: Chicago Public Schools.

Pressley, M., & Afflerbach, P. (1995). *Verbal protocols of reading: The nature of constructively responsive reading.* Mahwah, NJ: Lawrence Erlbaum.

Proctor, C. P., Carlo, M., August, D., & Snow, C. (2005). Native Spanish-speaking children reading in English: Toward a model of comprehension. *Journal of Educational Psychology, 97*(2), 246–256.

Quiocho, A. L., & Ulanoff, S. H. (2009). *Differentiated literacy instruction for English language learners.* Boston, MA: Allyn & Bacon.

Rasinski, T. V. (1998). How elementary students referred for compensatory reading instruction perform on school-based measures of word recognition, fluency, and comprehension. *Reading Psychology: An International Quarterly, 19,* 185–216.

Rasinski, T. V., & Padak, N. (2009). *Effective reading strategies: Teaching children who find reading difficult* (4th ed.). Upper Saddle River, NJ: Merrill.

Rea, D. M., & Mercuri, S. P. (2006). *Research-based strategies for English language learners: How to reach goals and meet standards, K–8.* Portsmouth, NH: Heinemann.

Reutzel, D. R., & Cooter, R. B., Jr. (2012). *The essentials of teaching children to read: The teacher makes the difference* (3rd ed.). Boston, MA: Pearson Education.

Reutzel, D. R., & Cooter, R. B., Jr. (2010). *Strategies for reading assessment and instruction: Helping every child succeed* (4th ed.). Boston, MA: Prentice Hall.

Routman, R. (2003). *Reading essentials: The specifics you need to teach reading well.* Portsmouth, NH: Heinemann.

Routman, R. (2005). *Writing essentials: Raising expectations and results while simplifying teaching.* Portsmouth, NH: Heinemann.

Rumelhart, D. E. (1980). Schemata: The building blocks of cognition. In R. J. Spiro, B. C. Bruce, & W. F. Brewer (Eds.), *Theoretical issues in reading comprehension* (pp. 33–58). Mahwah, NJ: Lawrence Erlbaum.

Salmon, A. K. (2010). Tools to enhance young children's thinking. *Young Children, 65*(5), 26–31. Available at https://www.naeyc.org/tyc/files/tyc/file/V4N5/Tools%20to%20Enhance%20Young%20CHildren's%20Thinking.pdf

Schickedanz, J. A., & Casbergue, R. M. (2004). *Writing in preschool: Learning to orchestrate meaning and marks.* Newark, DE: International Reading Association.

Schüler, A., Arndt, J., & Scheiter, K. (2015). Processing multimedia material: Does integration of text and pictures result in a single or two interconnected mental representations? *Learning and Instruction, 35,* 62–72. doi: 10.1016/j.learninstruc.2014.09.005

Shein, P. P. (2012). Seeing with two eyes: A teacher's use of gestures in questioning and revoicing to engage English language learners in the repair of mathematical errors. *Journal for Research in Mathematics Education, 43*(2), 182–222.

Shonkoff, J. P., & Phillips, D. A. (Eds.). (2000). *From neurons to neighborhoods: The science of early childhood development.* Washington, DC: National Academy Press.

Sidek, H. M., & Rahim, H. A. (2015). The role of vocabulary knowledge in reading comprehension: A cross-linguistic study. *Procedia—Social and Behavioral Sciences, 197,* 50–56. Available at www.sciencedirect.com

Simonsen, S., & Singer, H. (1992). Improving reading instruction in the content areas. In S. J. Samuels & A. E. Farstrup (Eds.), *What research has to say about reading instruction* (pp. 200–219). Newark, DE: International Reading Association.

Sleeter, C. E. (2011). An agenda to strengthen culturally responsive pedagogy. *English Teaching: Practice and Critique, 10*(2), 7–23.

Smartt, S. M., & Glaser, D. R. (2010). *Next STEPS in literacy instruction: Connecting assessments to effective interventions.* Baltimore, MD: Brookes.

Sousa, D. A. (2011). *How the brain learns* (4th ed.). Thousand Oaks, CA: Corwin.

Sousa, D. A. (2014). *How the brain learns to read* (2nd ed.). Thousand Oaks, CA: Corwin.

Spycher, P. (2009). Learning academic language through science in two linguistically diverse kindergarten classes. *The Elementary School Journal, 109*(4), 359–379.

Stahl, S. A. (1999). *Vocabulary development.* Cambridge, MA: Brookline Books.

Stahl, S. A., & Vancil, S. J. (1986). Discussion is what makes semantic maps work in vocabulary instruction. *The Reading Teacher, 40,* 62–67.

Svinicki, M. (1991). Practical implications of cognitive theories. In R. Menges & M. Svinicki (Eds.), *College teaching: From theory to practice. New Directions for Teaching and Learning* (Issue 45, pp. 27–37). San Francisco, CA: Jossey-Bass.

Swan, K. (2003). Learning effectiveness: What the research tells us. In J. Bourne & J. C. Moore (Eds.), *Elements of quality online education: Practice and direction* (pp. 13–45). Needham, MA: Sloan Center for Online Education.

Swinney, R., & Velasco, P. (2006). *Building bridges between language and thinking: Effective scaffolds to help language minority students achieve.* Handout from the Reading and Writing Project, Teachers College, Columbia University, New York, NY.

Tabors, P. O., Roach, K. A., & Snow, C. E. (2001). Home language and literacy environment final results. In D. K. Dickinson & P. O. Tabors (Eds.), *Beginning literacy with language* (pp. 111–138). Baltimore, MD: Brookes.

Tharp, R. G., & Dalton, S. S. (2007). Orthodoxy, cultural compatibility, and universals in education. *Comparative Education, 43,* 53–70.

Tharp, R. G., Estrada, P., Dalton, S. S., & Yamauchi, L. (2000). *Teaching transformed: Achieving excellence, fairness, inclusion, and harmony.* Boulder, CO: Westview Press.

Thomas, W. P., & Collier, V. P. (1995). Language-minority student achievement and program effectiveness studies support native language development. *NABE News, 18*(8), 5, 12.

Thomas, W. P., & Collier, V. P. (1997). *School effectiveness for language minority students* (NCBE Resource Collection Series No. 9). Washington, DC: National Clearinghouse for Bilingual Education. (ED436087)

Thomas, W. P., & Collier, V. P. (2002). *A national study of school effectiveness for language minority students' long-term academic achievement.* Santa Cruz, CA: Center for Research on Education, Diversity & Excellence. Available at http://www.usc.edu/dept/education/CMMR/CollierThomasExReport.pdf

Thomas, W. P., & Collier, V. P. (2012). *Dual language education for a transformed world.* Albuquerque, NM: Fuente Press.

Tillmann, A. (2012). What we see and why it matters: How competency in visual literacy can enhance student learning. *Honors Projects.* Paper 9. Available at http://digitalcommons.iwu.edu/education_honproj/9

Tomlinson, C. A., Brighton, C., Hertberg, H., Callahan, C. M., Moon, T. R., Brimijoin, K., et al. (2003). Differentiating instruction in response to student readiness, interest, and learning profile in academically diverse classrooms: A review of the literature. *Journal for the Education of the Gifted, 27*(2/3), 119–145.

Tompkins, G. E. (2007). *Teaching writing: Balancing process and product* (5th ed.). Columbus, OH: Merrill.

Tompkins, G. E., & Blanchfield, C. L. (Eds.). (2004). *Teaching vocabulary: 50 creative strategies, Grades K–12.* Upper Saddle River, NJ: Pearson Education.

Tompkins, G., Campbell, R., Green, D., & Smith, C. (2015). *Literacy for the 21st century: A balanced approach.* Melbourne: Pearson Australia.

Tovani, C. (2000). *I read it, but I don't get it: Comprehension strategies for adolescent readers.* Portland, ME: Stenhouse.

Turkan, S., Bicknell, J., & Croft, A. (2012). *Effective practices for developing literacy skills of English language learners in the English language arts classroom.* Research Report (ETS RR-12-03). Princeton, NJ: Educational Testing Service. Available at http://files.eric.ed.gov/fulltext/EJ1109828.pdf

U.S. Department of Education. (2016). *The condition of education 2016.* Washington, DC: National Center for Education Statistics.

Vacca, J. L., Vacca, R. T., & Gove, M. K. (2014). *Reading and learning to read* (9th ed.). White Plains, NY: Longman.

Vacca, R. T., & Vacca, J. L. (2008). *Content area reading: Literacy and learning across the curriculum* (9th ed.). Boston, MA: Pearson.

Vaughn, S., & Linan-Thompson, S. (2004). *Research-based methods of reading instruction, Grades K–3.* Alexandria, VA: Association for Supervision and Curriculum Development.

Vélez-Ibáñez, C., & Greenberg, J. (1992). Formation and transformation of funds of knowledge among U.S. Mexican households. *Anthropology and Education Quarterly, 23*(4), 313–335.

Violand-Sanchez, E., Sutton, C., & Ware, H. (1991). *Fostering home school cooperation: Involving language minority families as partners in education.* Washington, DC: National Center for Bilingual Education.

Vygotsky, L. S. (1978). *Mind in society: The development of higher psychological process.* Cambridge, MA: Harvard University Press.

Walqui, A. (2000). Strategies for success: Engaging immigrant students in secondary schools. *ERIC Digest.* Available at https://eric.ed.gov/?id=ED442300

Wessels, S. (2008). *IBA vocabulary framework: Ignite, Bridge & Associate vocabulary development for culturally and linguistically diverse students.* Unpublished doctoral dissertation, Kansas State University, Manhattan, KS.

Wessels, S., & Herrera, S. (2014). Drawing their way into writing: Culturally and linguistically diverse students finding voice through mini-novelas. *TESOL Journal, 5*(1), 105–118.

Willis, J. (2006). *Research based strategies to ignite student learning: Insights from a neurologist and classroom teacher.* Alexandria, VA: Association for Supervision and Curriculum Development.

Wolf, B. J. (2011). Teaching handwriting. In J. Birsh (Ed.), *Multisensory teaching of basic language skills* (3rd ed., pp. 179–206). Baltimore, MD: Brooks.

Wolfe, P., & Brandt, R. (1998). Brain science, brain fiction. *Educational Leadership, 56*(3), 14–18.

Wong Fillmore, L. (2000). Loss of family languages: Should educators be concerned? *Theory into Practice, 39*(4), 203–210.

Wong Fillmore, L., & Valadez, C. (1986). Teaching bilingual learners. In M. C. Wittock (Ed.), *Handbook of research on teaching* (3rd ed.). New York, NY: Macmillan.

Wyatt, T. (2015). Understanding the process of contextualization. *Multicultural Learning and Teaching, 10*(1), 111–132.

Young, T., & Hadaway, N. (2006). *Supporting the literacy development of English learners.* Newark, DE: International Reading Association.

Zwiers, J. (2004/2005). The third language of academic English. *Educational Leadership, 62*(4), 60–63.

Index

Subjects

Academic dimension, ix, 4, 6, 10
  in Active Bookmark, 156, 158, 159
  in DOTS, 71, 72, 74
  in Extension Wheel, 139, 140, 142
  in Foldable, 81, 83, 84
  in Hearts, 147, 149, 151
  in IDEA, 120, 121, 122
  in Linking Language, 22, 24, 25
  in Listen Sketch Label, 51, 53, 54
  in Magic Book, 112, 113, 115
  in Mind Map, 46, 47
  in Mini Novela, 164, 165, 166
  in Pic-Tac-Tell, 89, 90, 91
  in Pictures and Words, 38, 39, 40
  in Picture This, 30, 31
  in Story Bag, 59, 61
  in Thumb Challenge, 106, 108, 109
  in Tri-Fold, 171, 172, 173
  in U-C-ME, 130, 132, 133
  in Vocabulary Quilt, 98, 100, 101
  in Word Drop, 178, 179, 181
Academic knowledge, existing, 5. *See also* Background knowledge
Academic language, 65, 67, 69
Accountability, 11, 185, 187, 189
  in DOTS, 73, 74
  in Foldable, 82, 83, 84
  in Listen Sketch Label, 52
  in Magic Book, 112
  in Mind Map, 45
  in Pic-Tac-Tell, 90
  in Pictures and Words, 36
  in Thumb Challenge, 108
  in Tri-Fold, 172
  in Vocabulary Quilt, 101
Activation phase, 3, 6–7, 15, 16, 67
  in Active Bookmark, 155–156, 160
  in DOTS, 13, 70–71, 75–76
  in Extension Wheel, 138–139, 142
  in Foldable, 80–81, 85
  in Hearts, 146–147, 151
  in IDEA, 119–120, 123
  in Linking Language, 21–22, 25, 26
  in Listen Sketch Label, 51, 54–55, 56
  in Magic Book, 112, 115
  in Mind Map, 45–46, 47, 48, 49
  in Mini Novela, 164, 167
  in Pic-Tac-Tell, 88–89, 92

  in Pictures and Words, 37–38, 41, 42
  in Picture This, 29–30, 32–33, 34
  in Story Bag, 59–60, 62, 63
  in Thumb Challenge, 106, 110
  in Tri-Fold, 170–171, 174, 175
  in U-C-ME, 129–130, 134
  in Vocabulary Quilt, 97–98, 102
  in Word Drop, 178, 182
Active Bookmark strategy, 154–162, 202
Activities as tool for learning, compared to strategies, 7–9
Affirmation phase, 7, 11, 15, 16, 67
  in Active Bookmark, 158–159, 160
  in DOTS, 13, 73–74, 76
  in Extension Wheel, 141–142, 143
  in Foldable, 83–84, 85
  in Hearts, 150–151
  in IDEA, 119, 121–122, 123
  in Linking Language, 24–25, 26, 27
  in Listen Sketch Label, 53–54, 55, 56
  in Magic Book, 114–115, 116
  in Mind Map, 47, 48, 49
  in Mini Novela, 165–166, 167
  in Pic-Tac-Tell, 90–91, 93
  in Pictures and Words, 40, 41, 42
  in Picture This, 31–32, 33, 34
  in Story Bag, 61, 62, 63
  in Thumb Challenge, 108–109, 110
  in Tri-Fold, 173, 174, 175
  in U-C-ME, 132–133, 135
  in Vocabulary Quilt, 100–101, 103
  in Word Drop, 180–181, 182
Alphabet knowledge, 25
Artifacts from strategy implementation, 15
Assessment procedures, 7, 11, 16
  checklists in. *See* Student academic behavior checklists
  confirming/disconfirming learning. *See* Confirm/disconfirm
  rubrics in. *See* Student assessment rubrics

Background knowledge, 3, 5, 11, 66, 67
  activation of, 3, 6–7. *See also* Activation phase
  in Active Bookmark, 155, 156, 159
  in DOTS, 13, 71, 74
  in Extension Wheel, 139, 141

  in Foldable, 79, 81
  in Hearts, 145, 147
  in IDEA, 119
  in Linking Language, 22, 25
  in Listen Sketch Label, 51, 52
  in Mind Map, 44, 46, 47
  in Mini Novela, 164
  in Pic-Tac-Tell, 87–88, 89, 90, 91, 92
  in Pictures and Words, 36, 38
  in Picture This, 30, 32, 33
  in Story Bag, 58, 59, 60, 61, 62
  in Thumb Challenge, 105, 106, 109
  in Tri-Fold, 171, 175
  in U-C-ME, 128, 130
  in Vocabulary Quilt, 96, 97, 102
  in Word Drop, 178, 181, 182
Biography-driven instruction, ix–x, 1, 2, 3–6, 8, 13, 14
  academic dimension in. *See* Academic dimension
  Active Bookmark strategy in, 154
  benefits of, 186–188
  cognitive dimension in. *See* Cognitive dimension
  comprehension strategies in, 15, 124–183
  democratic citizenship in, 186
  Extension Wheel strategy in, 137–138, 141
  Foldable strategy in, 79–80
  Hearts strategy in, 145
  image-based strategies in, 15, 17–64
  lesson planning and delivery in, 189
  linguistic dimension in. *See* Linguistic dimension
  Listen Sketch Label strategy in, 50
  Mind Map strategy in, 44
  Pic-Tac-Tell strategy in, 87, 89
  sociocultural dimension in. *See* Socio-cultural dimension
  Thumb Challenge strategy in, 109
  Tri-Fold strategy in, 169
  U-C-ME strategy in, 128, 133
  Vocabulary Quilt strategy in, 95, 96, 101
  word-based strategies in, 15, 65–123
  Word Drop strategy in, 177
Biopsychosocial histories of learner and teacher, 3–4

Center for Intercultural and Multilingual Advocacy (CIMA), 1
Checklists on student academic behavior. *See* Student academic behavior checklists
Cognitive academic language proficiency in Thumb Challenge, 107
Cognitive dimension, ix, 4, 5, 6, 10
  in Active Bookmark, 156, 158, 159
  in DOTS, 71, 72, 74
  in Extension Wheel, 139, 140, 142
  in Foldable, 81, 83, 84
  in Hearts, 147, 149, 151
  in IDEA, 120, 121, 122
  in Linking Language, 22, 24, 25
  in Listen Sketch Label, 51, 53, 54
  in Magic Book, 112, 113, 115
  in Mind Map, 46, 47
  in Mini Novela, 164, 165, 166
  in Pic-Tac-Tell, 89, 90, 91
  in Pictures and Words, 38, 39, 40
  in Picture This, 30, 31
  in Story Bag, 59, 61
  in Thumb Challenge, 106, 108, 109
  in Tri-Fold, 171, 172, 173
  in U-C-ME, 130, 132, 133
  in Vocabulary Quilt, 98, 100, 101
  in Word Drop, 178, 179, 181
Cognitive learning strategy, Picture This as, 28
Common Core State Standards, 2
Community influences in student biography, 4, 5
Comprehended input, 9, 79
Comprehensible input, 9, 79
  in Linking Language strategy, 21
  in Picture This strategy, 28
  transformative, 9–10
Comprehension strategies, 10, 15, 124–183
  Active Bookmark, 154–162, 202
  Extension Wheel, 137–144, 201
  Hearts, 145–153
  Mini Novela, 163–168
  Tri-Fold, 169–176
  U-C-ME, 127–136, 200
  Word Drop, 177–183
Confirm/disconfirm, 7, 10, 11
  in IDEA, 121
  in Magic Book, 113
  in Mind Map, 47
  in Mini Novela, 165
  in Pic-Tac-Tell, 89
  in Pictures and Words, 38, 39
  in Picture This, 31
  in U-C-ME, 131
  in Vocabulary Quilt, 99
  in Word Drop, 179
Connection phase, 7, 15, 16, 67
  in Active Bookmark, 156–158, 160
  in DOTS, 13, 71–72, 76
  in Extension Wheel, 139–140, 143
  in Foldable, 81–83, 85
  in Hearts, 148–149, 151

  in IDEA, 120–121, 123
  in Linking Language, 22–24, 25–26, 27
  in Listen Sketch Label, 52–53, 55, 56
  in Magic Book, 113, 115
  in Mind Map, 46–47, 48, 49
  in Mini Novela, 164–165, 167
  in Pic-Tac-Tell, 88, 89–90, 92
  in Pictures and Words, 36, 37, 38–39, 41, 42
  in Picture This, 30–31, 33, 34
  in Story Bag, 60–61, 62, 63
  in Thumb Challenge, 107–108, 110
  in Tri-Fold, 172, 174, 175
  in U-C-ME, 130–132, 134
  in Vocabulary Quilt, 99–100, 103
  in Word Drop, 179, 182
Consonant–vowel–consonant patterns in Listen Sketch Label, 54, 55
Critical care teachers, 13
Critical reflection of teachers, 187–188
Culturally and linguistically diverse (CLD) learners, 2, 3
  biography of, 4–6
  culturally responsive teachers of, 13–14
  early literacy experiences of. *See* Early literacy experiences
  framework for linguistic and academic development of, 6–7
  teachers as partners of, 9
  in technocratic–instrumental perspective, 185
  vocabulary development strategies for. *See* Vocabulary development strategies
Culturally responsive or relevant teachers, 13–14, 186

DOTS strategy, 11–13, 68–78, 186, 196

Early literacy experiences, 16
  Active Bookmark in, 159
  DOTS in, 75
  Foldable in, 84
  IDEA in, 122
  Linking Language in, 25–26
  Listen Sketch Label in, 54–55
  Mind Map in, 48
  Mini Novela in, 166
  Pictures and Words in, 41
  Picture This in, 32–33
  Story Bag in, 62
  Thumb Challenge in, 109
  Tri-Fold in, 174
  U-C-ME in, 133
  Vocabulary Quilt in, 101–102
  Word Drop in, 181
Educator contributors
  Abell, Anne, 105
  Berg, Amy, 60
  Blanchard, Lindsay, 111, 115–116
  Bowden, Jennifer, 145
  Bowman, Stacey, 110
  Burkhart, Courtney, 127, 134
  Burnham, Shilo, 58, 63

  Clark, Kathy, 91
  Cunningham, Susan, 19
  Darby, Reesa, 169, 175
  Donahey, Amanda, 34, 118, 123
  Euston, JoAnna, 68, 75–76
  Evans, Lara, 42
  Fisher, Kristin, 36
  Golden, Jessica, 177
  Hacker, Sabina, 154
  Hayes, Cathy, 85
  Hesse, Deborah, 151
  Langhofer, Lauren, 187, 188
  Larsen, Jessica, 163, 167
  Livingston, Beth, 186
  Metz, Kendra, 160
  Nicholson, Madison, 50, 56
  Peréz, Della, 182
  Ritter, Kari, 28
  Snyder, Nikki, 87
  Thomas, Dave, 188
  Valenti, Megan, 137, 142–143
  Wasylk, Kerry, 44, 180
  Werth, Cheryl, 79
  Wilhite, Stephanie, 49, 95, 102–103
  Wilk, Jenny, 92–93
  Winkler, Stacey, 26–27
English as target language, 4–5
Extension Wheel strategy, 137–144, 201

Family, in sociocultural dimension, 4
Figurative language, 50
Fluency, 124
Foldable strategy, 79–86
Funds of knowledge, 5. *See also* Background knowledge

Group configurations, *i* + *TpsI* mnemonic on. *See i* + *TpsI*
Guarded vocabulary, 9

Hearts strategy, 145–153

IDEA strategy, 118–123
Image-based strategies, 15, 17–64
  Linking Language, 19–27, 187
  Listen Sketch Label, 50–57, 194
  Mind Map, 44–49, 193
  Pictures and Words, 36–43, 192
  Picture This, 28–35
  Story Bag, 58–64, 195
Instructional conversations, 14, 18
i + 1 process, 9, 10, 186
  in Active Bookmark, 155, 158
  in DOTS, 69, 71, 72
  in Extension Wheel, 140
  in Foldable, 83
  in Hearts, 149
  in IDEA, 121
  in Linking Language, 24
  in Listen Sketch Label, 53
  in Magic Book, 113
  in Mind Map, 47
  in Mini Novela, 165
  in Pic-Tac-Tell, 90

i + 1 process *(continued)*
   in Pictures and Words, 39
   in Picture This, 31
   in Story Bag, 61
   in Thumb Challenge, 108
   in Tri-Fold, 172
   in U-C-ME, 128, 132
   in Vocabulary Quilt, 100
   in Word Drop, 179
i + *TpsI*, 10, 15–16
   in Active Bookmark, 156, 158
   in DOTS, 71, 73
   in Extension Wheel, 139, 141
   in Foldable, 81, 83
   in Hearts, 148, 149, 150
   in IDEA, 120, 121
   in Linking Language, 22, 24
   in Listen Sketch Label, 52, 53
   in Magic Book, 113, 114
   in Mind Map, 46, 47
   in Mini Novela, 164, 165
   in Pic-Tac-Tell, 89, 90
   in Pictures and Words, 38, 40
   in Picture This, 30, 31
   in Story Bag, 60, 61
   in Thumb Challenge, 107, 108
   in Tri-Fold, 172, 173
   in U-C-ME, 130, 132
   in Vocabulary Quilt, 99, 100
   in Word Drop, 179, 180

Knowledge, background. *See* Background
   knowledge

Lesson planning and delivery, 6, 188–189
Linguistic dimension, ix, 4–5, 10
   in Active Bookmark, 156, 158, 159
   in DOTS, 71, 72, 74
   in Extension Wheel, 139, 140, 142
   in Foldable, 81, 83, 84
   in Hearts, 147, 149, 151
   in IDEA, 120, 121, 122
   in Linking Language, 22, 24, 25
   in Listen Sketch Label, 51, 53, 54
   in Magic Book, 112, 113, 115
   in Mind Map, 46, 47
   in Mini Novela, 164, 165, 166
   in Pic-Tac-Tell, 89, 90, 91
   in Pictures and Words, 38, 39, 40
   in Picture This, 30, 31
   in Story Bag, 59, 61
   in Thumb Challenge, 106, 108, 109
   in Tri-Fold, 171, 172, 173
   in U-C-ME, 130, 132, 133
   in Vocabulary Quilt, 98, 100, 101
   in Word Drop, 178, 179, 181
Linking Language strategy, 19–27, 187
Listen Sketch Label strategy, 50–57, 194
Literacy, 4, 5, 6
   early experiences. *See* Early literacy
     experiences
   visual, 17–18

Magic Book strategy, 111–117
Memory in word-based strategies, 67

Metacognition, 67, 124–125
   in Active Bookmark, 154
   in DOTS, 69, 73
   in Hearts, 151
   in Linking Language, 25
   in Magic Book, 113
   in Mini Novela, 163
   in U-C-ME, 128, 130
   in Word Drop, 177, 178, 179
Metaphors, 50
Mind Map strategy, 44–49, 193
Mini Novela strategy, 163–168
Modeling, 7
   in Active Bookmark, 154, 156, 159, 160
   in DOTS, 74
   in Linking Language, 24, 25
   in Listen Sketch Label, 54
   in Magic Book, 115
   in Mind Map, 44, 47
   in Pic-Tac-Tell, 88
   in Pictures and Words, 38, 39
   in U-C-ME, 133
   in Vocabulary Quilt, 102
Morphology of words, 5

A Nation at Risk, 185
Native language, 2, 4–5, 66
   in DOTS, 70, 71, 73, 75
   in Foldable, 80, 82, 84
   in Hearts, 147, 150
   in IDEA, 121
   in Linking Language, 21, 22, 26
   in Listen Sketch Label, 50, 51, 54
   in Magic Book, 112, 114
   in Mind Map, 45, 48
   in Pic-Tac-Tell, 88, 89, 92
   in Pictures and Words, 37, 41
   in Picture This, 29, 32
   in Story Bag, 62
   in Thumb Challenge, 106, 107
   in Tri-Fold, 170
   in Vocabulary Quilt, 95, 96, 97, 101, 102
   in Word Drop, 179, 180

Oral language skills
   in DOTS, 75
   in early literacy experiences, 16
   in Foldable, 84
   in IDEA, 118, 119, 122
   in linguistic dimension, 5
   in Linking Language, 25
   in Pictures and Words, 41
   in Picture This, 32, 33
   in sociocultural dimension, 4
   in Thumb Challenge, 105, 106, 109
   in U-C-ME, 129, 130
   in Vocabulary Quilt, 97

Parents, strategies recommended for
   DOTS, 74, 75
   Foldable, 84
   IDEA, 122
   Mind Map, 48
   Mini Novela, 166
   Pictures and Words, 41

   Story Bag, 62
   Thumb Challenge, 122
Peers in group configurations, *i* + *TpsI*
   mnemonic on. *See i* + *TpsI*
Phonemic awareness, 124
   in Linking Language, 25
Phonetic spelling in Listen Sketch Label, 54
Phonics, 124
   in Linking Language, 25, 26
   in Magic Book, 112, 113, 114
Phonology, 5, 25
Pic-Tac-Tell strategy, 87–94, 197
Picture Me a Story version of IDEA strategy, 122
Pictures and Words strategy, 36–43, 192
Picture This strategy, 28–35
Predictions
   in Active Bookmark, 154, 155, 156, 159
   in Foldable, 80, 85
   in Pictures and Words, 37, 38, 39, 41, 42
   in Story Bag, 58, 59, 60, 62
   in Thumb Challenge, 106
   in U-C-ME, 131
Prior knowledge, 5. *See also* Background
   knowledge

Question-and-answer process
   in Active Bookmark, 154, 155, 156, 157,
     158, 159, 160
   in Extension Wheel, 138, 141
   in Hearts, 146, 147, 148, 149, 150
   in U-C-ME, 133, 134, 135

Reading skills, 2, 4, 65
   in Active Bookmark, 154–155, 157
   comprehension in, 124, 125
   in early literacy experiences, 16, 32
   in IDEA, 122
Reflective–transformative perspective, 186
Revoicing, 7, 10, 11
   in Active Bookmark, 157
   in DOTS, 70, 74
   in Extension Wheel, 140
   in Foldable, 79, 81
   in Hearts, 149
   in IDEA, 119
   in Linking Language, 26, 55
   in Listen Sketch Label, 51
   in Mind Map, 48
   in Pic-Tac-Tell, 88
   in Pictures and Words, 37
   in Picture This, 29, 30, 33
   in Story Bag, 60
   in Vocabulary Quilt, 97, 99
Rubrics, assessment. *See* Student assessment rubrics

Scaffolding, 3, 11, 14
   in Active Bookmark, 154, 156, 157
   in DOTS, 13, 69, 71, 73
   in Extension Wheel, 141, 143
   in Foldable, 80, 84
   in Hearts, 151
   in image-based strategies, 17, 18
   in Linking Language, 21, 25

in Listen Sketch Label, 50
in Magic Book, 113
in Mind Map, 45, 47
in Mini Novela, 163
in Pictures and Words, 36, 39
in Tri-Fold, 170, 173
in U-C-ME, 128, 132
in Vocabulary Quilt, 96, 98, 99, 100, 103
in word-based strategies, 66
in Word Drop, 179
Schemas, 124, 125
in Tri-Fold, 175
in U-C-ME, 128
in Vocabulary Quilt, 96, 99
Second language acquisition, 9, 32
Semantics, 5
Sequence of information, 3
in Story Bag, 61
in Tri-Fold, 169, 170, 174
Socialization, 13
Sociocultural dimension, ix, 4, 10
in Active Bookmark, 156, 158, 159
in DOTS, 71, 72, 74
in Extension Wheel, 139, 140, 142
in Foldable, 81, 83, 84
in Hearts, 147, 149, 151
in IDEA, 120, 121, 122
in Linking Language, 22, 24, 25
in Listen Sketch Label, 51, 53, 54
in Magic Book, 112, 113, 115
in Mind Map, 46, 47
in Mini Novela, 164, 165, 166
in Pic-Tac-Tell, 89, 90, 91
in Pictures and Words, 38, 39, 40
in Picture This, 30, 31
in Story Bag, 59, 61
in Thumb Challenge, 106, 108, 109
in Tri-Fold, 171, 172, 173
in U-C-ME, 130, 132, 133
in Vocabulary Quilt, 98, 100, 101
in Word Drop, 178, 179, 181
Spanish language, 2
Spelling skills
in DOTS, 75
in Listen Sketch Label, 54–55
in Word Drop, 181
Standards for Effective Pedagogy and Learning, 14
Story Bag strategy, 58–64, 195
Strategies, 7–9
artifacts from, 15
compared to activities, 7–9
teacher testimonials on, 15
in vocabulary development. See Vocabulary development strategies
Student academic behavior checklists, 16
for Active Bookmark, 202
for DOTS, 196
for Listen Sketch Label, 194
for Pictures and Words, 192
for Thumb Challenge, 199
for Vocabulary Quilt, 198
Student assessment rubrics, 16
for Extension Wheel, 201
for Mind Map, 193

for Pic-Tac-Tell, 197
for Story Bag, 195
for U-C-ME, 200
Summarization
in DOTS, 13, 69, 73
in Extension Wheel, 141
in Foldable, 83, 85
in IDEA, 123
in Mind Map, 44, 47
in Mini Novela, 163, 164, 165, 167
in Pic-Tac-Tell, 88, 91, 93
in Story Bag, 61
in Thumb Challenge, 105, 108
in Tri-Fold, 169–170, 173, 175
in U-C-ME, 133
in Vocabulary Quilt, 101, 103
in Word Drop, 177, 180, 182
Syntax, 5

Target language, English as, 4–5
Teachers
as agents of change, 185–186
critical reflection of, 187–188
culturally responsive or relevant, 13–14
joint productive activity of, 14
lesson planning and delivery by, 6, 188–189
as partners, 9
in reflective–transformative perspective, 186
revoicing by, 11. See also Revoicing
strategies of, 7–9
in technocratic–instrumental perspective, 185
testimonials of, 15
Technocratic–instrumental perspective, 185
Templates, 16
for Active Bookmark, 161–162
for DOTS, 77–78
for Extension Wheel, 144
for Hearts, 152–153
for Listen Sketch Label, 57
for Pic-Tac-Tell, 94
for Pictures and Words, 43
for Picture This, 35
for Story Bag, 64
for Tri-Fold, 176
for U-C-ME, 136
for Vocabulary Quilt, 104
for Word Drop, 183
Thumb Challenge strategy, 105–110, 199
Tri-Fold strategy, 169–176

U-C-ME strategy, 127–136, 200

Video clips of exemplary teaching, 16
Visual cues, 9
in image-based strategies. See Image-based strategies
Vocabulary development strategies, 2, 3, 6
Activation phase in. See Activation phase
Active Bookmark, 154–162, 202

Affirmation phase in. See Affirmation phase
cognitive dimension in. See Cognitive dimension
for comprehension. See Comprehension strategies
Connection phase in. See Connection phase
DOTS, 11–13, 68–78, 186, 196
Extension Wheel, 137–144, 201
Foldable, 79–86
Hearts, 145–153
IDEA, 118–123
image-based. See Image-based strategies
linguistic dimension in. See Linguistic dimension
Linking Language, 19–27, 187
Listen Sketch Label, 50–57, 194
Magic Book, 111–117
Mind Map, 44–49, 193
Mini Novela, 163–168
Pic-Tac-Tell, 87–94, 197
Pictures and Words, 36–43, 192
Picture This, 28–35
sociocultural dimension in. See Sociocultural dimension
Story Bag, 58–64, 195
teachers as partners in, 9
Thumb Challenge, 105–110, 199
tier system of words in, 65–66, 95
Tri-Fold, 169–176
U-C-ME, 127–136, 200
Vocabulary Quilt, 95–104, 187, 198
word-based. See Word-based strategies
Word Drop, 177–183
Vocabulary Foldable strategy, 79–86
Vocabulary Quilt strategy, 95–104, 187, 198

Website resources, 16
Word-based strategies, 15, 65–123
DOTS, 11–13, 68–78, 186, 196
Foldable, 79–86
IDEA, 118–123
Magic Book, 111–117
Pic-Tac-Tell, 87–94, 197
principles of, 66–67
Thumb Challenge, 105–110, 199
tier system of words in, 65–66, 95
Vocabulary Quilt, 95–104, 187, 198
Word Drop strategy, 177–183
Writing skills
in Foldable, 83, 84, 85
in Magic Book, 112, 113, 114
in Mini Novela, 163

Young CLD students, early literacy experiences of. See Early literacy experiences

Zone of proximal development, 3, 5, 7, 9, 186
in DOTS, 69
in Pic-Tac-Tell, 90
in Picture This, 32

Cited Authors

Afflerbach, P., 61
Aisami, R. S., 19
Almeida, P. A., 127
Amanti, C., 5
Ambrose, S. A., 69
Anderson, N. J., 9, 125
Anderson, R. C., 124
Anderson, V., 111
Arndt, J., 51
Au, K. H., 59
August, D., 65, 66, 75, 118
Ausabel, D. P., 79

Bailey, K. M., 41
Baker, S. K., 170
Baquedano-López, P., 189
Bartholomé, T., 51
Baxley, T. P., ix, 4
Beaty, J. J., 84, 122
Beck, I. L., 65, 66, 177
Benson, C., 18
Bett, H. K., 185
Bhattacharya, J., 2
Bicknell, J., 137
Blachowicz, C. L. Z., 28, 65, 128
Blanchfield, C. L., 65
Bobe, G., 105
Boerma, I. E., 50, 51
Borman, K. M., 185
Bortnem, G., 101
Boston, G. H., ix, 4
Boyd-Batstone, P., 54, 159, 181
Boyle, O. F., 69
Braden, R. A., 17
Brandt, R., 96
Bransford, J., 9, 96, 119, 128
Bridges, M. W., 69
Bromme, R., 51
Brown, A. L., 128
Brown, C. A., 11
Brumberger, E., 18
Burkman, A., 96, 128, 155
Buzan, T., 44, 48
Byers, H., 171
Byers, P., 171

Cabral, R. M., 3, 4
Calderón, M., 9, 65, 66
Campbell, R., 50
Carlisle, J., 108
Carlo, M., 66, 118
Casbergue, R. M., 54
Center for Research on Education, Diversity & Excellence, 14, 145
Chamot, A. U., 163
Chen, C., 137
Chick, N., 128
Chin, C., 127
Cho, K. H., 11

Coady, M., 111
Cocking, R. R., 128
Collier, V. P., 4, 5
Cooper, J. D., 69
Cooperstein, S. E., 174
Cooter, R. B., Jr., 65, 66, 124
Council of Chief State School Officers, 2
Coyne, M. D., 66
Croft, A., 137
Cummins, J., 5, 84
Cunningham, J. W., 69
Cunningham, P. M., 69
Currie, P., 181
Curtis, A., 41

Dalton, S. S., x, 4, 145
Darling-Hammond, L., 119
Davoudi, M., 128
Dewey, J., 3, 69
Díaz-Rico, L. T., 87, 88, 169
Dimino, J., 65
DiPietro, M., 69
Donovan, M. S., 9, 96
Dressler, C., 66
Duke, N. K., 58, 108

Echevarría, J., 111, 124
Edwards, B., 11
ERIC Clearinghouse on Languages and Linguistics, 5
Escamilla, K., 4
Estrada, P., 145

Feldman, K., 128
Fisher, D., 65, 66, 87
Fisher, P. J., 28, 65, 128
Flavell, J., 125
Flynn, K., 44, 88, 96, 154
Forman, E. A., 11
Frei, B., 105
Frei, S., 105
Frey, N., 65, 66, 87
Friedlander, B., 155

Gambrell, L. B., ix, 4
Gay, G., 4, 58, 89
Gentry, J. R., 54
Gersten, R., 65, 170
Geva, E., 118
Gipe, J. P., 5, 6
Glaser, D. R., 155
Goldenberg, C., 2
Gonzalez, N., 5
Goudvis, A., 18
Gove, M. K., 69
Graesser, A. C., 128
Graham, S., 155
Green, D., 50
Greenberg, J., 5

Gregory, G. H., 96, 128, 155, 169
Gunning, T. G., 36, 66
Guthrie, J. T., ix, 4
Gutiérrez, K. D., 189

Hadaway, N., 67
Hakuta, K., 65
Harris, K. R., 155
Harvey, S., 18
Hattie, J., 65, 66, 79, 111
Herrera, S. G., ix, 1, 2, 3, 4, 5, 9, 11, 13, 32, 36, 44, 66, 69, 75, 89, 119, 124, 128, 137, 145, 154, 163, 170, 178, 185, 186, 187, 189
Hill, D., 185, 186
Hill, J., 44, 88, 96, 154
Holmes, M. A., ix, 3

Irvine, J. J., 58

Jackson, T. O., 185
Jayanthi, M., 65
Jensen, E., 36, 105, 128
Jolles, J., 50, 51
Ju, M. K., 11

Kapp, S., 66
Kavimandan, S. K., ix, 3
Kim, J., 65
Kinsella, K., 66, 128
Kocevar-Weidinger, E., 174
Kraemer, J., 137
Krashen, S. D., 7, 9, 69, 79, 90
Krussel, L., 11
Kucan, L., 65
Kumar, R., 185, 186
Kuzmich, L., 169
Kwon, O. N., 11
Kyle, D. W., 137

Lado, A., 58
Ladson-Billings, G., 58
Langer, J. A., 36, 66
Larreamendy-Joerns, J., 11
Lent, R. C., 20, 69
Leopard, D., 185
Linan-Thompson, S., 65
Loftus, S., 66
Lovett, M. C., 69
Lunt, J., 18

Maria, K., 9
Marzano, R. J., 3, 65, 66, 69, 105, 133, 145, 181
Mason, L. H., 155
McCoach, D. B., 66
McGee, L. M., 32
McIntyre, E., 137
McKeown, M. G., 65